Seeding the Process of Multicultural Education

An Anthology

EDITED BY

CATHY L. NELSON & KIM A. WILSON

Minnesota Inclusiveness Program
Plymouth, Minnesota

FIRST EDITION, 1998

Library of Congress Catalog Card Number: 98-67732

ISBN 0-9636822-3-7

Production Coordinator: Pamela Rizzi
Cover Illustration: Perry Andrews
Cover and Book Design: Claudia Smelser
Printing: Banta Information Services Group

Printed in the United States of America

10 9 8 7 6 5 4 3 2

TABLE *of* CONTENTS

OPPRESSION

AUTOBIOGRAPHY

FRAMING MULTICULTURAL EDUCATION

TEACHING & LEARNING

ACKNOWLEDGMENTS

OUR DEEPEST THANKS AND RESPECT GOES TO EACH AUTHOR who was willing to write for this book. Whatever merit and use this anthology ultimately has will be because of what each author committed to paper. Their writing is insightful, important, and appreciated. It has been a pure joy to read their work and imagine the articles and poems bound together between two covers.

This book would not have been possible without the creative genius, commitment, and attention to detail of Project Coordinator Pamela Rizzi. Her willingness to undertake this project in addition to the multitude of responsibilities she has with the Minnesota Inclusiveness Program was critical.

We also thank Judy Logan for paving the way; Rob Peick for his willingness to proofread on a moment's notice; David Mura for his immediate, unconditional support; Perry Andrews for artistically capturing the book's title for the cover of the anthology; and Claudia Smelser for cover and book design.

We also want to acknowledge the efforts of many people in our network who attempted to respond to our call for articles or poems, but who for one reason or another were unable to craft on paper their considerable knowledge and experience. It was not for want of stories to tell but a testament to the difficult process that writing is.

We would be remiss if we did not acknowledge the legacy of the National S.E.E.D. Project on Inclusive Curriculum (Seeking Educational Equity and Diversity) and co-directors Peggy McIntosh and

Emily Style. Our work in Minnesota continues and extends the work they have done nationally.

The vision of this compilation was translated into self-imposed deadlines and a myriad of decisions. Early on we decided to request previously published articles from Bill Bigelow, Carl A. Grant, David Mura, Emily Style, James A. Banks and Peggy McIntosh. These writers, as well as others, have informed our work over the years and we wanted to include them in this anthology. We broadly invited participants in the projects of the Minnesota Inclusiveness Program to submit a poem or article to us for consideration, trusting that a diverse range of stories would result. We also relentlessly encouraged those people who called our office, crossed our paths, or who had ever indicated an interest in writing about multicultural education. Our decision to trust that a diverse range of stories would emerge leaves us with a book that is not as inclusive as we had initially hoped. We acknowledge those absent voices and look toward a second volume to gather an even broader range of stories.

The process of pulling this collection of articles and poems together was, at times, a delicate dance between honoring the stories and writing of the authors and accepting our role as editors. Mistakes were made along the way on both sides of that dance, and for that we apologize, trusting that the strong network that binds us can withstand our learning process.

INTRODUCTION

THE PURPOSE OF THIS INTRODUCTION IS THE SAME AS THAT of the book: to engage readers. Housed between the covers of this book is a diverse range of voices. Most of the articles and poems were written by people currently working in preK–12 education in Minnesota. The writing reflects the individual author's experiences and invites the reader to accompany them on their journey.

Fundamental to the work of the Minnesota Inclusiveness Program (MIP) is the recognition that we all have stories to tell, learning to do, and work to get done. As we tell our stories in this anthology, we also have the opportunity to hear the voices of others, contributing to our own learning. And we hold ourselves accountable for translating that learning into concrete practice and action. Motivation to change requires that we hear with more than our ears, imagine more than what has been, and take risks in order to become the teachers that can make a difference in the lives of all students. If one more person calls and asks us to do an "awareness training," we swear we will not be responsible for our actions! Information and knowledge, quite frankly, do not get the job done.

In Minnesota we had the good sense to replicate a nationally-recognized staff development project, the National S.E.E.D. Project on Inclusive Curriculum (Seeking Educational Equity and Diversity), and to make it our own. Since 1992 we have developed, planned, and facilitated seven Minnesota SEED Leaders' Workshops, preparing over 250 people to facilitate monthly, 3-hour seminars with their colleagues on multicultural education. Over the years we developed other, corollary projects as we identified ways to support the work we were already doing. These include: *Voices of Experience,* a play written and performed by a dozen teachers to illuminate the ways bias manifests itself in hallways, classrooms, and staff lounges; the Community of Leaders as Advocates for Inclusiveness (CLAI) Project which works with parents and community members; the Administrators' SEED Institute (ASI) which provides diversity leadership training for administrators; and publishing the book *Teaching Stories* by Judy Logan.

This book is further evidence of the growth and development of MIP. In what has become our typical way to generate ideas for a new project, we looked at each other on the "porch" (where meetings are held, weather permitting) and said, "Why didn't we think of doing this before?" As soon as we were done laughing at ourselves, we rolled up our sleeves and began to get the job done. Getting the job done began with calling people in the Minnesota SEED Network for their reaction to our latest proposed venture. Typically the response was, "What took you so long?"

The title of this book, *Seeding the Process of Multicultural Education,* was carefully and deliberately chosen. It sends the immediate message that this book is about multicultural education which, simply defined, recognizes that students from traditionally marginalized, under-studied, and under-represented groups have not been served well by educational institutions. Likewise, traditional education has not prepared students who have flourished in those systems for the "real" world. Creating a learning community where all students are respected and encouraged to succeed academically requires that we examine and transform curriculum, school climate, staff development, policies, practices, and resources (human and financial).

It is also our belief that process is as or more important in this work than product. Having spent our lives attending or working within educational institutions, we do not use the word process lightly or broadly. The process we honor is committed to creating safe space where people may engage in the difficult, often painful internal and external work that is part of this journey. Educational diversity work needs to be a process which respects and trusts that teachers have the capacity to inspire, motivate, and learn from and with one another to improve education. In our experience, attention to the quality, integrity and on-going nature of the process is often missing in diversity work, particularly in preK–12 schools where we live and work daily.

And the book title begins with the word "Seeding," which captures a sense of new planting, tending, and beginnings. We envisioned our readers encompassing a wide range of experiences and knowledge of multicultural education. This book can provide an entry point, a turning point, a crossroads, or an extension. By including people's stories and personalizing knowledge, we hope to convey to the reader that this is important and doable.

It is not our intent to simplify complex territory. The book is organized thematically, capturing areas useful for educators, parents, and community members to consider as we imagine education that is multicultural: "Voice & Identity," "Oppression," "Autobiography," "Framing Multicultural Education," "Teaching & Learning," and "Building Community." And to question: Whose stories are told? Whose voices have been missing? What is the role of identity formation in our work with an increasingly diverse student population? What can we learn by hearing the stories of those who are from traditionally marginalized groups? What writers and theorists can provide us with useful frameworks as we work to imagine, develop, and implement multicultural curriculum, strategies, and policies? And finally, how do we build community in schools so that all students can achieve?

There are many voices that have not been center-stage in conversations about multicultural education, including those of preK–12 educators. While there is abundant scholarship and writing in the field, there are far fewer "teacher-generated" articles. To engage preK–12 educators in working toward education that is multicultural, it strikes us as essential to provide writing that reflects their experiences and scholarship. This book was intended to be both an impetus to empower preK–12 educators to write their stories and an anthology that would be useful to educators as they continue to construct their own personal and professional identities.

Let the journey continue.

Cathy L. Nelson
Kim A. Wilson

PROSPECTIVE IMMIGRANTS PLEASE NOTE

Adrienne Rich

Either you will
go through this door
or you will not go through.

If you go through
there is always the risk
of remembering your name.

Things look at you doubly
and you must look back
and let them happen.

If you do not go through
it is possible
to live worthily

to maintain your attitudes
to hold your position
to die bravely

but much will blind you,
much will evade you,
at what cost who knows?

The door itself
makes no promises
It is only a door.

1962

VOICE & IDENTITY

It is far more constructive to . . . learn to create classroom communities that grant voice and legitimacy to the perspectives and experiences of those who are different from themselves—communities that do not require students to surrender personal and cultural identity in exchange for academic achievement.

—*Sharon Nelson-Barber and Terry Meier*

Growing Stories

Gene-Tey Shin

I REMEMBER THE FIRST DAY MY MOTHER DROVE ME TO Montessori school. I turned from the door after walking the whole concrete way from the car where she stood, watching. I looked back. She waved to me, smiling, and said, "Learn something!" in a happy, vibrant voice. Terrified, I realized that she was going away, and I was going to go through that door alone. The rest of that time has faded, but my mother's parting became a ritual that daily sent me into the world of Education. "Learn something."

Never "Get good grades," or "Make me proud," or even "Do a good job." She always left me with that cheerful, determined reminder and wish. "Learn something."

∾ ∾ ∾

It is very hard to write about multicultural education, about what it means to include other voices, other visions in the teaching of our children and our own learning. I cannot restrict my thoughts about how and why to include other voices to the structure of the traditional essay, because the traditional essay cannot hear those voices, does not speak with their tongues.

"Learn something," my mother says, and so I do. Leaving the car and the warm embrace of her voice, of her hopes, to face the demands of

3

the public school system is the transition of half a step to a very particular frame of mind. Even though there are many things about school that I love, and there are many teachers whom I adore, I never forget that somehow this is not a place where I belong. And so while there are many things that I remember with fondness, it is not fondness which drives the need for change, and it is the need for change that I want to explore.

I cannot recall a time when I am not being given a model to follow, some example to emulate, some huge, inhuman person to look up to and admire: Columbus, the Pilgrims, Thomas Jefferson, George Washington, Abraham Lincoln, Jesus, Benjamin Franklin, Lewis and Clark, Andrew Jackson, Paul Revere, Thomas Paine, Theodore Roosevelt, Shakespeare, Homer, Milton, Hawthorne, Poe, Emerson, Melville, Joan of Arc, Dickens, Hemingway, Avogadro.

I love the Pledge of Allegiance. My heart pounds every time I give it. What a great thing. What a wonderful thing, to live in this country!

In sixteen years of formal schooling, I never had an Asian American teacher. In sixteen years of formal schooling, I never read a book by, about, or containing an Asian American. Can you imagine that? For yourself, I mean? Not having one teacher who looks like you, not reading one book which reflects your embodied experience or the world view your father and mother taught you from before you could crawl?

"Learn something!" and so I do.

I learn to see Homer, Shakespeare, and Dickens as authors whose works contain the universal truths of humanity. It means hard work every day, struggling with texts that are utterly opaque, but I do not question this opacity because every other kid says the same thing. "Who actually reads this stuff?" we ask instead, full of the disdain of the desperately ignorant. But the test depends on it, so we study. I study. And I read, and I write papers, trying to come up with the right combination of words which will elicit the magical appearance of that blessed A on my paper. Only it doesn't come.

Of course, I think, no one gets this; I'll just have to try harder. So I write and I study and I read and I think, until I become expert at seeing myself as the character. That is the only way, you see, that I can develop any understanding of him at all. And it is what I have always loved about reading all my life. I love to be Batman, John Carter, Conan, D'Artagnon, the Count of Monte Christo, Bilbo, Thor, and Hercules. I want to be them all. I want to wear a sword and fly through space, rescue maidens, and battle evil wherever it can be found.

The Green Hornet. Now there is a cool show; Kato is the best. He is so fast, but there is something else about him . . . I can't put my finger on it, but he is . . . hypnotic. Then they take the show off the air and I can't watch him any more, but there are always a hundred, a thousand other heroes to take his place, so I am happy.

That is the secret to my success in English. I can read because I always loved reading, always loved where it could take me, and the more I lose myself in a character as I read, the better grades I get on my papers. Besides, I have a great vocabulary; everybody always said so. "It's all that reading he does," they said. And so I don't just read the *Iliad* and the *Odyssey*, I am Achilles, I am Odysseus. These stories are about me and they tell the truth about what athletic competition is really about. Yes, here is truth I could know, I do know, and as I look in the bathroom mirror at home, I find myself unable to recognize the boy who looks out at me. He is so . . . Why can't I . . . I wish I had blonde hair and blue eyes and sharp, narrow cheeks. I wish I were good looking.

Did I say that I never forgot that school was a place where I didn't belong? Well, I guess I did.

Belong, that is.

I mean forget.

Didn't I?

~ ~ ~

My Father was never my hero.

He didn't ride a horse, wear a cowboy hat or shoot bad guys.

He didn't watch a mugger kill his parents, wear a cape, or terrorize crooks at night.

He didn't wear tuxedos or have a license to kill.

He didn't invent bifocals or chop down cherry trees.

He has never written a sonnet, a novel, a play, or metaphysical poetry. My father is not a puritan, a colonist, a settler, a slave holder, a priest, a farmer, a statesman, a policeman, a general, a boxer, or the President of the United States.

My Father was always too busy to be my hero. Sixteen hour days with my Mother kept the business going and paid gas bills, electric bills, grocery bills, hospital bills, book bills, and taxes, taxes, taxes.

My Father is short and has slanted eyes. When he was a boy the Japanese occupied Korea, made Japanese the official language, and forced all children to learn it. So my Father is trilingual but his English is still broken. Even today when we talk, I break my English, too, so we can understand each other.

My Father taught me that Judo is the Gentle Way, but it is also a painful, frustrating search for perfection that takes a lifetime to travel. It never helped against the three who beat me in the schoolyard, calling me chink, nip, gook, and slant. It didn't make me popular. It didn't get me the girl.

In fact, nothing Koreans ever did was important. What did they do to build this country? They just worked in their little shops all day. They didn't fight their own war. MacArthur did that. They didn't even star in the TV show.

How could my Father be my hero? We didn't speak the same language, love the same art or learn the same history. How could we? He was too busy working so I could be free.

So I could be an American.

∽ ∽ ∽

I loved comic books as a kid. I still have hundreds of them, stored alphabetically in two large boxes in my closet, waiting for the next time I feel the urge to relive the days I spent poring over them, totally absorbed in the endless battles between Good and Evil. My father came in one day—I must have been sixteen—and I could feel his anxiety over the money I was spending on something he considered a useless waste, so I was surprised when he asked me, "Why you spend so much time on these comics, eh?"

Telling him simply that I loved reading them was no use, that they took me places I couldn't go otherwise, that when I read them the world, for a time, made a simple, clear sense I found beautiful and stirring, that quickened my heart and made me smile. None of that would have made any sense to him, so I spoke instead of the investment these books represented. Pulling out one of my favorites from a series about mutants, people whose physical and mental abnormalities gave them great powers to fight evil while struggling with the loneliness in their souls at being outcasts, shunned and feared by the very society they risked their lives to protect, I said "Look, this one cost seventy-five cents when I bought it; now it's worth almost three dollars!" He was very receptive to this. "Really?" he asked. Seizing the moment, I showed him several more that had appreciated similarly.

I held this instant of connection carefully, this sense of closeness with my father which had become so rare. We didn't enjoy the same things; he was as married to his business as he was to my mother, and I detested the Store and the drudgery it represented to me, an endless, gray and gritty process of moving boxes and dealing with customers I thought of as slightly crazy. A continual tension between us grew out of his desire for me to come in and work at the Store and my own intense dread of the moment he would ask me or order me; not just because he asked me to, but because he wanted me to want to be a part of something he built up for my brothers and me, but me especially because I am his oldest son. To have this tension ease, even for a moment, was to relax a breath I had held for so long that I forgot I was holding it at all.

Excited and hopeful, I went from talking about the financial investment my comics could represent to the qualities I loved most about the art and the stories, how the layouts had changed radically, breaking away from straightforward sequences of six or eight self-contained panels per page to wild explosions of action, characters leaping out of their little boxes to extend across entire pages. Plot had enjoyed a similar liberation, with romantic relationships developing across previously uncrossable lines. Even character development had matured to the point that figures central to major lines were being killed, bringing an element of tragedy to the stories they never had before. But the moment faded; my father was not interested in these types of details, and he went back to his room to finish getting ready for work.

Comics were not the first stories I loved. Reading the Greek myths as a child in my grandparent's house, I was enthralled by Theseus, Icarus and Daedalus, Jason and the Golden Fleece, Arachne and her pride, Pandora and the box that could not be closed again, and Hercules, of course. My favorite characters were the gods themselves. I couldn't get enough of Athene, Poseidon, Apollo, Hera, Hephaistos, and especially Zeus. From these characters with their fantastic adventures and superhuman powers, it was only a short step to comics, and as silly as it may sound, as silly as it sounds to me now, comics were not simply entertainment to me; they were a source of wisdom and virtue as profound and stirring as any story from ancient Greece.

I remember one in particular, a special double-sized issue of Superman where he had to go to a planet which revolved around a red sun which, as everyone knows, being of the same type as the one which warmed his native Krypton, would rob him of the powers he gains from living on Earth, in the light of our yellow sun. There the Man of Steel would have to face their champion, a huge, fearsome warrior, greatest of a warrior race, with the outcome of the battle deciding the fate of the planet Earth. Fortunately, being the challenged race, humans could choose the contest; we selected boxing (how, I don't recall).

To prepare, Superman had to train under the greatest boxer of all time, Muhammad Ali. I can still picture the scene where Superman is walking down the street of a big city, resplendent in his brilliant blue tights and flowing red cape, a shining figure in a neighborhood darkened by poverty and filth. He stood out for another reason, too. Perhaps for the first and only time in the thousands of comics I have read, everyone on the page was anything but White, except for Superman, and it was for this as much as for his clothes that he was noticed. Two Black men watched him as he walked by, and one remarked on how Superman was lucky to be the Man of Steel, being White in their neighborhood. His friend admonished him and said that, among all the White men he knew, Superman was the only one who was "cool" because, despite his ability to see through walls, he was blind in a very important way: "There's one cat who's blind my way—colorblind." ·

Of course, Superman, with Ali's help, went on to win the day and the Earth went on uninvaded, and everything went on as before. That line has stayed with me through the years, not only because of the comic book, but because being colorblind was an extremely important facet of my life. I remember my mother teaching me that color was incidental to who I was, that the real worth of a person was inside, where everything that mattered was kept: his thoughts, his feelings, his character. Color is only skin deep, after all. From this I inferred that to be colorblind was the way to really see a person, and this made enormous sense to me because I knew many people who used horrible words, kids who beat me up on a fairly regular basis. There were three boys in particular who made harassing me in the playground a daily event. One winter day, they caught me on the way home at the very edge of the schoolyard and beat me until I couldn't stand. Then they kicked me for a while as I lay in the snow, calling me names which made no sense: "Fucking chink." "Goddamn nip." "Jap." When they were finished, they walked away, laughing, and I cried for a while. When I looked up, I saw that a crowd of kids had gathered, had watched the whole time, and had done nothing. They continued to do nothing as I got up and walked home. This was how I knew racism, and naturally I wanted nothing to do with it, so being colorblind became my firmly established view of the world and of everyone around me.

This fit in perfectly with school, of course, facilitating the idea that we were getting the best possible education, that the people we were studying—Lincoln, Washington, Franklin, Dickens, Hawthorne, Shakespeare, Avogadro, Planck and Euclid—all of these men through their brilliance, courage, and heroism exemplified the best of human knowledge and experience. To bring up race in regard to these men was simply unthinkable. It would be in the worst possible taste to focus on something so superficial and petty, and obscure what men such as these could teach us. Truly, race and color were utterly irrelevant concerns. I certainly never thought about it, being colorblind.

And then I called Steven a "nigger."

It was during wrestling practice, and Steven was one of only two Black kids on the team. He wasn't very good, and I used to ride him really hard, shouting at him to work harder, scorning him when he lost. By this time, I was one of the major powers on the team, and I felt it was my responsibility to push everyone to do his best. I remember now, though, that I was always harder on Steven than I was on the others, always angry with him and ready to be disgusted with his failure. I poured all this out in my voice as I helped him work harder. "GET UP! You're holding us all back! C'mon, you . . ." and I would trail off, my eloquence exhausted.

One day our positions were reversed. Having one of those days all athletes know when nothing works and the world is an awkward, disjointed place, all my reactions were totally off, and I couldn't hit a single move. Guys I normally tied in knots were holding me down as though I were a baby, or, as I thought at the time, a girl. And Steven was ecstatic. Using precisely the words I had always used, he lashed me, taking every chance to return what I had given him for weeks. Finally, my mind broke open and I turned to him in rage and hate, knowing that something horrible was coming up out of my mouth, out of my eyes, out of a place deep below my belly, and I couldn't stop, couldn't hold back but could only vomit up at him with every drop of red anger in my body, "SHUT UP, YOU NIGGER!"

And even now, more than fifteen years later, my shout pounds at the walls of my skull, a hammering wave of shame and guilt, throwing me off balance and I sit dizzily, trying to blink away my sorrow.

My coach grabbed me and threw me out of the room, shouting that he didn't care how good I was, if I ever said anything like that again, I was off the team. I could only nod, horrified by what I'd said, agreeing with him even as I wanted to die right there. But I didn't die. And I didn't die when I apologized to Steven as fast and as strongly as I could. He just brushed it off and, gratefully, I let him, and I buried that incident quick and deep.

~ ~ ~

I was the teacher. They were the students. I was there to teach; they were there to learn. I planned my strategy in my first year of teaching with this definition of my relationship to my students and by thinking about my favorite teachers from high school and college. These were teachers who listened to me, and in doing so, encouraged me to develop in ways no others had. In their classrooms, I developed confidence in my ideas and began to see the world in a larger way by making connections with great works: *The Scarlet Letter, The Crucible,* Homer and Descartes. This was Learning. They embodied what a great teacher was, and I wanted to be the perfect amalgamation of everything I saw in them.

I wanted to give my students the opportunity to develop for themselves everything I valued in myself: independence, thoughtfulness, intellectual curiosity, and passion. I would develop these qualities in my students the way my teachers had, through strong, energetic discussion, even argument. I never felt more involved and important than in the middle of good, deep debate. I wanted to wake my students up, get them talking, get them to defend their ideas and, in so doing, develop them fully and clearly. In this way, I planned to follow as best I could the adage: "We don't teach you what to think. We teach you how to think." It didn't occur to me then to wonder at the fact that this was something my favorite teachers never said or the absurd paradox it presented.

I assigned a list of vocabulary words, requiring the students to build their own definitions based on how they were used in the reading. They failed the quiz miserably. To "teach them a lesson," I scolded them for their wretched performance and warned them that study habits like these would never get them into college. Two girls started crying, and I was a little worried I had gone too far, but I thought that, finally, I was getting their attention.

In the first week, a boy half my size looked up at me as he left class and said, "You have to learn how we do things around here. We got a teacher fired we didn't like."

I didn't know what to say.

∿ ∿ ∿

"Do you consider yourself a person of color?"

"No!" I declare, shocked at the sudden question in the middle of the morning. I have given some thought to the phrase, but it seems so unwieldy to me, divisive. But, come to think of it, it never occurred to me to apply the term to myself. I have my hands full just trying to figure out what a good teacher is; I don't have time for this kind of thing.

And teaching is such a mystery.

I don't argue so much with my kids, now. In fact, it seems that the less I argue with them, the less they go crazy. I guess I must have learned something over the past couple of years. Grammar is boring no matter what I do. And what does it take to make poetry interesting anyway? We're reading the best, everything that everybody gets. Of course, I didn't like it much either when I was in high school. And grading! I hate grading papers. I write all those comments and all the kids do is look at the grade; sometimes I feel like I'm drowning, only there's no water,

it's like

I'm drowning in the air.

∿ ∿ ∿

"What am I doing here? What is the point of multicultural conferences anyway? I just don't see the use of going into all this. Why does she have to talk about all that Asian American stuff like that? I never thought of myself that way. I never thought of myself as effeminate or invisible and never as a victim. Sure I was called names as a kid, but who wasn't? But, but, but, but . . . ."

Thoughts run through my head on bare, bleeding feet, until red anger forces my jaws open, and I challenge what the woman in the front of the room is saying. My words are incoherent and thoughtless, full of too much rage for memory to hold. Maybe it's because she's Japanese American; maybe Korean experience is different. All I know is that what she has to say strikes me as so much whining that I can no more identify with than . . . than what?

Now this man makes sense, and it's amazing how much we have in common. He grew up in a Chicago suburb not five miles from me. We knew the same places, ate the same food. Sure he's Japanese American, but as I listen to a poem he has written about dating, I hear thoughts I have had in my own head come out of his mouth: "What will happen if I ask her out? Will she like me? What will her friends say?" But the last one catches me completely by surprise. "Why don't I ever want to go out with any Asian girls?"

And I remember.

In high school, every time I saw one of those Korean calendars, with a Korean model on it, how strange she always looked to me. Was she supposed to be beautiful? In college, as a man, those discussions about women which men have, talking about women, and saying that I didn't find Asian women attractive. In fact, I thought them rather plain. And it strikes me now that I was never talking about their faces, the faces of these women.

I was talking about my own.

I am an Asian American. But why couldn't I hear this the other day? Why couldn't I hear this from . . .? Ah. Her.

∽ ∽ ∽

"And all this business of you changing your name from Gene to Gene-Tey," my colleague said to me. "By focusing on your Asian half, denying your White heritage, you have obscured everything in you I can identify with!"

How can he say this? He's
a teacher
What do I say? I'm
a teacher

Why can't we learn together?

I haven't changed my name
I've just decided that I'm sick
of hiding it
hiding from it
pretending it doesn't exist
that the love my father
and my mother shared
isn't complicated
doesn't cross a boundary
a line visible
in my face.

I'm just so tired of being blind.

∼ ∼ ∼

In my last two years of teaching, I offer a senior elective, American Identity, a multicultural literature course which examines works in the context of dealing with the question: "What is an American identity?" It is a demanding course; we read four novels, several short stories, articles, and poems in roughly twelve weeks. In addition, there are at least two compositions a week. Aside from this, the subject of the course itself is most challenging in that it requires students to deal with extremely difficult questions concerning race and gender and how these influence the development of identity. While I conform to the traditional practice of compiling a reading list beforehand, it is the most culturally and racially diverse range of American authors I can compile.

About halfway through the novel, *Ceremony,* we watch *Winds of Change: A Matter of Choice.* This video documents the dilemma many Native Americans face in having to choose between reservation life and city life, of how they endure and integrate profound changes in their most basic definitions of identity and world view. Even something as simple as having a grocery store on the reservation has dramatic repercussions in the very conception of family, of how the tribal members relate to and depend on each other. Off the reservation, the change is seemingly more superficial but is no less severe. Living in the city, leaving tribal life behind, leaving behind language and ancient definitions of mother-child relationships, people go from being Hopi, Navajo, Lakota, or Cherokee and become Indians. With no way to maintain the identity unique to one's individual tribe, Indians attempt to retain some sense of identity through intertribal gatherings, multi-tribal powwows, competitive dances, and festivals.

Afterwards Rikki, one of the White students says, "You know, I watch this and I get so jealous; I don't feel I really have a culture."

As I watch the video, I can't help but be struck by the depth of the differences I see in dress, in speech, in relationships, in ways of being. On the reservation, English is a rich, brown language, spoken with the rhythms and music of Hopi life. "Ceremony is the center of life," one man says. This life mixes T-shirts and football, computers and a modern high school, with an ancient twenty-one day birthing ceremony held in a room lit by incandescent light bulbs. It is strange to me, this cultural combining, even as I recall my own family dinners, where we ate Kalbi and kimchee, drank coke and poricha, stuffed ourselves with chopchae, bulgogi, and yaki mandu, all the while watching the Bears play football on TV.

I am more familiar with the images presented in the second half of the documentary, the big competitive powwows, the fantastic costumes with feathers, bells, buckskins and face paints. These are the Indians I know, the ones I grew up with on television and in the movies. But as I compare them with those who live on the reservation, trying to maintain the Hopi way of life, there is a palpable and dangerous sense of loss. It is not my place to judge which of these lives is more valid, more genuine, to decide which is more truly "Indian." Yet I feel the loss of language, of connection, of a way of life. Of a matriarchal society where the woman is sole owner of the house and all the property of the family. Of a conscious understanding between culture and identity, between the substance of ceremony and the substance of self. Of the richness of words spoken with a distinct flavor, words like family, daughter, Hopi, and identity. All of this is lost, replaced by what I have always known as Indian but now I see as only gaudy costumes; pathetic, fragmentary speeches parroted by children who have no comprehension or attachment to what they are saying; and a son whose parents quietly, but desperately, admonish to "marry Indian," but who admits he finds White girls far more beautiful.

All this, and then Rikki says, "I watch this, and I get so jealous. I don't feel I really have a culture." And she is not alone in her response. Many others agree with her, talking about how they feel their lives are basically empty of any cultural richness. There are no rituals, no ceremonies like this which define their lives. What do they have? Fast food and T.V.

Reading further, we begin to find that Silko's *Ceremony* speaks to us and gives us ways to speak to one another that we sorely need. As we read Tayo's story and we share our own stories about what we do and what we have come to accept as "natural" parts of the high school experience, we begin to see that our lives are rich with ceremonies. What's more, we see that we have not just received them, but that we create them as we go along; they are constantly changing, just as Betonie said. Our ceremonies grow out of who we are so that the life of identities and ceremonies is a continuously dynamic, cyclical event.

So we decide to continue to tell our stories, and what's more, we decide to make them as much a part of the course as the books we read. It is an idea I had originally planned on as basic to the concept of the course but had been forced to drop by administrative pressure.

Now I see that not only was it a good idea but that it was vital to make just such a change. They need to know, I need to know, that our stories are a part of who we are, not just as individuals outside of the school, but in our lives as students and teachers inside the school as well. This need strikes me as so powerful that I make the writing of personal stories part of every class I teach. We write about our families, our histories, meals which represented friendship, the first time we realized we had racial identities, what it means to be a person, and suddenly English is not an imposition on life; it is life.

∾ ∾ ∾

During the last couple of days prior to the final exam, we return to the central question of the course, "What is an American identity?" to see if an answer can be formulated which is applicable to all the works we have read. We find that the works were too diverse to say that there is a single American identity, but that they all illustrate the struggle to define one's self, and they all conclude with a strong sense of being only part of an ongoing process which was much larger than the individual; the struggle for self definition never really ends, and it is influenced by all aspects of one's life. "But how is that different from just trying to be a person?" Rob asks.

A few days after the final, Rob comes to me and explains that when he first came into the course he had two definite thoughts: first, he really wanted definitive answers to questions concerning race, gender, and American identity; second, because of his own experience growing up in an Iranian household and a predominantly white independent school simultaneously, he believed he could speak with authority on books such as *Ceremony,* even though they dealt with cultural experiences different from his own. Instead, he found that the course was not providing him with simple answers, and he was as much at a loss over the novels as anyone in the class. He described how he would come into the class with headaches and would leave confused. The harder he struggled, the worse it got.

Then, he says, it finally hit him that he was experiencing exactly what we had been reading and discussing. His own struggle to find The Answers was exactly what was causing him so much difficulty because he was not taking the time to examine his own assumptions about race, about gender, about his own questions. This realization was so amazing, he said, that he couldn't get to sleep that night; it was astounding and frightening that literature could so closely mirror his own experience. This had never happened to him before.

But that isn't all. He also lets me know how the course has shed some light on his own personal debate about being Iranian American; he hasn't arrived at an answer, but now he is able to deal more clearly with the question of labels and how they can both confuse and clarify an issue. Realizing that he had come into the course seeking The Answers allowed him to change his focus; the frustrating scramble for answers became the satisfaction of clarifying questions.

∾ ∾ ∾

I remember the first day my mother drove me to Montessori school. I turn from the door after walking the whole concrete way from the car where she stands, watching. I look back. She waves to me, smiling, and says, "Learn something!" in a happy, vibrant voice. Terrified, I realize that she is going away, and I am going to go through that door alone.

But she isn't going away, and I have never really been alone. I carry the stories of my teachers, my students, my friends, my family, my father and mother with me all along. I have the stories of many cultures in my blood, growing out of me with my hair. I carry them in my brain, in my belly, in my bones, and in the pores of my skin. They are in the shape of my eyes and in the smiles of my sons. They are in my partner's kindness and warmth of her song.

"Learn something!"

Sounds like good advice.

ABOUT THE AUTHOR

It's really very difficult for me to explain why I wrote a particular piece, because there are usually multiple reasons driving my writing. One of the most significant though, is similar to what Gloria Anzaldua describes in her own process as taking images suggested by her unconscious and making sense and meaning out of them through writing. For me, writing is a way of exploring and discovering the connections between who I am and who I have been, and how these layers of identity operate in and with and through the world around me. In this way, writing has been an increasingly valuable and marvelous key to understanding my experiences growing up a biracial Asian American male in mainstream America, teaching in an independent school environment, and pursuing a doctorate in English Education.

Changing Expectations:
Shifting Narratives on Disability

Melinda Morrissey

M ARTHA JUST TOLD ME THAT HER SON HAS BEEN DIAGNOSED with muscular dystrophy—she doesn't yet know what type. I don't have MD, don't know the first thing about it, but because I am disabled, friends and colleagues often informally consult me about these issues. I don't really mind. I just don't always know what to say, especially when it isn't the person directly affected doing the asking. Usually I try to listen more than offer advice. In this case, I am struck by Martha's sense of loss and her pain. Her son will not be the person she imagined him to be, that is most certainly true. I can empathize with the sudden sense of chaos, the loss of control that has come over her.

When I first began having seizures and other symptoms of what would eventually be diagnosed as lupus, suddenly nothing in the world made sense anymore, nothing was predictable, everything was dissonant. It was about that time that I first read Joan Didion's *The White Album* (1979). In it she says, "We tell ourselves stories in order to live" (p. 11). That is, we impose narratives on disparate events and images in our lives in order to make sense of the world. The trick is that these narratives are never really fixed.

Take some of the narratives I had twelve years ago, before lupus. I expected continued success as a graduate student in art history and I was certain the internships I held would lead to a career in museum education. On a more basic level, I never questioned my ability to articulate my thoughts. When I needed to speak, I could express myself; when I wanted to write, my hand could form the letters. I also assumed that I would go through each day without losing consciousness. Then the narrative shifted. For about eight months I averaged a major seizure every two or three weeks. I left my apartment each day not knowing whether I would come home that night or find myself regaining consciousness in an emergency room or on a street in downtown Chicago (a fact that strangely enough is only truly frightening in retrospect). Since it is extremely difficult for me to communicate after a seizure, I could rarely tell paramedics who I was or whom the hospital should contact. Life became an unpredictable series of good days and bad days. On a bad day I had difficulty articulating my thoughts and using my right hand. It seemed that my body was spinning out of control.

But then again, I never had complete control over my body or my abilities. I only had expectations of what my body should be like based on past experience and what the world—through schooling, film, books, and the media—had taught me was "normal." I just happened to fit in with society's notion of physical normalcy for the first twenty-seven years of my life. Sure, the rest of my life was pretty abnormal and I did have a variety of illnesses during those years, some of them relatively serious. But those illnesses were finite and didn't permanently affect my physical state. They didn't affect the essence of who I was, or at least they didn't affect how other people perceived me and related to me.

This was different. I was assigned new labels—new limits—in discussions with everyone from doctors to friends to the folks in the Department of Motor Vehicles. I was an "epileptic," or in the new terminology, "a person with a seizure disorder." I was disabled but only in the sense that I was on disability leave; disability was linked to the ability to work. And I was incurable, a label that causes extreme frustration in the medical community. Actually, I was becoming a disabled person with an unpredictable, chronic illness that has its ebbs and flows. Over the years some symptoms have progressed while others rarely see the light of day.

In *The White Album* (1979) Didion refers to being diagnosed with multiple sclerosis. She juxtaposes the unpredictable nature of her symptoms and physical future with the social and political upheaval of 1968. This is, to me, a particularly eloquent way of demonstrating that disability is closer to the uncertainties and change which make up "reality" than most of the narratives society creates to form "normalcy." Perhaps that is also why disability and disabled people are often so feared. We not only violate people's notions of how the world (and bodies) "should" be, we are a reminder that anyone can become disabled at any moment.

Unfortunately, I don't think this insight, which speaks so directly to my experience, will bring Martha much comfort right now.

So what do I say? My heart goes out to her, but being on the other side so to speak, my primary concern is how her son will respond to her view of what he has become. After all, he is only becoming who he is. I'm thirty-nine and still fight off taking responsibility for how other people react to my condition. My identity as a disabled person has had eleven years to evolve and it is still evolving. Eric is four. So I struggle to support Martha while trying to somehow express that Eric still has a very real life to be lived, albeit dramatically different than she had ever expected. I offer to ask friends about resources she and Eric might access and, most importantly from my point of view, to see if someone with MD might talk with both of them along the way.

But that still doesn't get at what I really want to tell her, what I want her to know and to believe. Although her son and I currently have little in common, I try to relate how I am coming to experience disability and its ever changing meaning for me. Ultimately that is all I really can do. As I mull it over, I begin to wonder: When did I begin embracing what disability has added to my life, even as others seem to only comprehend the loss?

John Hockenberry (1995) talks about the "harrowing twinge" he gets when thinking that he might have missed the moment of the accident in which he became a paraplegic: "I might have missed what my life has become" (p. 69). Most people would agree that becoming a paraplegic is life-altering but Hockenberry seems to be saying more than that: he is saying that given the opportunity to miss the accident and never be disabled, he chooses the life experience afforded him as a person with a disability. Having a chronic illness, I can't pinpoint a set moment in its onset that would be parallel to Hockenberry's, the critical moment I might have missed. There are, however, moments and encounters that forever altered my perceptions of disability—that changed the narratives I impose on disability experience. To have missed these moments—now that's a harrowing thought.

～ ～ ～

It's the end of a long first day of a summer institute on multicultural education. A group of local performers is on stage. I only remember the final actor. She is in a wheelchair and going through the rigors of applying for disability insurance. The success of her efforts will be in her proving how little she can do. I'm in the back of the room, stunned, sinking into the wall, looking around at the teachers in the workshop and wondering if they can see that this is me on stage, that it took me over a year to fill out the damn application forms because I was so ashamed, that I'm crying and laughing and thankful to be heard, even if it is in someone else's voice.

∿ ∿ ∿

I'm in a large university cafeteria waiting for the disability arts center planning meeting to begin. It's the first I've attended and I have no idea what to expect. I listen to the varied speech patterns and the hum of electric wheelchairs as the group of artists, arts administrators, professors and disability advocates get settled in. I mull over whether I should ask the woman next to me if she needs help opening her boxed dinner, but a man I will later find out is her personal assistant steps in. I eat my sandwich and feel oddly out of place.

When I called Carol Gill out of the blue a couple of months ago, I couldn't imagine that I would end up here. I ran across her comments in an interview on the Internet; I remember thinking how much I would like to meet this person but somehow assumed she lived somewhere like Berkeley. Fortunately for me, she directs the Chicago Center for Disability Research, a unit of the Department of Disability and Human Development at the University of Illinois at Chicago. We met and talked about my interests in disability and art and my uncertainty as to where to go with it. At the time, she was working on getting a doctoral program in disability studies underway. Our conversation sent my head spinning with possibilities. It also provided me with the new experience of being understood when talking about how disability has changed my life for the better. Among other recommendations, Carol invited me to this planning meeting.

But now that I'm here, I wonder, do I really belong? Do I fit in? Will I be accepted? Do I want to be accepted? My disabilities aren't always visible so I feel like I should wear a sticker saying, "I qualify." I try not to worry about this and hope my association with Carol will be enough to establish some legitimacy.

The meeting is finally getting underway. The topic of the day is "disability culture." A facilitator (who makes it clear that she doesn't have a disability and needs us to educate her) begins taking us through a brainstorming exercise on characteristics of disability culture. Words come out slowly at first but then the momentum builds: "talent," "humor," "risk-taking," "resourceful," "joyful," "creative," "frustrating," "opportunity," "active," "possibility," "awareness of other perspectives," "alive," "painful," "proud," "ambiguity," "celebration," and "community."

The words lead to a discussion of who should be exhibited and served by this art and culture center. Should people with and without disabilities be represented? I quietly implode, my inner voice wondering what we would then call it, the "culture center that disabled folks can get into?" But if we don't compromise, will we get funding? Will we offend the nondisabled supporters in the group? Would we, god forbid, appear to be excluding nondisabled people? It's an insidious power play. My head is spinning.

The facilitator tries to bridge the gap: "Aren't we all disabled in some way? There are many things that I can't do. We all have different abilities."

That does it. We all feel compelled to speak at once.

"But it doesn't limit your rights!"

"You aren't considered 'abnormal.'"

"You aren't discriminated against because of it!"

"No one is suggesting that you would be better off dead!"

The voices go on. Carol talks about the medical model of disability in which physical variation is viewed as defect, as deviance from the norm. She compares the disability rights movement with the women's movement, citing the credo, "biology is not destiny," and she notes that an important part of the women's movement early on was simply the act of coming together to share stories and experiences. The conversation is boisterous and rich. One of the voices is mine.

And I realize that I have never been with so many disabled people outside of a hospital; that is, I've never been with an entire group of disabled people as *people*. I've been with groups of disabled *patients*. I see how isolated I have been and I don't want to leave. I am both exhilarated and outraged; most of all I am stunned at the utter certainty of my own feelings. As I tell Carol later, I am realizing that I have "strong opinions that run deep."

Thoughts start racing through my head. I feel so naive, not quite knowing how to explore this new territory and wondering why I hadn't found some of these folks earlier. I want to get to know these people better but I don't know how. I feel that there is a whole world of disabled people out there that I have to get to know NOW. Suddenly I am very invested in this art center; I want it to be a center *of* disability art rather than simply *for* people with disabilities. I want a place to congregate and create that is led by disabled people. How can we know what will result from our center unless we try it? How can we know what conversations will be had, what experiences shared, what paintings, theater, dance, and writing will be created or perhaps, more importantly, which of these will not be produced if we can't gather with one another? For that matter, what might have been said or learned about disability culture at this meeting if only disabled people had been present and, as important, facilitated the conversation? When I get home I call my friend Gail and tell her, "Now I understand why the African American students in college wanted their own floor in the dorm!"

∾ ∾ ∾

"It isn't my responsibility to educate you!"

I've just exploded, in my own quiet way, in a disability studies seminar. I'm not even officially a part of the class; the professor generously offered to include me as I try to learn more about the future doctoral program.

Somehow what I am beginning to call the "full disclosure" law has become a topic of conversation. We were discussing the miscommunication that often occurs between disabled and nondisabled people simply because the visual and aural cues may vary from that of social interactions between nondisabled people. It was noted that the more open a disabled person is to explaining their condition, the more educated, comfortable and eventually, accommodating others are able to be. It all sounds so simple, so clear—so impossible. In practice, this usually means that if nondisabled people ask about the whys and whats of a disabled person's condition, disabled people must dispense information. I find myself trying to explain that this can quickly become an invasion of privacy, that "full disclosure" usually comes back to haunt you in lowered expectations in the workplace and in school, and that for me it is incredibly tiring to constantly interrupt work or play to revisit seizures or lupus and why the sun and certain artificial lighting aggravates both. Add to this the fact that most disabilities vary in some way from day to day, and simple explanations only create more confusion.

Worse still, listing aspects of disability in terms of "what is wrong with you" or what you "can't do" only serves to cast disability in terms of pathology or defect. Although disability is not being viewed in the seminar within the framework of a medical model, the questions that arise from this discussion certainly have me feeling a bit defective. As I try to give an example to support my viewpoint, I realize that I am avoiding any mention of how difficult it can be for me to communicate at times. I suddenly realize that I have been trying to mask these difficulties in this setting while I don't in others. Is this because I may want to apply for the doctoral program and don't want to appear to be deficient or weak?

I had expected to be challenged by this seminar, but I didn't expect how central my identity as a disabled person would become as I read the material, participated in discussions, and formulated research questions. On the one hand, this is incredibly invigorating and exciting. Disability studies allows me to wander through books and articles on art, psychology, diversity and education with new eyes. Writers like Anne Finger, Nancy Mairs and Jean Stewart can be revisited while the work of Rosemarie Garland Thomson, Simi Linton and Carol Gill can be discovered. My training in art history is resurfacing as I become intrigued by representations and themes of disability in the arts and the media. I wonder how artists with disabilities represent physical, psychological and sensory variation in their work. What meanings are assigned to disability by disabled people? How does this compare with the traditional iconography? If there is a disability culture, how is it reflected in the art and media produced by disabled people? How has it been shaped by other representations throughout history?

The joy of this inquiry, however, is balanced by the intensity of my reactions to some of the course material. Approximately half of the required readings for the class are written by nondisabled people. In and of itself I don't object; there will always be a variety of people engaged in this work, and there should be as long as we all take time to acknowledge the subjective lenses through which we view the world. The writers I take exception to seem to analyze with little direct consultation with the subjects; that is, the voices of disabled people often seem to be missing or are easily dismissed in favor of the "objective" interpretation of the researcher. At times it seems that my words need to speak for the entire disabled community (at least it feels that way). But how can my experiences speak for such a diverse range of people?

I wonder about the reactions to my comments and analyses of the course material. If I become angry, are disabled people overly sensitive? If I relate readings or support my opinions with my own experience, do disabled people take things too personally? Are we too close to the situation to do credible research? If I reveal specifics about my disabilities, will I appear to be less promising as a doctoral student? Or worse, will I become the object being studied? And how do I not offend the professor? Do nondisabled people spend as much time considering how their subjective experience impacts their research in disability studies as I do mine (I know my assumptions about disability were certainly different before I became disabled)? It strikes me how different this experience might be if more people who identify as disabled were a part of the class, how important it is to have a sense of connected knowing in situations like these, simply to be understood and to avoid being relegated to the margins.

What really pisses me off is that I am grateful to have experiences of disabled people included and valued (why don't I simply expect this?). It actually goes far beyond that in this case. The professor has welcomed my input, my feedback; the time we have spent hashing out my research question has been invaluable. He truly wants to assist me in defining what I want to study and has made it clear that my contributions are critical to a mutual learning process. He doesn't pretend to have the answers, is able to say "I don't know," a rare thing indeed. Ultimately, I suppose I am learning how naive I have been, assuming that by entering a world where disability studies is central that I would be entering a world where disability is never pathology.

∾ ∾ ∾

My immunologist is struggling to fit my chart under his arm while holding both crutches. "Want me to carry anything for you?"

"No, I've got this part down." I follow him to his office for my first appointment since his accident.

"You're probably sick of people asking, but what happened?"

"I wiped out on a patch of ice on a mountain bike. A real mess; my ankle got the worst of it. I couldn't get around at all for six weeks."

"Well, at least you're up and around for spring." I catch myself. "Sorry, you're probably tired of people pointing out the bright side."

"Oh god," he says, tossing my chart on his desk and leaning back in his chair. "My wife made one comment too many like that the other day and I just lost it. Everyone wants to tell you how grateful to be and won't let you just be in a bad mood. I had to tell her to just let me feel rotten for awhile."

I nod and say, "Yeah, sometimes people don't think it's okay to be angry."

"And I must do the same thing. I've probably pointed out the 'bright side' to you a thousand times over the years."

Well, actually yes, I think to myself. I take the opportunity to point out another annoying habit. "The comparisons to other people 'worse off' don't help either." I resist the temptation to point out the "no whining" sign on his wall. He already knows how much I hate it.

Some kind of role shift seems to be happening here. It isn't the candor of the conversation; that's been a norm over the years. With a chronic illness, it's definitely an advantage to be able to joke around with your doc. It also helps that he remains focused on helping me to achieve and maintain a quality of life as defined by my goals and expectations. And much to the dismay of some other physicians I have had to encounter, he taught me to read reports on my blood work early on and fully expects treatments to be discussed and negotiated. No, he was already a holistic, laid-back kind of guy who didn't pretend to have all the answers. So what is different?

Perhaps the shift here is that he is visiting disability.

"At least I can move my knee now but you know in physical therapy you see a lot of progress and then you hit plateaus where nothing seems to be happening. I'm hoping this is just a plateau right now with my ankle." He pauses. "The scary thing is that it might not be; this might be as good as it will get. Or it might get a whole lot better, I just don't know. That's the hardest part, not knowing."

Did he really say that? Does he realize that, to me, the loss of control, the "not knowing" of chronic illness has been both a source of fear and of possibility? And I think, maybe he is afraid that he isn't just visiting disability. Maybe he is afraid he is here to stay.

We get on to the business at hand, going over my recent close encounters of the medical kind, and my concerns about new variations in the way lupus is affecting my central nervous system. I try to explain my frustration.

"It isn't that I think that something acute is acting up right now; that's not what concerns me. It's the changes over time that don't improve. I can't help but wonder what things will be like five or ten years from now. It's the not knowing."

When my doc nods in agreement, I know he understands what I am saying in a way he could not possibly have before his accident. And

I realize that perhaps our conversation would have been different, perhaps I would not have been quite so candid with him about my concerns and his ability to place them in a larger context, had there not been that moment of connected knowing.

∾ ∾ ∾

In my experiences working with teachers in university/school partnerships, I am occasionally struck by the similarities between the defect/deficit models of traditional doctor-patient and teacher-student relationships. One diagnoses and prescribes treatment to "fix" (teach) and the other is healed, or at least complies with treatment (learns or at least follows the rules). Needless to say, the doctors I benefit from the most don't go along with this "prescription." They don't pretend that medicine is an exact science (usually they don't think there is ever one "right" answer) and they seem to approach each new situation as a joint learning opportunity. They often share some of their experiences, acknowledging their humanity. They don't presume to know what I am experiencing and therefore take a genuine interest in what I have to say, the information I have gathered on my own, and my activities and life priorities. In other words, my lived experience, goals, and knowledge are as important a part of the process—are just as respected—as their research and knowledge. Shouldn't the same be true for the lived experience, goals, and knowledge that students bring to the classroom?

Developing a tolerance for ambiguity and "not knowing" is fundamental to learning, to problem solving, to any form of meaningful creation whether you're disabled or not. I know I'm more inclined to experiment and take risks in all aspects of my life since I became disabled. I think that part of what disability has done for me (when it hasn't been cast as defect), is to resurrect improvisational skills I used in theater and in play when I was younger. For me, "not knowing" is now as much about possibilities to explore and outcomes to eagerly anticipate as it is about anxiety or fear of the unknown. Perhaps that's why the relationship between disability and the arts is so intriguing to me; the arts hone these same improvisational skills, albeit in a disciplined way. It's an odd paradox. Although disability is usually viewed in terms of limits, in many ways it also liberates.

I began writing this essay just before I went to a colloquium on disability studies and the humanities at Ohio State. As always seems to be the case when coming together with other disabled people, I found common language, common experience and a level of comfort that I don't seem to find elsewhere. It's as if a part of me relaxes that I don't even realize is tense. Mark Willis (1998), a writer and storyteller, gave a talk at the colloquium in which he shared stories of his family whose genetic heritage has led to multiple disabilities. Four generations of experience in living with disabilities led him to consider his family members' lives in terms of improvisation: "We improvise our lives out of what we have, composing the score as we go." On my best days, that is the beauty of disability—rigid expectations set aside for the art of improvisation.

～ ～ ～

I'm sometimes asked why I often use the term "disabled person" rather than "person with a disability." Although I am amenable to both, given the choice between the two I feel that "disabled person" is a far more accurate term. As Simi Linton (1998) outlines in *Claiming Disability: Knowledge and Identity*, disability and my experiences arising from it are an integral part of my identity that can't be separated from my "person." To do so is to cast it as something negative that I want to separate from the assumed-to-be whole or normal parts of myself. In many respects I think I would remain disabled whether I still had disabilities or not. The limitations might be lifted, but my view of the world and myself would remain forever changed. And although being disabled can be extremely difficult and frustrating, I believe that change is for the better.

I don't really know why or when this shift in identity occurred. When I consider the moments highlighted in these brief vignettes, a recurring element seems to be simply being with other disabled people outside of medical settings. Reading and discussing literature and research by disabled authors; gathering to begin a new organization; attending conferences on disability studies; and developing friendships with disabled women have all enabled my current understanding of disability to be based on who disabled people really are—what we really do—and how we represent ourselves. This is, I believe, a much more authentic sense of disability experience and identity than that generally represented by the media, medical community and society at large. To return to Hockenberry, I experience a "harrowing twinge" at the thought of not having had these experiences, of having possibly remained isolated in an "able" world.

～ ～ ～

And finally . . .

A couple of years ago a colleague from New Jersey told me something that she had heard on the radio. Apparently in some Native American cultures, health is defined as a "willingness to participate." From this perspective, the majority of disabled people, regardless of the nature of their disability, are probably quite healthy; it certainly casts aside the misguided belief that equates disability with disease and defect. But what of a society that can't seem to tolerate the presence of disabled people, that sets up barriers to participation, and views disabilities as defects to be eliminated? Aren't these barriers and attitudes the real defects in need of treatment? To paraphrase Trickett, Watts and Birman (1994), perhaps it is time to move from a mode of "person fixing" to one of "context changing."

REFERENCES

Didion, J. (1979). *The white album*. New York: Simon and Schuster.

Hockenberry, J. (1995). *Moving violations: War zones, wheelchairs, and declarations of independence*. New York: Hyperion.

Linton, S. (1998). *Claiming disability: Knowledge and identity*. New York: New York University.

Trickett, E. J., Watts, R. J., & Birman, D. (1994). *Toward an overarching framework for diversity*. San Francisco: Jossey-Bass.

Willis, M. (April, 1998) Improvising on the genome. Presentation given at the colloquium, Enabling the Humanities, at Ohio State University, Columbus, Ohio.

ABOUT THE AUTHOR

Putting these moments in time on paper reminds me how much I learn about myself when I share even a small part of my story. I have moved past the issues and struggles of some of these moments and am currently in the midst of others. For the past fifteen years, I have worked with teachers and students in a variety of programs at universities, museums and social service agencies. These have included seminars on inclusive curriculum, museum education and art history, and an NEH Teaching with Technology Initiative focused on teaching history through the study of architecture. I am also the current board president of a newly formed organization, the Disability Arts and Culture Center, and am actively involved in learning more about the expanding field of disability studies.

Listening for Myself

Scott Lowery

MEMORY FOR ME IS A FLOW OF VISUAL IMAGES AND shifting waves of feelings, but there are also sounds which drift back through time like ghosts. Looking for my sources of identity, I find them compressed into one of these sounds, a very particular sound which I can call up and hear in my memory forty years later. The sound (or, more accurately, the sequence of sounds) is a metallic squeaking of the pivot points in my father's lunch box as it swings in his hand coming through the back door, the screen door swooshing shut, and the clank as the lunch box is placed on the linoleum top step and heard from elsewhere in the house. Somehow my various meanings of class and gender, of being and becoming a man are held inside that lunch box sound, waiting like DNA to be opened with the passing of time.

To be male was to be a father. Fathers give horseback rides, down on all fours on the living room floor, neighing loudly. Fathers drive cars and have misshapen leather wallets with money and other official items inside. Sometimes fathers are glad to see you, and sometimes they are too tired to notice. Fathers know about baseball and tools. Most importantly, fathers work.

My father's lunch box was steel, painted battleship gray with a glossy white interior. There was a springy piece of wire on the top half, which held one or two sandwiches that he made the night before

29

(probably bologna or meat loaf on white grocery store bread) wrapped in waxed paper. In the lower half he carried heavier items: a Jonathan apple, a couple of sweet pickles in tin foil, maybe a hard-boiled egg or a piece of cake. Along with a thermos of coffee, this made him as self-sufficient as he could manage. There were no vending machines in the shops where he worked then, and he wouldn't have wasted the money if there were. Sometimes, if I was sleeping lightly, I would hear him go out into the dark morning, carrying only these two things. He had on his work clothes and was fortified for the day. When he returned he was tired, and the lunch box was empty.

My father never loved his work, or even enjoyed it during that time, but he clearly believed in it more strongly than anything else in the world. After a day at work, empty lunch pail resting on the step, he would take his jackknife and coax black dirt from under his finger-nails. He believed in the honor of getting dirty, of making something well, of touching the product of his labor. During sour times at work, as technology pushed craft aside, his anger was that of a person de-serted by his gods. Outraged at the breakfast table on Saturdays, he pointed out to his boys the flaws of the new offset printing used on their cereal boxes or fumed about mistakes made by incompetent bosses. If my mother tried to join in and take his side, calling his com-pany a sweat shop, he would snort and dismiss the notion. He didn't want to share his religion with his wife. She didn't really understand, and maybe he didn't want her to understand. He did want love, and to have fun with his kids, and to eat well and plentifully. Work was his business, plowing ahead, unappreciated but undefeated.

My father is now in his late sixties. He has retired but is still work-ing almost full-time, freelancing in sales, largely out of spite toward his former employers and to give him a reason to get out of the house and out around town. He has turned down chances to do the things he thought he would do now, like golf and fishing, in order to keep his lit-tle business going, and he is making good money that he doesn't really need. Despite arthritis, carpal tunnel, back problems, emphysema and high blood pressure, he is driven forward by the power of work. This is more than a script or a role and more particular than a work ethic. It has to do with what a man does, at least in his mind, and perhaps in mine as well.

When I got a job in a cabinet shop after dropping out of college the first time, I found his old lunch box in my parents' basement and used it myself for a couple of years. For a long time it has been retired to a cardboard box along with other odd items that I keep for no particular reason. If I went and found it in the garage, took it in my hand and swung the handle, I would hear the sound of the power of work, and I would feel like smiling and crying at the same time.

ABOUT THE AUTHOR

My piece about my father's lunch box started as an exercise related to sources of my own gender identity. As it developed, that sound in my memory emerged as a personal seed that had been waiting to germinate. For me, writing is my most productive method of meditation. Specific details can become enigmas to unravel, suitcases to unpack. My recent involvement with SEED work has re-fueled my writing, as both move me toward trying to develop a healthy Euro-American identity (at least to the extent that that is possible until such time as the wheel of oppression grinds to a halt). I am a special education teacher at Winona High School in Winona, Minnesota.

Circle of Letters: Voices of Parents

Erika Thorne with Selma Twigg, Linda Larson,
Teresinha Bedi, Rita Williams, Adam Ahmed,
and Deborah Stark

"This letter is the simplest way to introduce you to my child, my most precious treasure, someone who is cherished and loved by us, unconditionally."

It was Friday night. The thirty-two public school teachers and twenty parents sat together in a circle. They had met each other for the first time two hours earlier, checking into the conference center and eating dinner together. They are attending the mid-year conference of the Minnesota Inclusiveness Program, a non-profit educational corporation that works with teachers, parents, administrators, and community members. This is the third year such a gathering has taken place. The purpose of this conference is to bring together the adults who are shaping the education of our young people to work together toward multicultural education.

These were parents of children of color, parents with disabilities and/or of children with disabilities. Most were working class, all were hard-working, dedicated people whose children had experienced blocks or setbacks in their public school: curriculum which neither reflected nor respected their child's culture, field trips and activities which excluded a child using a wheelchair, technical courses which assumed girls would fail, reduced expectations and increased discipline for African American children. In addition, many of the parents brought painful memories of their own growing up years in public schools.

These meetings with school teachers are important in their empowerment. To speak from the heart to individuals who appear to have power over both them and their children, to sit in these circles outnumbered and with less formal education, is an exercise in leveling the playing field. Speaking and acting tonight as if they can be equal partners with school personnel in creating their children's education brings them that much closer to playing a vital role in their school district.

Now the moment the parents had prepared for had begun. Most had written a letter to a teacher, telling them those things they would want a teacher to know about their child or children. Some had not written but were ready to speak. Their messages were not addressed to a specific teacher, but intended to voice their concern, love, and nuanced knowledge about their offspring. Speaking in this circle was an act of hope.

∾ Selma Twigg ∾

Selma Twigg is an immigrant parent from Brazil. Her ethnic heritage includes ancestors who are indigenous to Brazil, Angola, and Portugal. She combines them in her Brazilian identity, which she proudly calls her "unique root." Selma and her husband are raising their daughter and two sons in an upper middle-class suburb. Selma read a letter about her daughter, who was six years old at the time.

> This letter is the simplest way to introduce you to my child, my most precious treasure, someone who is cherished and loved by us, unconditionally. Someone fun, smart, sensitive and very, very special in our lives.
>
> She is heading to your class with the deep belief in her magical powers and how she is able to magically change wrongdoings into peaceful solutions just by snapping her fingers or with a wink of her eye.
>
> She is heading to your class with a mind that she will be able to change the world into a much better place, with more conscientious minds, more justice and wider chances for everyone.
>
> We, as parents, believe in her abilities, love for learning and also in her motivation and curiosity to find answers, find new ways to solve problems, find better approaches to make sensible choices.

We, as parents, also believe that she has the right to reach her highest potential and to have it done in a sensitive, progressive, and rewarding manner so that her learning is not hampered by obstacles of any nature.

We, as parents, expect that her education should involve ways for her to be seen as a valuable human being, with emotions, determinations, unique thinking abilities that would allow her to learn from her mistakes and actions.

And you, dear teacher, only you, can assure my precious child that you will not fail her, that all the early printings that you stamp her life with will be proof of her ever-growing confidence, knowledge and empowerment which she was only able to develop and acquire with the understanding, deep concern and love from you.

∾ Linda Larson ∾

Linda and her husband raise their two daughters in a working-class suburb. They each have a visible physical disability. One of their daughters has an invisible physical disability. The entire family is of European descent. Linda begins with her own experience, believing this would enhance understanding of her daughter.

I identify myself as a person with a disability because I recognize that society and the medical profession have labeled me that. Even though my husband has a physical disability that is visible, he does not call himself disabled. My daughter has found that in order for her to be accepted and comfortable, she has had to consciously choose not to bring recognition of her disability to the surface. They haven't had the early life experiences I have, and that makes a difference. It's not so much my particular disability, rather it's being part of a cultural group that has been discriminated against. I use this term because of society's issue with this. There's not something wrong with me for having a disability.

As a child, I was stripped down and looked at by a dozen people to be assessed. We wouldn't handle any other child this way. My surgery happened at a time when people told children nothing about surgery. So when I was six and the gas mask was put over my face, I had no idea if I'd live.

I would have surgeries done during the summer so I wouldn't miss school. There's always that letter at the beginning of school, "What did you do in the summer?" I couldn't put that I'd been in the hospital for three months. I had a couple good friends in junior and high school, and I was too afraid to tell them. So I just had no contact over the summer, and they thought I was weird.

The only kid I ran into with a disability was in junior high. He used a wheelchair, and I did everything to avoid him. He was lower on the acceptability scale. Especially with polio . . . the big thing was to get them walking, no matter how uncomfortable. If I could walk with crutches and a brace, I was better.

It is very difficult to be female and disabled. Any type of abuse is 50% higher for women with disabilities than for the general population. Women with disabilities have a very hard plight. When only one's loss of function is seen, a lot of discrimination happens.

There are more things I recall: books on persons with disabilities. The only ones I found were on Helen Keller, who didn't have my particular disability and couldn't answer my questions. There is the book *Heidi*, with Claire as a character with a disability. Over the years I've realized that she got better and her personality and her disability got better at the same time. Then I felt that if I could become a better person, my disability would go away. That puts quite a burden on a child. I didn't realize that other children have the same unrealistic expectations, especially when it comes to physical disability. When I go into the classroom to give a presentation, they want it to go away, too. The concept of disability as permanent is a real hard concept. We need to get beyond that this happens to an individual, to know that this is a part of our world; disability is a part of life.

As a parent, my fear is that it's easier to label my child, harder to seek out what is unique about her. Find out about my daughter as an individual. If you begin to see the child only as a particular label, it's harder for the child to understand themselves as individuals.

I hope you will explore different cultural groups in your classrooms. That opens up so many doors for children. There's a large chunk of history I don't know because I was only taught one facet of it. That is so essential for these children for issues which may come up in their workplace or neighborhood. A person of western European background needs to be able to know Native American history and African American history to function in the real world.

My wish for my daughters is that they're comfortable with themselves and their world. That they feel they have skills to deal with their world. That they have skills to keep physically, mentally and emotionally stable and well. That they're able to feel happy in their world, saying, "Oh, cool, this is a good place to be."

ᕓ Teresinha Bedi ᕓ

Teresinha is Brazilian and of African descent. She is raising her children with her husband, an Asian Indian, in a working class suburb. Her children identify themselves culturally as Black and Asian.

My children are scared on the first day. You'll be a new person in their lives. I'd like you to make life easy for them and respect them as individuals. Be patient with them. Remember they are just children. Any problem, please contact me right away. I'm available any time for any kind of volunteering you need at the school, with my children and any other kids. I make sure I'm available.

It is important to me that my girls develop self-sufficiency. I want them both to be doctors or something else that would make them enough money to support themselves, not depending on a husband. Though I married for love, I feel that if I had had enough support I would be in a different place in my life today. I don't want my daughters to be in the position I was in.

Every student in every class has a cultural background. Talk about diversity, the background of each child. Even if they say it isn't "cool" to talk about, make sure they know that where they came from is beautiful and important.

I hope you would help educate us parents on things like computers and math. We can volunteer our time, then. Give us the basics so we can help the children learn math. It's hard when your kid looks at you and you feel like crying because you don't know the answer.

Open communication between the child, parent, teacher, and all who surround the kids is important. So is meeting with other parents to share concerns, ideas, and plans.

Be my friend, and we can both work as partners for the kids.

ᕓ Rita Williams ᕓ

Rita Williams identifies as Black and prides herself on being very involved in her culture. She is a single parent raising her son, Paris, in a Minneapolis suburb. He was twelve at the time Rita spoke.

The number one thing I want teachers to know is not to stereotype Paris because he's Black. Try to understand his culture, view him as being unique, not negative or threatening. That's the value I instilled in Paris and what I teach him.

Yesterday he came home crying because of what a teacher said. He has had problems with a teacher. I had to talk to a teacher who was treating him different. This is very disappointing, since teachers are mentors to kids. Two of his teachers seem to perceive my child as always doing something wrong. If he was acting out with other students, the teachers would belittle him.

I let Paris know, "If you're playing and are called out, remember that it takes two to make an argument." If it seems like he is being singled out by a teacher or treated differently than others involved, I question it. On one occasion Paris and another child were acting up. The other child did it three times, when my son did it once. I asked the teacher, "Why did you allow the first child to have three chances and my child one?" She couldn't answer the question. The most she said was, "Well, what the other child did was different." But it was worse. When you have your child walk a straight line and a teacher says they're not going to change or even try, it defeats a parent's purpose. It makes it harder to teach and correct your child. The best thing to do is to tell the child, "You've got to do what you're supposed to do to get through class," especially if he's being treated unfairly.

A lot of stereotypes are taught to Paris and to other children by how my son is treated in school. If he's being told, "You're not as good as the other kids. You can't perform as well," then he fulfills that expectation and that's what he thinks about himself.

When I went to talk to another teacher about how Paris felt he was being treated, the teacher said, "I wasn't aware how I was treating Paris. Please let me know if it happens again, and I'll take a different approach." That was so nice! We all have these prejudices, but the teacher was trying to reduce hers.

At the beginning of the year, I speak with the teachers to let them know I'm a firm parent, and if you know there's a problem or you find something wrong, let me know immediately. Don't wait until the situation escalates and gets out of control. It doesn't make sense to wait, but some teachers do. All I need is a phone call, and then we can work together to solve the problem. Most teachers do call, but some teachers can't because of their own prejudice. Most don't know how to handle a situation involving my son because they're not used to it. There are only two Black children attending the school. They may think, "Why should we accommodate them or make anything different?" Since the school doesn't have many Black children, they literally don't try to know what to do.

When I spoke with the district administrator about any concerns, they acted on it immediately. When I spoke with the principal, I wouldn't get a reply. That's why I decided to go to the district.

Each evening I sit down and do homework with my son. He would like for me to tell him the answers, but I don't. When I don't understand, I will call the teacher to get help. When Paris attends high school, I will need help. I'm his tutor, and I depend on the teachers to explain to me so I can explain to Paris in a way he can understand. I communicate faithfully to all the teachers. That's what it takes.

As a parent, I believe you need to know your child. If people say, "He's this way and that way," you have to know your child to know if their claims are true. When he was in third grade, his teacher said, "Have him tested for attention deficit disorder." I did not get defensive. I remembered that he *is* squirmy, like myself. He was tested and, sure enough, he needed medication. I appreciate the teacher 's concern. If I didn't know Paris, I might assume that her prejudice was getting in the way.

I want Paris to be able to stand up for what is right and what is fair. I try to teach him to take a stance and be proud of who he is. I didn't go through any of this at his age because my environment was different. I grew up in a Missouri community where the majority was Black and the minority White. Though the teachers were mostly White, they had experiences and knew how to respond.

For the future, of course, I'm hoping he'll be encouraged to stay in school and go to college. Beyond that, I try to just get him through each day.

❧ Adam Ahmed ❧

Adam Ahmed, his wife, and children all identify simply and proudly as American. They are of Asian Indian descent. He asks teachers to understand several things:

I want to tell you that the important things to me are the food and the culture. I need you to know right away that my children don't eat pork, that they're not used to junk food. And also not pork products, including jello.

Culturally I would like to inform you that we are of a religion that is important to me. Our belief is that there is only one God, not a trinity— that goes against our belief.

My children are used to a second language, and a second language is spoken at home most of the time. If they can't verbalize things, it's not because they are dumb, but that they are speaking a different language at home. It's important to us that they are surrounded by that language. Sometimes it is looked at like a drawback—I'd like you to look at it as a strength. People who have two languages have that much more to be proud of, and have more confidence.

Most of the education is European based. I would want them to know that that's not the only possible base to education.

I'm still struggling with that eternal question: How do I approach the principal or district administrators? I don't want to sound like I'm different, yet I want them to incorporate other things in the curriculum. Approaching school personnel can be difficult because of stereotyping. No matter how long I live in this country, I am treated by many people as a foreigner. Other people assume when they see me that I am a programmer or an engineer. Assumptions can go both ways but are not based on knowing the individual.

There are good things in the system, too. You're not completely isolated in ethnicity. There are some people who are more accepting. But there is a lot of room for greater understanding of ethnicity.

My hope for my children is that they'll be accepted so they can excel. I have a lot of friends who have computer professions. They'll always be working behind the scenes, and their boss gets the credit for what they do. They contribute a lot toward the good of the company, but they don't have direct input or interaction with the company. Somebody else interacts on their behalf. I want my children to be recognized for their work.

➷ Deborah Stark ➷

Deborah is a member of the Cree nation, born and raised until age eight in Canadian Cree country. Her daughter and son also identify as Native American, and her teenage son, through extensive involvement in Buddhism, additionally identifies as Buddhist. Deborah's mother, who has psychic abilities validated in the context of her culture, was certified mentally ill and taken away from her children. Deborah was taken from her homeland and raised in a series of foster homes until being adopted by a European American couple at high school age. She has raised Alexis and Damieon largely as a single parent, in an upper-middle-class house made possible by her adopted parents.

I want the teachers to know that I thank them for doing what they do. It is of most importance. It's with great gratitude for the service they do that I tell them: These are children who live in two worlds, with one foot in their

Native culture and one in the mainstream culture. The awareness of their walk and balance is important in the understanding of relating to them.

Their eyes may see differently, their ears may hear differently, but there is a place that bridges, which is the heart. So when you teach my children, teach them from a point of loving. Remembering that it's not exactly what the mind learns, but what the heart carries into the world that becomes what kind of students they are. Listen to their needs and their wants, share with them what yours are, thus creating the circle and the community that allows them to grow. Hold them gently but not too tightly. Allow for them and you the sovereignty to stand as beings connected to a greater whole, remembering that we are all one tribe.

I ask of school administration that you stand next to the child, and not above them. Nor above the parents.

The school system can support me as a parent best by knowing, feeling, sensing, experiencing that we hold the circle of the community together. You can make it different for them than it was for me in one simple way: Teach the truth.

My sweetest dream for my children is that as they walk as adults in the world, they can hold their sovereignty . . . because they were loved that much.

∾ ∾ ∾

There were many other stories shared as parents voiced their experiences and concerns: the low expectations on the part of some school personnel for African American children; getting notes from teachers when progress is being made, rather than only when problems are observed; a school that has a board right at the entrance with children's and parent's photos with the message, "Parents are a part of our school here."

On this night, parents harbored hope that by using their voices and speaking passionately, truthfully and lovingly on their children's behalf, they would be heard. On this night, both parents and teachers cried. The space had been created where parent voices could be heard and experienced as valid without defensiveness on the part of teachers. They also laughed together, asked about each others' lives, and made commitments to work together. How rare this exchange is and how important it is to multicultural education!

Emerging from the power of that circle, Selma Twigg's letter held the closing thought which, perhaps, could speak for all present:

So my dear teacher, on you lies a great responsibility to help my child fulfill her capabilities of seeing a bright star even when you look up to the sky and just gray clouds cover that quiet, still night. But she believes in her own magical powers! And we are positive that she would be thrilled to share the magic with you.

ABOUT THE AUTHOR

My hope in writing this article in collaboration with parents is that parents and teachers can better connect with each other and work together toward an educational system which reflects and nourishes children of all cultures and backgrounds. I am an organizational consultant, activist, and lesbian passionately committed to fostering anti-racism work among us European Americans, and to building coalitions—especially across racial, cultural, and sexual identity lines. I am part of a worker-owned collective, *Future Now,* dedicated to training and consulting on social change issues.

Hollywood, My Children and the (New?) Kung Fu

David Mura

L AST FALL, SAMANTHA, WHO'S SEVEN AND OUR OLDEST CHILD, talked about how Disney and the movies were not making films with Asian or Asian American heroes. Therefore, she and her friend Diwa—who's Thai-Filipino American—were going to shoot a video about Asian Americans. They decided to film the story of Ruby Bridges, one of the young black girls who desegregated the schools in the South (Samantha has a book about Ruby's story). Sam and Diwa played the crowd, picketing with signs saying, "Whites Only." Then they played Ruby and her teacher as Asian Americans desegregating a school.

I said to Diwa's mother, a Filipino American film scholar, "Maybe we're doing something right."

My childhood consciousness of identity was quite different from Samantha's and Diwa's. Growing up in the melting pot fifties, with the media of *Leave It to Beaver* and *Father Knows Best,* and stereotypes like Hop Sing or Charlie Chan, living in a midwestern suburb with few

---

This article was first published in *The Journal of the Asian American Renaissance,* Volume 2, 1996.

Asian Americans, I spent my childhood denying any ties with my ethnic identity. It took me many years to realize the fallacy in such thinking. I didn't understand how the culture had led me to repudiate my
ethnic background, nor how my parents' silence about the internment
camps had affected me. I had no language to talk about the issues of
race or how I'd internalized the message that to look the way I did
meant there was something wrong with me.

Obviously, I don't want my children to grow up the way I did. I've
read to my daughter books about Japanese Americans and the internment camps, about African Americans, Native Americans and Latino
Americans. I want her to have a sense of the rich tapestry of peoples
and experiences that make up this country. More than simply teaching
her about Japanese culture, I want her to understand what it means for
her to be Japanese American and a person of color in this country.

Still, there are complications here I don't know what to do with. My
wife is three quarters WASP, one quarter Austria Hungarian Jew. In
many ways, I assume my children will learn about their WASP background, since that background is deeply embedded in the school curriculum and media. When Samantha turned three, though, it became
apparent that she thought her mother, as well as Susie's mother and father, were Asian American. Asked who the whites were, she replied,
"The bad guys?"

It's difficult to separate my feelings toward the dominant culture
from the ways I talk about American history or my children's WASP
background. When my wife and I first visited her WASP grandparents,
her grandfather crept into the room where she was sleeping—we were
unmarried at the time—and whispered, "Don't make a mistake with
your life, Susie."

Not surprisingly this same grandfather was also prejudiced against
Jews and was never told that his daughter had married someone who
was part Jewish.

Recently, we've learned new facts about the Jewish side of my wife's
family. One is that distant relatives died in the Nazi death camps.
Samantha's immediate response was, "I had relatives who were in the
concentration camps in Europe and in the camps in America." These
past few months she's been especially interested in books about Ju-
daism, and she asked that we celebrate Sedar this spring.

Will my daughter one day accuse me of teaching her to neglect her
WASP background? Will she find silences and gaps in my pictures of
her family's past and who we are? When I look at her, I want to see her

as Asian American; that's an identity I've worked very hard to learn about and accept. And yet I know she'll have to come to terms with her multiracial, multiethnic and multireligious heritage. She will have to face questions of identity that I have not. She will find her own answers.

Still, I do have my own opinion on these questions.

I know that many people would want to look at her identity as simply a colorful mosaic, as if all the parts of her heritage should be regarded as equal, blending in harmony. However ideal this sounds, it doesn't reflect the world she'll live in. Given the way she looks—her Asian features are noticeably visible—the world will respond to her as a person of color. She will grow up amid a welter of stereotypes which still persist about Asian and Asian American women as exotic, submissive and sensual. She will also find that many whites will want to see her as an "honorary white," part of the "model minority" that is placed in opposition to other people of color. This is merely another way the deep seated problems of race in this country are denied.

To me it's important that she see the history and presence of racism as a crucial part of her identity. It's important that she see links between the struggles of Ruby Bridges and African Americans against racism and similar struggles by Asian Americans. It's important that she realize that the great-grandfather who was prejudiced against Japanese Americans was also prejudiced against African Americans and Jews. It's important to me that she understand the reasons behind the internment camps—racism, war time hysteria, a desire for the property of Japanese Americans—and also the way that racism permeates more subtly the portrayal of that experience in a mainstream media vehicle like *Come See The Paradise*.

These historical connections are, of course, part of her WASP heritage, and there are whites who do acknowledge them. But at present I do not see a WASP identity which finds the history of racism central to its own understanding of itself. Instead, the tendency is to see that history as an unfortunate sidelight. It is what that WASP heritage wants to forget, not remember.

The images and stories produced by the mainstream media reinforce a sense of white supremacy that most whites and even many Asian Americans are not always aware of. It's important for us to teach our children to view that media critically, to question who is telling our stories and creating images of us, and to what purpose.

That struggle of education seems to me part of the building of an Asian American identity. We must help our children both to combat the negative media images around them and to create their own images and stories themselves.

A couple years ago, on a week long business trip to Philadelphia, I found that each night I turned on the television I could find a movie or program with Asian gangsters or kung fu fighters. Each time an Asian man's face appeared, I said to myself, "I bet within a half hour, he's going to get beaten up or killed by the white hero." For five nights in a row, my prediction came true.

For me the problem of such movies runs deeper than my dismay at negative stereotypes. My three-year-old son's favorite game now is hiding beneath the covers, waiting for the "bad guys." What will the "bad guys" look like to Nikko? Who will my sons identify with—the white hero or the Asian villains?

Growing up, I watched war movies with John Wayne and Richard Widmark mowing down row after row of Japanese or Korean soldiers. I watched Hop Sing cook for the Cartwrights on *Bonanza*, Peter the cranky Chinese housekeeper kvetch and clean for *Bachelor Father*. I watched white men play the buck-toothed, thick-glassed Mr. Moto, and the bovine eunuch detective, Charlie Chan, while Keye Luke played Charlie's bumbling number one son. I knew Ming the Merciless was somehow related to Fu Manchu. And I came to feel that there was something wrong with looking the way I did; only by denying who I was could I become a hero.

Will my sons feel the same? And will the temptation to deny their Japanese American background be even greater given the fact that they are half white? Nikko is starting to understand there's a difference between Asian Americans and whites. "Daddy's Asian and you're white," he said to my wife the other day. But in our culture, the two halves of his background are not equal.

To combat media stereotypes, I read Nikko the story of Momotaro, the Japanese folk tale of a boy who is found inside a giant peach by an old childless couple. The boy eventually goes off to fight the Ogres on Ogre Island who have stolen and oppressed his village. Nikko loves the parts where Momotaro vanquishes the Ogres, where the Japanese boy acts heroically.

Unfortunately, he'll find no images like that in American movies or television. Momotaro the Peach Boy can't compete with James and the Giant Peach.

But it's not just that Batman or the male heroes of Disney movies are always white. Recently, when Hollywood filmed the internment of

Japanese Americans in World War II, the hero of the movie, *Come See the Paradise*, wasn't a Japanese American man. It was Dennis Quaid, who played an Irish American married to a Japanese American woman. I've shown the film to my children because I want them to learn about the internment camps. And yet the message such films send to my daughter and sons is: If a hero is needed, he'll be white, and he'll always be the sexiest, most intriguing character. Moreover, the Asian or Asian American heroine will always choose him over the Asian man.

Still, this movie was benign compared to the countless movies where Asian men are villains, as in *Rambo II*, *Rising Son* or figures of ridicule, asexual bumbling nerds or robotic businessmen as in *Sixteen Candles* or *Gung Ho!*

There are some who might see the recent spate of American martial arts films as a promising way for Asians and Asian Americans to make it to the big screen. Given my experience in the hotel room with the kung fu cable hell, I don't feel this way. Almost invariably such films present a view of Asians and Asia filled with faux orientalisms and a melange of stereotypes from the exotic east. The Chinatown of *Showdown in Little China* resembles more the Little Tokyo of *Showdown in Little Tokyo* than any actual Chinatown; the movie versions are both rife with secret back alley rooms of gambling and drug trade run by tong gangs or yakuza who still cling to the "ancient" ways; nowhere in these films do you find anything resembling a real American born Chinese or Japanese, nor do you get any hint of the complex processes of generations and assimilation or the political and regional layerings within an actual Chinatown like the one in San Francisco. (Compare, for instance, the Chinatown of *Year of the Dragon* or *Kung Fu: The Legend* with the Chinatown of Wayne Wang's *Chan is Missing*.)

Just as importantly, these American made martial arts films invariably reinforce notions of white male supremacy even as they make a titular bow to the "east." Yes, there may be Asian fighters in these films, but from Chuck Norris or Stephen Segal blockbusters to the cheapies like the "Showdowns" to the kid versions like the Karate Kid series or the Three Ninjas, it's the white males who are shown to be the ultimate martial artists and who take up center screen. The Asians or Asian Americans are relegated to the role of the best buddy or the kindly "Wisdom Tooth" teacher. And even here their relative goodness is predicated on their association with the white hero (echoing, of course, the good colonial native, who doesn't rebel against the white masters). Moreover, the "good" Asian character is offset by the hideous portrayals of the Asian villains, whose portraits still go back to the stereotypes of Fu Manchu, World War II movies, and the opium and gambling dens of the decadent "east."

What are we to make then of the recent success of Jackie Chan? In certain ways it's a little too early to assess what the Jackie Chan phenomenon means, other than the fact that it will almost certainly inspire Hollywood rip-offs, where white actors attempt badly to imitate Jackie Chan. It's important to note that Jackie Chan comes to us by way of Hong Kong rather than Hollywood. There are no American made films like Jackie Chan's, with an Asian man at the center, or, as in the recent *Supercop,* with an Asian man and an Asian woman at the center (what an unusual concept). Then too Jackie's success has much to do with his hard work and daredevil stunts and his comic genius; he's a unique figure, an exception to the rule as it were, that a large mass American audience cannot stomach an Asian male at the center of the screen. And having given Jackie his due, we should observe that Jackie's genius is comedic. His martial arts persona is one laced with irony and self-deprecation. Unlike Stephen Segal, Jackie never takes himself or his martial arts skills too seriously; he's modest; he smiles a lot. "I act the clown," Jackie says in a GQ interview. "I fight hard, yes, but when I get hit, I show that it hurt." As one Chinese American friend remarked to me, "He's non-threatening. Sure, he got on Jay Leno. But what does Jackie do there? He makes fun of his accent. At the Oscars, he makes fun of his height. On Rosie O'Donnell he and Rosie do a mock fight and he lets Rosie smash a chair up his crotch. Isn't that a little too obvious? Even though he's a martial artist, he lets white people feel they're still in charge. He lets them bust his balls."

Don't get me wrong. I love Jackie Chan. My wife loves Jackie Chan. I'm sure my boys and even my daughter Samantha will love Jackie Chan once they see his movies. And his presence on the wide screen does mark some sort of change. And yet, as I was watching *Supercop* recently, even as much as I was thrilled by both Chan's Harold Lloydesque stunt-jokes and Michelle Kwan's kick-ass style, I suddenly flashed on another star of color from my childhood: Cantiflas, the diminutive Brazilian comic who appeared in such films as *Around the World in Eighty Days* and the eponymous *Cantiflas* in the fifties. It's easy for white Americans to eat up a star of color who's funny and whom they don't have to look up to. And because of his Hong Kong origins, Jackie's films don't really grapple with the issues of race, and if such issues do appear briefly, as in *Rumble in the Bronx,* they're quickly exiled. Which is exactly how the white audience wants it to be.

The one possible exception to the white men as master in the martial arts genre is *Dragon: The Bruce Lee Story.* This is not to say that the film is great art; it's definitely a work of mass culture, titillating the masses with high energy, over the top, kung fu choreography, along with bits of hokey Orientalist mysticism, playing on the supposed curse that hung over Bruce Lee and his family. Still, to my eye, there is something subversive about this movie, despite its divigations to the fantasy mysteries of the "orient." For one thing, in the whole film Bruce Lee never gets beaten up by a white hero; instead, very early on, he dispenses a group of prejudiced white attackers, along with one black attacker, with ease, proclaiming proudly, "I'm not a gook. I'm Bruce Lee." (Tellingly, it is the black attacker and the least macho white attacker who sign up for Lee's martial arts school.)

Beyond this, what made the movie remarkable for me when I first saw it were things the mainstream white audience probably saw as secondary or didn't even notice. For one thing there was the uncanniness of seeing the relationship between Bruce Lee and his Caucasian wife on screen. I am so used to never seeing anything in large scale films which could provide even a corollary to my relationship with my wife that I felt a certain amount of anxiety or discomfort during the first scenes between Lee and his wife, as if some part of my own psyche were being exposed, as if I were somehow naked up there on the screen during the love scenes.

At a certain point in the film, Lee and his white girl friend go to see *Breakfast at Tiffany's.* When the buffoonish Japanese photographer comes on the screen, played by Mickey Rooney, everyone in the movie audience is laughing, including Lee's girl friend. She turns to look at Lee. He is not laughing. "Let's get out of here," she says, and this incident marks a new stage in their intimacy. As I watched, I was struck by the uncanny use of *Breakfast at Tiffany's,* since I had used a parody of the Mickey Rooney character in my first performance piece, a parody which underscored the ways I'd felt humiliated by the images of Asians in American pop culture.

And this, beyond the bi-racial romance, is why the movie struck me. For Bruce Lee lived this humiliation not simply in seeing stereotyped figures on the screens of American movie houses, but in his own struggles to make it as a film star, in his own frustrations and disappointments fighting the racism and glass ceiling of Hollywood. Like many Asian Americans in corporate America, Bruce Lee was not struggling at the bottom of the social or economic ladder. He was struggling to break through at the top. His frustrations were those of an Asian American who finds out that despite his wealth of talent, despite his abilities, despite his hard work, he will never reach the level he knows he deserves to reach; he will never break into the mainstream; he will always be a foreigner, an "other," a "gook." Ironically, Lee came up with the idea for the martial arts series, *Kung Fu,* and saw it as a vehicle to move him into a leading role and stardom. But the role was given to David Carradine, a white actor with none of Lee's martial arts background or charisma. Lee left Hollywood and America for Hong Kong, where he could obtain leading roles and where he managed to make the films that have created his reputation.

In one of the last scenes of the movie, there's a disturbingly authentic scene where Lee's wife asks him to leave Hong Kong and come back with her to America. Lee bursts out in fury and shouts that he's not going back. He talks of how America is pictured as the promised land, the Gold Mountain, but what you don't know until you get there, is that that promise, that gold, is only for the whites, and you don't see this until you read the fine print, and if you don't read, well, you don't even see the way you're shut out. He says he's not going back to play gooks, and goes into a monologue where he imitates Oriental stereotypes with a manic fury, exaggerating his accent, making his teeth look like buck teeth, and screwing up his face, just like Mickey Rooney in *Breakfast at Tiffany's.*

The initial time I saw *Dragon,* I told my wife: "That's the first time I've ever seen something on screen which reflects the rage inside I feel over race, the anger I have over how I've been humiliated by mainstream American culture, the ways I feel shut out. It was scary seeing that. And affirming. It helps me see I'm not crazy."

A film like *Dragon* reaffirms for Asian Americans that our experience of America does involve the issues of race; our experiences here do not solely involve the clichéd conflicts of East vs. West or the "bi-cultural" dilemma. There is a racial hierarchy in this country which is as American as apple pie, and one of the most telling examples of it takes place week after week on the screens of American theaters and on the cathode tubes in our living rooms. I want my children to see *Dragon* not only because it provides them with a true-life Asian American hero, but also because it will give them a glimpse into the Asian American psyche and Asian American feelings about this racial hierarchy.

What does the media future bode then for my children?

With all too few exceptions then, Hollywood and the mainstream American media continues to appall and astonish me by their lack of creativity and sensitivity, their blatant and unthinking regard for the complexities of Asians and Asian Americans. Whether in kung fu vehicles or in mainstream "serious" dramas like *Rising Sun* or *Miss Saigon*, we get the same stereotypes and Orientalist plots repeated over and over again. Recently, Hollywood has even decided to resurrect Charlie Chan, although with the small improvement of having a real Asian American actor, Russell Wong, play the lead role. Our choice still seems to be either total absence or racist dreck. The only exception is the work of Asian American independent media artists, with their limited financial resources and their resourceful creativity. Documentaries like *History & Memory* about the memory of the internment camps, or *A.K.A. Don Bonus* about the life of a young Cambodian American, or small budget narratives like *The Great Wall* or *Dim Sum*—this is the media our children need but seldom have a chance to see.

When I recently asked my children what they wanted to be, Samantha said she wanted to be a visual artist. Nikko, only three, said he too wanted to be an artist and also a "karate guy." Talking to a friend, Samantha once said that when she grows up and becomes an artist, she'll become a member of the Asian American Renaissance. Nikko talks more these days about Ninja Turtles and superheroes like Batman and Robin than anything really about art; his remarks about art were just echoing his sister's desires. Certainly he evinces a desire for fighting and physical prowess that Samantha has never shown, and though I can name all the reasons, including sexism, why that might be, I don't ultimately know the cause of this difference. At the same time, I sense in Samantha already a rejection of many of the clichés of girlhood. Inspired in part by Maria Cheng's performance piece, Samantha recently created an installation of chopped up Barbie parts. She hates pink and dresses, doesn't see much in Disney's Jasmine, and favors quirky white girl heroines like the title character in *Harriet, The Spy*. At three, Nikko's imagination seems to me more conventional, mirroring my obsession with cowboys and six guns when I was a child (I wore a holster everywhere I went).

At any rate, they both know they are Japanese American and Asian American, and each night before they go to bed, they say prayers to Buddha. They know about the internment camps, and Sam can even tell you why the hero of the internment camp movie, *Come See the*

Paradise, is a white guy rather than a Japanese American. They both know that the pictures of Native Americans in *Peter Pan* and *Pocohantas* aren't accurate, though they probably don't perceive the exoticism in something like the Ninja Turtles.

And yet, I sometimes wonder if I spend too much time inoculating them against the racial supremacy inherent in the media, too much time fostering their critical mind, and too little time emphasizing their own ability to create new visions, to bring their own subjectivities and stories into the world. I emphasize defense rather than offense, skepticism rather than initiative, skewerings of present works rather than the possibilities of future works. This, I suppose, is evidence of my ties to the past, my inability to project myself into the unforeseen that will unfold, openings I can't conceive. In this, I too, like Hollywood, show a lack of imagination and creativity.

I want my children to go beyond me, to reach some other summit, enter some new land. And, of course, they will. But whether they will still find Disney's Snow White myths and Hollywood's kung fu clichés there or creations to reflect their own stories and community, I don't know.

ABOUT THE AUTHOR

As a parent of three bi-racial children, I'm concerned with the effect of the media on the way they look at themselves and at those of other races. I think that people often underestimate the effect of the media on the self-image of both children of color and white children. I want my article to help teachers and students understand the complicated ways through which the media perpetuates racial stereotypes and the effects such stereotypes have on Asian Americans, who are sometimes left out of or neglected in discussions concerning race. I am a *Sansei* or third generation Japanese American poet, creative nonfiction writer, critic, playwright and performance artist.

in a "different" voice

memry roessler

why do we mark the changing of a young man's voice while the
loss of the young woman's voice passes unnoticed?
why do we celebrate the young man's "finding" his
voice yet fault women for attempting a parallel search?
how did we come to lose our voices so that they
must be found?
why does our search begin so late and take so long?

throughout my life i have thought often about voice—about the
changes in my semantic self.
i have thought about my pre-contact voice—that is to say, the
voice i used prior to negotiating a speaking space in this man's
world.

> a voice melodic and abrasive
> a voice fluid and erratic
> a voice sensual and innocent
> a voice connected and distinct
> a voice imperative and yielding
> a voice passionate and discontented

when did i lose these voices?

maybe i lost them when my first grade teacher frowned at my out-
burst
maybe i lost them when my father said i should be seen and not
heard.
maybe i lost them when my report cards said "she talks too
much!"
maybe i lost them when i discovered that boys don't bother with
girls who "talk too much."
maybe i lost them when i saw that silence in class was rewarded.
maybe i lost them when i let others speak for me.

i have listened to a symphony of these lost voices—unchained
melodies at once empowering and bittersweet.
i have heard voices that

> celebrate, deliberate, elaborate, accentuate, exaggerate, stimu-
> late, alleviate, communicate, intoxicate, invigorate, reverber-
> ate, interrogate, extrapolate, speculate, congratulate,
> penetrate, investigate, integrate, commiserate

such a conglomerate! it makes my heart ache!
i hesitate to contemplate the splendor of it all
i wish only to luxuriate and not debate
listening to my lost selves resonate!

ABOUT THE AUTHOR

I came to teaching through an alternative licensure program that targeted
underrepresented populations. I stay in teaching because of the students.
I am a mother, mestiza, mediator, and "midwife." I see my work with students as helping them to become critical thinkers. I currently teach high
school English and serve as a multicultural resource specialist at a private
school in Minneapolis.

OPPRESSION

Not everything that is faced can be changed, but nothing can be changed until it is faced.

—James Baldwin

Humor As Armor

Lillie Pang

I HAVE A CHILD. MY CHILD IS A CHILD OF COLOR. A GIRL. Adopted. As she enters the world of peers and playgrounds, daycare and preschool, I watch with trepidation. And I can't help but think I want to send her out into the world in a suit of armor. I can't help but think she'll need a suit of armor!

I worry about what life will be like for her. How can I protect her? I want to give her the gifts of toughness, assertiveness, common sense, fairness, and most of all humor as a way to deal with painful experiences.

When I was growing up and life became too oppressive, it was a sense of humor that buoyed me up and kept me going.

"Hey, Chink!"
❧ And Other Greetings from Junior High ❧

After my third-hour English class, I would have to walk past Mr. Santano's door and down the hall to get to Ms. Johnson's science class. It would never fail that as I rounded the corner, my thoughts of how to avoid dissecting an eighteen-inch bullfrog were interrupted by, "Hey, Chink!"

Oh no, not again. If I keep my head down and walk as fast as I can, maybe I can avoid this idiot.

"You, Ching, Chong!! Speaky the English!"

I thought of saying, "I'll show you English, you @#@$$%!!" No, no, just keep walking, don't look at him, it only gives him satisfaction. Keep walking.

It's hard being one of fifteen non-Black students at my high school of 2500. I guess students like to take potshots at other students. Being a minority within a minority is hard. I thought my classmates would understand how hurtful such comments were. Why was I being picked on? All I want is just some common human decency. Not this race crap. And if it's not race, it's "Fat Mama" this and "Fat Mama" that.

Damn! I can't take this anymore. Where are the teachers when you need them? Where are my friends? "Hey, Carey, wait up for me." Let's see . . . only 300 more days of school left. I've got to find a better way to avoid this guy. I've tried being the first one out of English class. I've tried being the last one out of class. I've tried a curt response. I've tried yelling. Just a few more weeks and the semester will be over and I won't have to walk down this hallway again. Just a few more weeks. I can do it. I can make it until next semester.

"Hey, Chink, go back where you came from!"

Well, where I came from was Newark, New Jersey. I had a teacher in ninth grade who asked me to tell the class about China. I was so embarrassed. I didn't know anything about China; the farthest east I'd been was New Jersey.

She was mean, Ms. Y. She was so mean she would brag that "Nobody can move me. I'm the Rock of Gibraltar!" She would belittle and embarrass students into silence. I guess that's the form of behavior management she found effective. I hated her class. She was an equal opportunity demoralizer.

She would call on Mimi Chang. Mimi's dad and my dad knew each other. They came from the same province in China. Her family owned a Chinese restaurant in the northeast section of the city; my family owned one in the northwest section. Ms. Y would zing one at Mimi, and Mimi would just smile and nod her head, lower and lower and lower, and if you dared stare long enough, you could see the tears. But I didn't want to draw Ms. Y's attention to me, so I would just stare at the picture of Mesopotamia in my text book.

My friend Tamika was sitting in the front row and Ms. Y was trying to get us to talk about some country's exports. She went to Tamika, put her hand on her afro and patted, saying, "I'm giving you a hint." Then she would yell, "WOOL!" Bam!! Another student smacked down into submission.

❧ Check the Box, Any Box ❧

It was up to me to get all the forms in I needed to go to college. My dad thought it was a waste of time for a girl to go to college. I would just get married anyway and my husband would take care of me. Well, that was his plan for my future, not mine. I wanted to go to school to be a teacher. I had read a novel about Helen Keller and her teacher Anne Sullivan in fourth grade, and I knew then and there I was going to be a teacher.

The vision was there; now I needed to make it a reality. My grades in high school were good and I was very involved in community service projects, from volunteering in hospitals to camping as a senior Girl Scout. I would be the first one in my family to go to college directly from high school. That's if I could get my parents to sign all the forms for admission and financial aid. It would be important to catch my parents in a good mood.

Boston College, Catholic University, Boston University, Seton Hill—all East Coast schools were on the top on my list. Let's see, four financial aid forms, four grant forms, four loan forms, four scholarship forms, and four physicals. That's a lot of signatures. I think I'll start with the easy ones, the application forms. Name, date, street number, street name. OK so far. City, state, zip code, schools attended, clubs, organizations. Pretty easy form. Race: White, Hispanic, Asian, American Indian, African American, OTHER . . . . Yipes! A land mine. Other, other, white . . . no, Chinese . . . no, other, other, other. I would just freeze for a while and think . . . .

Let's see, my mom is second generation Italian and my dad is from China. They met at the steak house where my dad worked. They fell in love and broke the law. Whether it was an official law or an unspoken one, I'm not really sure, but my mom "married outside her race."

When my mom would take us to New Jersey to visit our Italian cousins, they would tell us not to leave the car while they went into a store to buy something. We were to stay in the car. It would be embarrassing for them to explain they had Asian cousins. Other . . . Other.

I had two older sisters—one who embraced her Asian heritage; another who didn't. I found myself somewhere in the middle. I could not pass for Chinese. I could not pass for white. I tried to pass in college but at every turn was asked, "Are you Indian?" "Are you Tahitian?" "Are you Eskimo?" DAMN, I wanted to yell, can't you see I'm trying to pass!!! So I learned I couldn't pass. I also couldn't be just one exclusive of the other. I was a blend of two cultures, Asian and European. I was mixed. So I checked "Other" and next to it wrote in "Chinese-Italian." If there were any questions about this choice from the application makers, they would have to deal with me directly. I had a strong suspicion that whoever was asking this question would just add a tally mark to the "Other" category and call it a day.

∾ The Downfall of a Liberal Arts Education ∾

It was hard to leave the inner city of Washington, D.C., and find myself smack dab in rural Pennsylvania. I went from Motown to hoedown in one long summer car ride. Why did I choose to go to *this* college? All my friends were in schools in Massachusetts. I, too, could have been picking up a Boston accent, but Boston College couldn't offer the financial package I needed to attend.

Catholic University in Washington, D.C., offered me a full ride with one hitch—I would have to live at home for my first two years of college. That would have been impossible with nine sibs and two parents eager to wed me off in an arranged marriage. This bolted me into the flight part of the freeze-flight syndrome. So, it's off to this all-women's Catholic college in rural Pennsylvania and Sister Mary.

I was enrolled in my first class of the semester, first class of my whole college career: Speech and Communication. Was I prepared for this? I who had just graduated an honor roll student from a public high school. I was beginning to panic. What was I doing here with all these rich, Catholic school girls?

I stood before the class with my three-minute speech ready to go. My topic—Catholic Pentecostals. After the speech I stood by the podium in my three-inch chocolate brown platforms and matching shirt dress while Sr. Mary proceeded to rip me up one side and down the other. I felt humiliated, out of place, ridiculed. But this was college, this was hardball. I knew I would have to improve my speech. I waited until after class to speak to Sr. Mary about it.

She was on her way out of class and surrounded by her theater major groupies when I mustered up enough courage to say, "Excuse me, Sr. Mary. You said to make our speeches in a conversational tone. That's how I did my speech."

"Yes, I did. And your conversation is wrong. You have an impediment," she hissed back at me, never breaking her stride. Hmmm, I have a speech impediment. I never knew that. I went to the counselor on campus to find out who I needed to see about this impediment.

The counselor told me to see the speech therapist on campus. So I did, and after four sessions, she told me I had no impediment. This was reassuring. With this information I felt I had a chance to pass my course. I had two strikes against me: one, it was rumored that Sr. Mary was not fond of Catholic Pentecostals (my topic of choice), and second, what she thought was an impediment in my speech was really Black vernacular.

An African American student from Maryland told me she was in the gym and heard someone "talking Black." She went to find what she presumed was another African American student but instead found me talking to my friends. And as she put it, "Imagine how surprised I was to see this Chinese girl talking Black!" Having attended a school with Black students, "talking Black" was the language of communication.

It's Sr. Mary who was the uneducated one here. She was so sheltered that she didn't know I was speaking Black English and that it wasn't an impediment but another way of communicating.

∾ Reality Check ∾

My first year of teaching was a real challenge. I was teaching at a central city school in Milwaukee. I was a volunteer with a religious order. My life that year consisted of teaching kindergarten half the day and bringing communion to the elderly and infirm the other half of the day.

In November of that year, a kindergartner taught me a valuable lesson—listen to the student; each child comes into the classroom with a wealth of knowledge and experience; tap into it and honor it. My experience as a student had been void of this honoring of my experience and culture.

I was teaching the hand-print turkey art lesson where children trace their hands and turn the shape into a turkey. All the kindergartners were listening intently to my instructions. They started working and I did what all good teachers do; I walked around and gave them encouragement and praise.

I came to the desk of a child who was busily coloring. I looked down at him and he looked up at me and said, "Chicken!" I responded, "Turkey." "Chicken!" he said again with delight. "Turkey," I said, then stopped and really looked at what he was drawing. Sure enough it was a very beautiful cartoon-like chicken. "Chicken!" I said. And I thought to myself, "That's right, kid. Don't let me tell you what your reality is!"

But it is not only students who find others willing to falsely define their reality. Spring is the time when the snow starts to melt in Minnesota, and the district issues teachers' contracts. Susan, a white teacher, and I were hired the same year. Every year around contract time she would start to get nervous. At the time, our district had a policy to lay off all non-tenured teachers and then hire them back in the fall. It was a nerve-wracking formality that we all had to endure.

Each year Susan would say, " You don't have to worry about being hired back." "What do you mean?" I would ask. "You know, you're a teacher of color." I was stunned. If the district was going to hire me back, it would be because I'm a damn good teacher. She seemed to feel that all the jobs in the district were for white teachers and that if a teacher of color got a teaching job, s/he was taking it away from someone white.

Teachers of color were not taking white people's jobs. We were applying for jobs that were posted and for which we were qualified. I needed to check my reality with other teachers of color in my district.

Sure enough, the teachers of color that I spoke with were hearing this same comment during their lunch periods. White teachers would make outlandish, racist comments about hiring practices. This wouldn't be the last time someone made an outlandish comment to me.

❧ Hello! ❧

A teacher once asked me if my daughter knew who her real parents were. HELLO! We are her real parents. She entered our family through adoption. We love her, change her diapers, feed her, clean gooey spaghetti from her hair and delight in her discovery of the world around her.

"Mama, I'm thirsty. Mama, read me the comics. Mama, stay with me til' I fall asleep."

"Who do I love?" I ask her.

"ME!" she shouts with a hug.

Yes, you are my darling daughter. You are in awe of life's simplest pleasures. You who make frequent stops during our walks to pick up a leaf, rock or flower that has caught your eye. You who turned my world upside down and I landed on my parenting feet.

Our home shelters, shapes, nourishes and supports you. As you enter the world of peers and playground, daycare and preschool, I watch with trepidation. And I can't help but think I want to send you out in a suit of armor because that's what I know you'll need. As a girl. As adopted. As a child of color.

At dinnertime in our house, we ask each other how the day went. "So, how was your day? Did you get to the zoo?" I asked my daughter.

With a very serious face she says, "No."

"No," I say. "I thought you and Mommy were planning to go to the zoo. You were really looking forward to it."

"No, we didn't go," she says seriously and then she breaks into a smile and says, "Can you see my dimples? I'm just teasing you, Mama."

I had to laugh and think—she's beginning to develop a sense of humor. She'll be able to use that sense of humor to help protect herself from thoughtless and hateful comments. And that's no joke!

ABOUT THE AUTHOR

Through this article I hope that teachers will understand how important it is to know and respect the gifts that our students are to us. Each student, no matter what age, comes to our classrooms with experiences that are to be valued and honored. As I reflect on what I have written, I realize there were harsh times during my school years. If it weren't for my humor and my faith, I would have lost myself to self pity or have been stymied by blind rage. I currently work with students in a Minneapolis public school. My partner (also an educator) and I are raising our daughters in Minnesota, with hope and lots of humor.

Targets of Oppression: GLBT Students

Michael Williams, Matt Nielsen, and Janet Bystrom

OPPRESSION TAKES MANY FORMS IN SCHOOLS, AND YET often those who work in schools overlook, avoid, or feel "there are more important things to do" than to address them. While many go through everyday life pretending that problems don't exist, there are people being continuously hurt by being the target of oppression. One group for whom this is a constant experience is gay, lesbian, bisexual, and transgender (GLBT) students.

In my experience, these students often feel they need to be silent, to keep "it" hidden in order to fit in with other students. I choose to work with my colleagues on this issue, not because I want to but because I have to. I have heard the personal stories of students who are gay, lesbian, bisexual, or transgender—stories that rip through my heart. It is important to listen to the experiences of our students, and I have found that inviting former students to return to their school and share their stories with former teachers can help us begin to address these issues.

Two people who have shared their story with me and other teachers now share their story with you.

❧ Matt Nielsen ❧

I was one of the lucky ones who had it figured out early. I didn't know what to call it or how to claim it, but I knew it was me. And I knew the world didn't like it. So early on, I walked in two worlds: one full of expression and truth; the other a young man hiding. I showed the world a normal kid doing everything the right way, the best way, so that no one would ask questions or notice, or if they did notice at all it was to compliment an achievement or behavior that proved to them I was OK. I feared that if anyone found out, I wouldn't be welcome on the team, in the house, in class. The worlds were born in fear and stayed apart in fear. But things change, entire worlds change with the landmarks of experience, and the decision to be different. These are my landmarks. This is my story.

My earliest memory of sexual separateness happened in grade two. Beth, the second grade diva, had cornered me in the gym during recess. We were on four-wheeled scooters, and she and her gang of giggling girlfriends trapped me in a corner as she planted a wet one full on my lips. Even then, as the girls gushed and my buddies sheepishly grinned, I didn't get it. It wasn't titillating or even interesting. But I recall wishing it had been my best buddy John instead of Beth.

I did well in grade school and was busy. I read a lot and won contests. I liked to be in plays, I played soccer and sang in choirs. I heard the words "fag" and "queer." I hurled them. Even played "Smear the Queer," not knowing what a queer was or did. But I knew I didn't want to be one. The worlds stay apart.

Gays made the news now and then, usually portrayed in drag and partying during a pride celebration. The images were far from the docile suburban neighborhood I was accustomed to. My stepdad made a comment about Adam and Steve. With each image I learned. Gays are strange, wear weird clothes, live in the city, and make the news.

We learned quickly from Bibles in the church basement the passages which spoke of the "sin" of homosexuality but didn't understand them. It certainly wasn't me. In a rush of hormones and curiosity, I learned of sex. "How bodies function" was an uneasy class discussion. The guys on the soccer team talked of girls and their body parts and growing expectations of kissing and sex. There was excitement and anticipation that I couldn't participate in. The worlds flew apart. Kissing girls, touching them held nothing for me. But I didn't tell anyone that either. The words "fag" and "queer" were beginning to mean something to me. I stopped using them. I avoided any talk about girlfriends and sex, topics that were beginning to dominate my buddies' lives. I felt isolated.

High school was filled with activities, school, work, music, theater, soccer, anything. I made friends easily but stayed mostly on the edge, accepted by lots of folks but never really having a group of friends. I stayed separate. I was the perfect son and student because, if I wasn't and if they knew, I would be more alone.

I was a sophomore in high school when I first began to think of myself as gay. I discovered a gay newspaper at a local theater during the intermission of a play my English class was attending. In a coatroom rack, I found a newspaper filled with stories and pictures and news about gay men and women. All of the images and thoughts that I thought were stuck only in my head were laid out in black and white for everyone to see. I wasn't alone. Here, in my city, were other people like me, normal people, with a paper. I put one under my coat. Read it. Hid it. Read it again.

I went back to that coatroom every two weeks to get the next issue. I felt that it was at least possible for some people to walk in one world.

In my junior year of high school, full of hormones and libido, and a spark of confidence born of the new image of gays I had found in the paper, I found myself interested in a guy from my school. He was a year younger; we both sang in the choir and played soccer together. I recall writing a note to myself: *a guy loving another guy, what would people think?* I was afraid. I became depressed and let things slide: schoolwork, relationships, everything. I wore dark clothes, wrote bleak poems about death, and dreamed of running away. Teachers, parents, friends, all became concerned. I stopped eating, planned suicide. The loneliness was all encompassing. Dying seemed to be the only way to quiet the struggle, to protect myself. Dying was the way to keep the truth hidden: the son, brother, student wanted to touch and love another guy from the soccer team.

During my struggle a teacher sat me down in her office and asked a laundry list of questions. She asked if there were problems at home, with drugs, with friends. She asked about sexual identity. It might have been the moment when despair turned to possibility. Someone opened a door. Someone had made a space in the world for me to be a young man with a sexual identity that wasn't assumed or taken for granted. In that space and time the two worlds could come together, but I wasn't ready.

I really liked John. We were friends, and I sought as many opportunities for us to be together as I could. He was cute, athletic, nice, well-liked. I wanted to tell him I liked him. He had had girlfriends but something in me wondered if he had thoughts like mine about guys. I didn't know.

Late one night, while he and his family were on vacation in late winter, I put an unsigned letter in his mailbox. It explained I was a guy he knew, a guy he liked, and that I had feelings for him.

In the weeks after his return I just watched him, looking for signs of safety, of discomfort, uneasiness, anger. Anything that would provide some clue about his feelings about gays, about a friend being gay, about a gay friend attracted to him.

A month later, on our high school choir tour, John and I stayed with two other friends in our hotel room. It had been a long, hot spring day and there was a weird tension. John and I tussled for a quarter that had fallen on the floor. We wrestled with an intensity that held an undercurrent. Not anger. Not sexual. More like business. In a headlock, it ended.

Two hours later. Quiet and heavy. Our friends asleep between us. He whispered, "Risk it."

My heart pounded. My mind raced and my eyes filled. All the years of being alone, ashamed, afraid came crashing into the present. It seemed like forever, but in the dark I whispered back, "I think I am in love with you." My worlds were coming together.

I went away to college and found many other men and women who, like me, shared what still felt like a secret. Those relationships, tribal and full of community, gave me confidence and a new, stronger voice. Stories were told of first crushes and families. For the first time there were friends to walk with and eat with and talk to. The labels "queer" and "gay" became Erica and Joel and Jason and Jack and countless other people whose lives intertwined with mine.

In my sophomore year of college, with a new boyfriend and a supportive group of friends, I came out to my family. I wrote each of them a letter and stood trembling on a warm spring day as I dropped them in the blue postal box by the campus student center, uncertain of the response they would bring. Friends were coming out to their families. Some had had support. Others lost it entirely. One even withdrew from school as hurt and angry parents withdrew financial support. I had been honest and respectful in my letters and I took the task seriously, wishing to no longer hide the truth from these important people.

I told my family that I am a gay man. My secret heart. I told them how hard it was keeping it from them. I told them how hard it was not to tell them about my first crushes and the discoveries I was making. I told them I grieved with them the loss of their expectations for what they wanted for me. I told of happiness and excitement and the pride I felt about the truth. I told them there was an open door to me and that I loved them and hoped they could understand.

Two days later I stood in the student center retrieving messages from my machine. After the beep was my mother's voice: "Matt, we love you. No matter what." Another beep. "Matthew. It's Grandma. This doesn't change a thing. Grandpa and I love you." The fear behind a lifetime of hiding and control disappeared. My sister's first words to me were a comforting, "Oh, that." She claimed she always knew.

I walk in one world now. I am still afraid sometimes, but the truth really did set me free. My family astounds me with their acceptance. Community abounds and relationships rise and fall. I am whole, blessed by this lens of mine. Every once in a while I am asked if I would change if I could. I wouldn't change a thing. Who else gets to walk in two worlds and bring them together? Nope. I wouldn't change a thing.

∾ Janet Bystrom ∾

The question people usually want to have answered but are too afraid to ask is, "How does a person get gay?" As a lesbian, you'd figure I'd be able to help answer that one, but I'm afraid I'll have to disappoint. There was no moment at which I became a lesbian anymore than there was a defining moment you "became" the sexual orientation you are. Regardless of my sexual behavior at any given point, my sexual identity has always been a part of who I am.

There was, however, a defining moment in which I knew the rest of the world would begin to consider me a lesbian. That was the moment I first kissed another woman. A junior in college, I found myself very drawn to my friend. We would go out for coffee study dates, and the only thing we'd end up studying was one another. I never said out loud how I felt, to her or anyone else. I was too scared. We would hug good-bye when she dropped me off at home, and I had the unmistakable feeling that something was missing.

One evening, in my room, we talked late into the evening. She had shared some personal things and I was comforting her. She laid her head upon my chest. As my heart raced, I pondered the consequence of a kiss on my life. In living color, I saw my mother's face, heard her voice, "Now, it's just not normal for two women to be holding each other like this!" I saw my father's disapproving frown. I spoke to them, "But what's the big deal? One kiss doesn't necessarily make me a lesbian! Why can't I just do what feels right to me?" I saw my own dreams of husband and children vanish before my eyes. We kissed. There was stunned silence. I cleared my throat and asked, "Have you ever kissed a woman?"

"No," she replied. "Have you?"

"Well, just my mom, but it wasn't anything like that."

Think of a time you've met someone really special and how you talked about that person so incessantly that people want to smack you, but you're in such bliss you fail to notice. Well, the telling is a privilege. I was on cloud nine but couldn't share it with anyone. I needed time to sort all of this out for myself before coming out to anyone else. Despite my silence, I figured people could tell, like I had a big scarlet letter "L" on my chest.

I did tell my parents two months later. My educated, liberal parents, mind you. My mother wept. "Are you sure?" she said. "What will our friends think? I know I never should have sent you to that college! She made you that way, didn't she?" My dad said he felt persecuted as his sister is a lesbian, too. Hmmm, sorry Dad. That wasn't my intent. Really, it wasn't.

I wasn't sure what to make of it all myself. I'd had good relationships with men all through high school and college. And now this. My parents struggled hard the first few years but have grown much more comfortable with the idea of my being partnered with a woman.

One moment sticks out in my mind as especially meaningful. My mom was raised in Missouri, the daughter of a Baptist Bible Belt preacher. She was taught that wearing lipstick was a sin, not to mention homosexuality. Most of her family still adheres to those beliefs, so you can imagine she wasn't too eager to tell them about her daughter. One weekend, about three years after I had come out to my folks, my mom was visited by her brother and sister-in-law. I didn't think she would tell them about me, not wanting to rock the boat on such a short visit. I called her up prior to going over, wanting to confirm whether or not they knew about my sexuality. I said, "Mom, did you tell them?" She replied, "Yes, I did." I said, "How'd it go?" She said, "It went fine, just fine. You come out here, you be comfortable, and you love yourself." When I could finally speak again, I said, "Thank you. You have just given me a gift I will remember until the day I die."

The ironic part is that whenever I am reminded of that story, the two words that come to mind are family values. In that moment, I felt more valued than I ever had before. When my mom said that, it wasn't because she was totally accepting of my sexuality. It was just that she loved me so much, she was able to transcend everything else and love me fully for who I am. She touched my core.

I think people become teachers because they see that core of humanity in each kid and want to touch it and nurture it. They are in a unique position to create a climate in their classrooms in which each person will feel valued and respected regardless of or even because of his/her culture, class, ability, sexuality or religious beliefs. If you teach them any lesson at all, let it be that.

I know the demands on teachers are endless. You have tests to correct, classes to plan, and questions to answer. What do you do when you're rushing down the hall and hear someone say, "You faggot!" As someone who has worked with adolescents, I have sometimes let it go, unsure of what to say. I wonder if intervening will make things worse. I doubt my ability to say something without being shaming. And so I am silent.

One time, I wasn't silent. I saw these two guys in a mocking way doing the stereotypical gay lisp and limp-wrist routine. I had no idea what to say; I just knew it felt disrespectful, and I said as much. One of the guys just blew up in my face. He was over six feet tall with a short crew cut and weighed over 200 pounds. He stormed out of the room. He said, "Why are you on my case all the time!" I was stunned. After a few minutes, I followed him into the other room where he was hunkered over a table. A piece of paper he'd been doodling on was wet with tears. "Sometimes you just laugh about it to make it easier," he said. We ended up having a great conversation. He said the fact that he didn't "look" gay made it harder for him in some ways. No one ever suspected. It turned out he was suicidal, had been drinking a lot and driving his car recklessly, not caring whether he lived or died.

What that interaction taught me was that whether I feel armed with the perfect intervention or not, silence is not an option. Even if I am for some reason unable to respond in the moment, I will eventually address the people involved. Keep an eye out for the kids who get picked on day in and day out. Maybe pull them aside and let them know you notice. Ask them what they would like you to do if you ever witness them being harassed in the future. They may tell you to bug off, but they will know that you are an ally. It's amazing how many kids who say homophobic things have positive relationships with gay friends or family members.

People often panic when the word "gay" is brought up. Doesn't that mean the kid is destined to live a lonely life of torment and harassment? Not necessarily. People will only struggle with their sexuality as much as those surrounding them. If you go to District 202, the drop-in center for GLBT youth, you'll see lots of bright, talented, college-bound kids who love themselves. Their sexuality is an integrated piece of who they are. So be aware of the risks but don't panic.

Recently I began dating a woman who works across the street from where I work. I was encouraged by my co-worker to take her a flower. It would be romantic. I got all worked up about it, then realized I couldn't do that because I didn't know if she was "out" at work. How would it look to have another woman bringing her a flower? So I got her a latté instead. As I handed it to her, I said, "This is a flower." We laughed. It is funny and it's not. It is a perfect example of how the best and most innocent parts of someone can be twisted, squashed, and hidden. To me, that is a tragedy.

∽ ∽ ∽

My colleagues and I have heard other stories as well from former students—stories of being taunted, beaten up, talked about, teased, and laughed at. Stories of having students empty a fire extinguisher on them, all the while inviting other students to come and "look at the queer." The story of a student being beaten up in the hallway, summoned to the principal's office to discuss "her" problem, and finding the center of her homophobic universe—dear old Dad—waiting. Stories of being thrown out of the house and living on the streets until finding a safe place to live.

I have heard the stories of students, and I have to do this work. Listening to young people's voices, experiences, and suggestions about what we can do to make our schools safe for all students is a good place for this work to begin.

ABOUT THE AUTHORS

Michael Williams I am a 1990 graduate of Grambling State University, Grambling, Louisiana. I have been a resident of Minnesota since 1992. I received my M.Ed. from the University of Minnesota in Special Education. I am beginning my sixth year of teaching at Fridley Middle School in Minnesota.

Matt Nielsen I heard someone say that courage is not an individual act but an act of community. That it's somehow shared by those who have had a hand in creating you and standing by in those moments when you need to do the right thing. As a kid, a gay kid, and now a gay man, I thank those who have shaped me. Having felt courage's power, it seems only natural to speak and write on its behalf.

Janet Bystrom I have this idea that people will struggle with being gay/lesbian/bisexual/transgender only to the degree that those around them struggle with their identity. After all, you don't see too many people wrestling with their heterosexuality, do you? Thanks to a wonderfully supportive family, friends, and workplace, I sometimes have to remind myself that I am a member of a marginalized community. I feel called to write and speak on this issue on behalf of all of my sisters and brothers who have not known such safety.

Poor Folks Have Dreams

Etta Norwood

WE OPERATE OUT OF CLASS IN THIS COUNTRY, BUT WE DON'T talk about it. There's no acknowledgment that there's not a platform from which to speak about class, especially for the poor. And the poor are up against it already. So they don't confront and they won't push because that could create even more pain and that would be unbearable.

Maybe that's why there isn't a lot said about poverty when you're in it. You wait for things to change and look back on your experiences. There isn't any clout from that position, that's part of the not talking about class oppression: talking about it feels like exposure.

I grew up poor. I came from a legacy of people who refused to go on welfare. No matter what we didn't have, we figured out how to get by. The pride was in not taking welfare benefits. When we didn't have, we borrowed. When we had, we had to pay back. You're always underneath, never on top, trying to figure out how to be strategic, how to get through.

It sometimes looked like people on welfare had more than we did. They had when we didn't. There were so many times that we went without food that I still think in terms of food. I buy a book and come home and say, "I won't eat tonight. That's OK."

There are experiences that come out of poverty that are not seen as strengths. As a survivor of poverty I save everything that may be used again someday: the plastic forks, paper bags, envelopes, scraps of paper with surfaces not yet written on. I remember visiting a college friend at her home one weekend. I met her mom as we walked down a tiny, tiny little hallway. Piles and piles of stuff were all over the house.

I understood. When you don't have anything and don't know where the money will come from, you have to save everything. We save because we might need. Everything that you come across is important. So I felt at home in my friend's house because I understood they didn't have anything, either. They saved everything.

But there's a contradictory side to poverty; spending like there's no tomorrow, as though our happiness had to be consumed today. Who knows what hard time is waiting for us tomorrow? Worse, who won't survive another day?

Poverty builds some kind of character: to make judgments between the two—saving and embracing the immediate. The money may go in exchange for having joy. The respectability may go in exchange for a good belly laugh. The demure demeanor may go in exchange for a deep, mournful cry that needs to gush forward.

Money has all value and money has no value. It takes so much to fill what is needed, that, in a sense, it doesn't matter because if you have it, it goes. Money is the pin. It moves everything around. Enough is such a large amount, seeming so far out of reach, that you piss it away if you have any. There is no hope about saving because you're always at a deficit. In its place is an emphasis on the experiences of the day. That's what matters.

I notice that people with money talk about it a lot. I was sitting in a meeting with employees of my district and they began to discuss the "Rule of 90" as though everyone knows what it means. Their failure to acknowledge class in that room caused them to make this assumption. Then the words savings and annuity come up. It did not fit into my context of living: before, now, or in the future. I don't even think about those kinds of things. Because I started with not having enough, I didn't think about piling it up. Getting into neutral territory where you don't owe or you're not doing stuff to get around not having is as good as I can imagine it being.

> I couldn't let them know.
> I had to remember to lie
> and to make sure that nothing I said contradicted it.
> I had to keep the lie straight,

thinking through
each comment
no matter how trivial,
to make sure it didn't give away the truth.
I was afraid of being found out.
Sometimes I heard someone mention they had less,
didn't fit in well,
like I didn't.
But I couldn't let them know.
I shared the same feelings but because they were white,
that would usher in another kind of betrayal.

So there I was,
the only one;
Not the only one poor,
but the only one black.
And no one could ever come to my house
or they would find out.
Find out the shoes had newspapers in them,
the clothes were taken up
or pieces put in.
The clothes came in boxes.
The clothes came from May's, not Macy's.
Oh, don't misunderstand me.
I was schooled well at home:
what fork to use,
where to set my glass,
how to sit up straight at the table,
how to leave a small portion on the plate,
like it wasn't so good you wanted every bite
and could even lick the plate.

No, I knew how to "carry myself"
so that I was always comfortable among wealth.
But was I comfortable?
I learned how to lie and shut down,
shut down on every question,
how to skirt all issues
and how to be vague,
oh, vague, vague . . . vague as hell on a foggy morning.

I'm so clever at not telling the truth
that a dodging no-information-giving statement is liable
to come out of my mouth in response to a question like
"Where did you come from?"
Before I tell the truth I would tell a half truth
and have to clean it up.
Always keeping people at a distance
so that I am not found out.
Feeling like I'd like to be closer, but it isn't safe.
And every violation of that code of distance
is an entryway for betrayal
and the betrayal is only a question of when.

I would like to have more:
To go to the store and shop. Just shop.
I would like to live in a nice house, too,
with grass and wood and shiny things and my own room.
But it seems that that takes more money
than I can even imagine.
But I enjoy theirs. Their having.
I just know it's temporary for me.
At some point, I have to go home.

To feel the pain so keenly of not having the clothes one wants. Dressing without care of other's eyes, using whatever is there in the closet, thrift store racks, sales tables or give-away bins. To overdress when one feels it, not when the occasion calls for it. To underdress when one feels it, to be numb to the attention of others about clothing. Not concerned about the outside wrapping when the substance of the inner experience has become so important. The only thing to hang onto is the quality of relationships.

Relationships. That's the bond, the tie, that faith in the other person, not about money, or time, or land, or acquisition, or annuities. Believing that the person will come through for you. The will and desire to fulfill commitments to each other is so strong that someone or something else will come if they don't come through. That's how strong the commitment to relationships is.

To be concerned with my friends, my family, my community, my spiritual experience, my anything I can posses and hold—my relationship, my laughter, happiness, joy. Do I still fit? Do I still belong? No

matter how small poverty shrinks me or how wide wealth might in-
flate me—do I still have family, friends, community, neighbors, walk-
with-me-seekers and followers? Is it still *us*?

Us and we are what we hang on to. The togetherness of our experiences. The memories and everything that builds a memory is of value
to hang on to. Cast away any care of tomorrow and enjoy the moment,
the voice, the day.

> There was always room at the table
> in the home of the poor when I was growing up.
> Poor folks always had room for another dog,
> another mouth,
> another empty tummy that needed to be fed.

> But poor folks have no room—
> no room for rich folks who take,
> no room for selfish folks who eat in the presence
> of those who are hungry.
> Hungry for love, peace, joy—
> Hungry for a sense that it's going to be all right tomorrow.
> No room for children who won't share toys,
> adults who won't share their last dollar.
> No room for worry about things we can't change,
> that go on whether we are present or not.
> No room for care about politicians not elected with our money,
> a promised housing development project,
> another storm that may or may not come.

> No, what has importance is what's going in the soup.
> Do you have corn and a little bit of basil?
> A smile, a good laugh, and we have enough for today.
> And plenty more for whoever needs.

Poor folks have character if nothing else, character and dreams.
And what it seems most people know about people living in poverty is
what they don't have, not what they do have.

This is important. Children become the fulfillment of the dreams.
In the middle and upper classes, people talk about what they're going
to do with their parents' inheritance. It is understood that this is always something that is either given away, comes to them, or is divided

among them. But in poverty there is nothing left to the children. The children are the wealth. It is the children who take care of the parents financially. It is what children do with their lives that is the legacy of the parents.

> Some day it will be better
> it will get better.
> Poor folks have visions and dreams and desires
> tucked in tearful places
> too tender to be poked at
> by the fumbling hands of not caring.
>
> Poor folks have dreams of the somedays:
> someday when I finish school,
> someday when we can buy that car
> or house or land;
> someday when I can paint, write or play music,
> someday when I can play.
>
> Poor folks have dreams.

ABOUT THE AUTHOR

I was born and raised in the city. I wrote this piece to participate in the work that may help people recognize their own voice and hear the voices of others; to hear and articulate the voices of strength that come out of poverty; and to identify the qualities of character one can depend on and predict finding in survivors of adversity.

So Are You Gay?

Michael White

I KNOW THERE'S TROUBLE WHEN A TWELVE-YEAR-OLD GRINS AT me for no apparent reason.

I kicked this same kid out of my class two days before for repeated noises and other disrespectful behavior. While I called down to the office, he flashed a picture to the class as he walked out the door. I didn't see it, but I heard the tittering of the class.

"What was that all about?" I inquired in the most nonchalant voice I could manage at the moment. "I must have missed something." I've learned that the kids who can't keep their mouths shut while I give directions are the same kids who unwittingly turn in their friends. "Oh, Jason had a picture in his notebook he drew."

"Oh, great," came quietly between my lips. "Hmmm. What was it?" I say again nonchalantly and non-threateningly to Jason's classmate. I don't want to give him any reason to refuse my request by implying that Jason is in any more trouble with me than he already is.

"Oh, it was a drawing of a guy with a goatee and glasses and an earring." More snickers in the class. But they see the realization on my face. Hmmm. I hadn't had my picture taken that year, so maybe a student's drawing would fill in for the time being.

Two days later, the same class returned to my music room. And there was Jason, grinning in all his impish, spiteful glory. He prominently held his notebook up so I had a clear shot at the picture he drew during the previous class time, moments before leaving my room. There indeed was a man with a goatee and glasses and an earring. I also noticed the man parted his hair on the same side I did. How coincidental. The man apparently had a tattoo on his forehead—GAY. I took an internal deep breath to keep from chewing him out in front of his peers (a perfect set up) and went into my "inquisitive teacher" mode again.

"Jason, what's this?"

"Oh, that's a drawing I made." His grin widens in proportion to my annoyance with him. He was going in for the kill again. That tone was in his voice.

Jason had been quite adept at pulling me into power struggles that year. He'd make a noise and I'd shoot him a look. He'd wait until I'd start talking and make a different noise. I would ignore it once or twice and then give a warning. Jason would wait until I got started again with instructions, then he'd make yet another, different noise.

Jason would loudly contest my discipline approach in front of the class, others would attempt to intervene on his behalf, and within seconds I'd lose my cool. By this point I'm trying to tell myself that at least I'm aware of how easily he can push my buttons though I haven't been successful with my responses up to now.

"Who is that?" I inquire, straining that professional stoneface into a somewhat non-emotional look.

"Oh, this guy?"

I'm about ready to put him in a headlock and not ever worry about teaching again when I hear myself calmly reply, "Yes, him. The man who has the word 'GAY' on his head."

Now, I wonder if Jason thought that a teacher, me included, would just ignore "GAY" on the man's forehead—that it's a word that shouldn't be spoken in schools. And I catch myself hoping for the best even as I write this, knowing that Jason didn't do it to get me to say that word out loud. I believe he did it because he thinks I'll be scared of him. That he has found out about "my little secret" and that I may be too scared to say the word because I might implicate myself.

"Oh, that's just my uncle."

Wow, maybe we were separated at birth.

"Oh? And why did you put the word 'GAY' on his forehead? Is he gay?"

"Oh, that's the word he uses for happy! My uncle is happy in this picture."

This child is good! He knows how to use the system and that teachers are programmed to listen to his responses, no matter how far from the spirit of his actions his words really are.

I don't remember why Jason tore the picture out of his notebook, but he did throw it in the garbage can about a foot away. I guess I didn't conceal my glee enough when he did that.

"OK, I'll just take that out and have another look at it." Jason swooped his hand into the garbage can and retrieved the crucial evidence.

"Sorry, it's my property now. It was in my garbage can, so it's school property." Wow, I have no idea where that came from, but it worked! Jason handed over the picture, now slightly crumpled. Whew. I feel like I won something important. I have no idea what it was, though.

I put the paper on my desk and the "happy" tattooed uncle stares at my back for the remainder of that class and all of the next.

Jason actually does fairly well in my class that day. I'm a bit surprised and a little disappointed. I want to have a good reason to kick him out again. But I don't want to take our class time to confront him on this picture while my head is still swimming.

I all but forget about the picture until the final bell rings. I start cleaning up my paper-strewn desk and have to confront "Uncle Happy" again.

Up to this moment, the anger I had experienced about this drawing had more to do with Jason's manipulation of the story and bending of the truth than with the probable intent and actual impact upon myself.

I tell the story to my colleague who shares the room with me and show her the picture. Her eyes widen as she scrutinizes the picture.

"What did you do?" she inquires. I tell her the rest of the story and realize that I'm not so sure about what comes next. We talk a bit more about our day and I grab the offending paper and head out the door to the assistant principal's office. He had dealt with Jason earlier in the week and had needed to speak with Jason several times prior to that day.

I run into a colleague of mine who knows me, and I do my show and tell again. By this time, I found that I am becoming angrier, little by little. My assurance of a safe working environment has been violated. This child has attempted to intimidate me by exposing a part of my personal life I have kept hidden from him and the rest of his peers and the school.

My colleague advises me to consider holding on to the paper for a while, to sit on it until I've had a chance to think this all through. I considered that for a moment, and then it hit me; I needed to go directly to my assistant principal and state all pertinent facts about this incident. I was also covered by the same non-discrimination policies that I reviewed with all of my classes at the beginning of the year. I deserved the same protections that I gave my students.

I found my assistant principal, asked if we could discuss this in his office, and once again told my story. I found myself questioning my own conclusions about sexual harassment.

"Umm, I think this is harassment of some kind. It just doesn't seem right." I caught myself. Yes, I would press full charges, I thought. I deserve it.

"Oh, yes, this certainly is harassment. I'll speak with Jason tomorrow and go through the policy with him and write him up on step one of harassment charges. I'll put the drawing in his file."

Whew. It was done. No fight, no pain, no guilt. I asked to make some copies and found myself printing one after another until I had almost ten of them. I was not going to let this one slip away.

That night, I found my anger bubbling into a slow, burning rage. No twelve-year-old was going to intimidate me in my teaching environment! But I realized that I dreaded facing Jason again after the weekend. Therefore, he really had intimidated me.

This incident was about one month ago, and I have yet to inquire what exactly went into Jason's file. We now have an uneasy, unspoken truce, but Jason no longer intimidates me.

If we become defenders of other kids or say something about derogatory language being unacceptable in our classrooms, most gay and lesbian teachers probably dread the point blank question, "So, are YOU gay?" Part of it is dealing with the snickers and strange looks we will encounter for weeks after hearing that question and denying it to our students' faces. But for me, the most painful part will be the denial that tarnishes my own integrity. I am NOT ashamed to be gay. I don't want to change. In fact, I'm rather grateful that I'm gay. So denying all of that to a group of pre-teens will take its toll on me. Thinking about it, planning for it, replaying the possible scene and scripting my response, expression, and escape from the deer-in-the-headlights situation is taking its toll on me already.

I think it's ironic that we spend time and money providing students opportunities to discover fascinating details about other people from around the world when their own gay and lesbian teachers must hide the facts about themselves from these very students.

Yes, I hear you telling me, "You don't have to hide! You have supportive teachers, students, parents, and administrators just waiting for you to trust them!"

I know that I do. However, the unknown is something that I fear for good reason. I believe it would take only one fabricated story of sexual abuse or "homosexual recruiting" to end my career and my opportunity to work with children.

Yes, I know the union is behind me and Minnesota has a law protecting me, but that's all in writing only. No one has promised that I will be safe from parents spreading rumors about me. No one has promised that a teacher is innocent until proven guilty in the eyes and hearts of the community members. No one has promised me that my car and other personal property will not be vandalized because of my sexual orientation. No one has promised me that I won't be physically attacked after coming out. No one has promised me that the media would treat all of this fairly and objectively. I will be ready soon, but not yet.

I feel like I'm letting down all those students who would benefit from the knowledge that one of their teachers is gay. I know it would have made a significant difference in my own life. I spent far too much time feeling alone in my difference. Nowadays kids have Ellen, Elton John and Jamie Nabozny to look to as "role models," but how effective is this when these heroes are "out there"?

The explosion in media presenting lesbian and gay individuals as "regular people" certainly must help a kid who is struggling with his/her identity. But I know I needed more than a role model; I needed an ally who would defend me in school, be my mentor and just listen when I needed to talk. Fear and denial are such powerful forces to those who are struggling with their affectional/sexual orientation that few kids who question their sexuality ever feel comfortable trusting an adult.

As a teacher, I know I can count on having a few gay or lesbian kids in my classroom every year. I know that kids are looking to me to create a safe environment where they can be themselves. I want to create the kind of environment where students feel comfortable confiding in me. I want to be an adult in their life who makes their journey easier.

Toward that end, I use gender neutral words such as spouse or partner when referring to relationships. A lot of kids are part of families that don't fit the so-called norm of mom and dad.

I make reference to the fact that there have been well-known gay and lesbian individuals in our history. Children need to know this.

I know I risk being outed by students or at least challenged by parents and administrators when I mention that many of the most beloved musicians are gay or lesbian: Elton John, k. d. lang, Melissa Etheridge, and others who choose not to publically acknowledge their sexual orientation. I hear my students giggle as I slip this overlooked detail into the rest of the biography of these musicians. I can almost hear the collective question, "So, are YOU?!"

I was recently presented with an opportunity to agonize over my answer to that question. A special education teacher whom I am out to caught me on my way out the door to my next class and informed me that there was a student of hers who had been accepting dares from her classmates that week. One of the latest dares was to ask me if I was gay. She asked me what I would do if Melanie asked me.

I didn't have a reply for her. I saw this as an opportunity to finally be true to myself and yet I also could imagine the consequences of coming out. I feared I would lose all respect from the students, that I would not be able to teach effectively because of their ignorance and fear of me, and that their parents would rally to have me removed.

As I pondered all this on my way to my next classroom, I realized that I had a couple of options to consider. I could outright lie and deny it, but that hasn't been very effective in the past. A denial that's too strong looks like a definite cover-up. Besides, I didn't want to launch into lecture mode and remind her that I didn't ask if she was gay or about any other personal information. I expected the same level of respect from her. And I would have to joke that I really didn't want to know whom she liked or any personal information along those lines. Or I could come out right in front of the entire class and tell part of my life story. That was far too frightening, and I already feel like I talk too much while I teach. From my own experience, I couldn't expect the message I gave to be the one they carried home.

The option that dawned on me just minutes before this potential confrontation was to combine the two. I would say that I'm gay and just go right on with my lesson. Of course, they would all be stunned and then try to cover up their discomfort with laughter, but I would just keep on teaching and act like it was an everyday question.

"Oh, sure I'm gay," in a nonchalant voice. A little comedic rolling of the eyes (the international sign for "whatever!") and then, "Group one, get your notebooks," as the directive teacher voice is back along with the "we don't have time for this right now" look. I think they could be snowed. Acting is my passion and I pull it into my teaching every day. My sense of humor has helped me to defuse a tense situation more than once.

"So, what happened?" you ask. Nothing. Melanie was kept after class by another teacher and came late into my class. She had lost her potentially captive audience and didn't bother to ask me. I caught a couple of knowing looks aimed at Melanie during that class, but no one said a thing about "The Question."

I breathed a sigh of relief when that class was over, and yet I was a little sad that I had lost the opportunity to tell my truth in my place of work. I was at the same place I had always been—in the closet at work and quite out almost everywhere else.

I have a feeling that I'll have another opportunity all too soon. Every time I confront a student who blurts out, "That's so gay!" I know I just might hear, "So why do you care? Are you gay?" And I know that when I reply, I'll be watched very carefully by a couple of those quietly desperate kids in the back row.

ABOUT THE AUTHOR

In writing about this experience, I have come to realize that I must look for opportunities to be an ally for others as well as recruit allies for myself. My hope is that the reader will seek opportunities to be an ally for their students and colleagues. It's not an easy task, but school is a very scary place for those without an ally. Your students and colleagues really ARE listening and watching for any sign that you might be a safe person to confide in. I am a native Mid-Westerner and have taught elementary music for the past six years in the Minneapolis/St. Paul area. I am also a member of the Gay, Lesbian, Straight Educator's Network (GLSEN) and am currently volunteering at Project Offstreets, which reaches out to adolescents who are homeless.

Living LD

Jeff Offutt

SEVENTH GRADE. SECOND PERIOD. ENGLISH. WE ARE DISSECTING sentences. Mrs. Anderson calls it diagramming, but I think my term more accurately describes the process. Most of the class does not enjoy this section of the curriculum. I, on the other hand, hate it. I can't spell most of the words that go beyond four letters, my penmanship is not up to par, I do not do well in English, and I have an aversion to looking dumb in front of my classmates. Put this all together and I hate dissecting sentences.

That morning Mrs. Anderson asked me question after question and received back "I don't knows" and silences. I'm no mind reader, but I do know what she thought about students with learning disabilities: "If you would just try harder and not be so lazy you could do this." "You can't work the problem because you don't want to." "Of course you can do this! Both of your parents are teachers." I know she was thinking these things because she was saying them. Mrs. Anderson had apparently decided that it would be a good and helpful experience for me to hear these things. She must have also concluded that the rest of the class would benefit by being present when I heard these helpful words because she shared her remarks to me in front of the class, with everyone there to watch and listen.

Seventh-grade English was not the only time that I had a Mrs. or Mr. Anderson in my life. From these people I learned just how much a

86

teacher can influence a student. I learned that a teacher has an incredible amount of power to influence what students perceive as normal and right, the power to nurture or stifle the desire for and enjoyment of learning.

Although it was a painful lesson, I am glad that I learned it. I am a better teacher for having undergone Mrs. Anderson's unthinking tirades. I will never really know what it is like to be a student in my classroom, but I do understand what it is like to be different. I understand the problems and challenges of having a hidden disability. I empathize with students being seen by teachers as learning-disabled rather than as a student with a learning disability.

I remember sitting in life science and spending five minutes trying to remember how to spell the word *of* during a test. (Damn it! There's a *v* in there somewhere!) I remember Mrs. Elder, one of my teachers during junior high, telling me week after week, month after month for two years that even though I could hear the *a* when I spoke the word, it was spelled t-h-e-y. No *a*. I worked with Mrs. Elder for three years and I have no memory of her ever losing her temper, raising her voice or showing that she was frustrated by having to correct the word *they* and spell it to me over and over. I think of her when looking at a student and saying, "It sure does sound like there should be an *a* in the word, but do you know what? It's an *e*. T-h-e-y. They."

These things make me a better teacher because I understand what some of my students are going through. I understand when a student needs a little more time to process or would benefit from having the question stated in another way or simply needs to have his/her answer really listened to because it is not the rote answer from the book but an answer arrived at by looking at the problem in a different way.

I also have a feeling for when my students need a bit more pressure, not another, "Oh, that's OK not to be able to do that." I don't mean the student should be interrogated. Rather, all students can benefit from occasional persistence on the part of their instructors.

Recently I had this conversation with a second-grade student after he told me he did not know what to do on an assignment.

"Start off by reading the directions to me."

"I can't."

"Why not?"

"I can't read any of the words."

"Which word is the first one that you can't read?"

"I can't read any of them. I have a learning disability."

"So?"

"So, I can't read!"

"Having a learning disability does not mean you can't read. You can read. I have a learning disability and I can read. It was hard to learn but I read very well. Now, which word is the first word you don't know?"

"That one!"

"What does it say?"

"I don't know!"

"Sound it out."

"I can't."

"What letter does the word start with?"

"I don't know."

"You were reading very well earlier this morning, and I'm having a hard time believing that the whole alphabet has fallen out of your head. What letter does the word start with?"

"C."

"What sound does c make?"

"It says circle."

"Great. If you have any other questions, let me know."

Six minutes later Allen was finished with his assignment. Allen had said, "I'm too dumb to work," which we both knew was wrong and I had said, "It may be hard but you can do it," which we both knew was right. Now his work was waiting to be corrected. And all of this without leaving the immediate area of Allen's desk, where we could have a conversation that did not involve the other students in class.

As a teacher, I am able to remind students of the things that they do know and can do. This enjoyable task often reminds me of a high school English teacher whose class I was fortunate to be invited into.

I say "invited into" because Mrs. Hansen taught accelerated English. When I was first told that Mrs. Hansen had extended, to me, an invitation into her class for the next year, my immediate response was, "Does she know that I'm going to be in basic government next year?" I found out that she did, in fact, know that I was signed up for a basic class and that I was receiving help in the Resource Room. Mrs. Hansen had been talking to some of my current and former teachers and decided that she wanted to have me in her classroom. Even with the wonderfully supportive parents and teachers that I had had, it still was a shock that I would be asked to join an accelerated class in English!

With some encouragement, I decided to join the class and it was one of the best experiences I ever had. We did grammar and technical

work, but for the most part we read, wrote, and talked. Learn some vocabulary, read a chapter, think about it, and then discuss it in class.
This is work? It was wonderful to be in a class where the teacher
worked with me on the things I had problems with and let me be
proud of what I was doing well rather than dwelling on only the negative. There is a myriad of things I do not do well that a teacher could
choose to get upset about, but I fail to understand how pointing out
my weak areas in a negative way benefits the educational process.

As a teacher, I have even responded to "I can't do this" by saying,
"Great! Now we know what area to be working on." Any teacher can
find some thing to be negative about when working with a student
that has a learning disability. Any teacher can also look at the same student and find some things that s/he does well. Not all teachers look for
the positive in all of their students, and we know that when it comes to
people, we find what we look for.

I am thankful that I was able to spend time with teachers like Mrs.
Elder and Mrs. Hansen, and I am aware of the important lessons that I
learned from the Mrs. Andersons. I can only hope that what I say and
do in my classroom can be as helpful as the former and not as hurtful
as the latter.

ABOUT THE AUTHOR

After I was born, my parents named me Jeffrey Littleton Offutt. Like all of
us, I have many stories to tell about myself and my life. I believe personal
stories are an excellent way to share and to learn. The story you just read or
heard is not just about me or people with learning disabilities. It's about
the interactions we have with each other every day and the things we can
learn from one another. I am currently interacting with special education
students at Probstfield Elementary School in Moorhead, Minnesota.

Special Education and Students of Color: Time to Lift the Fog

Yvonne Redmond-Brown

I WAS ATTENDING ONE OF MY USUAL SPECIAL EDUCATION Individual Educational Plan (IEP) meetings where a parent was about to receive the results of an initial speech/language assessment. Our purpose was to decide if the student required additional services. As I entered the room I remember noticing how everyone was arranged around the table and how many professionals were there to talk to this one parent. The ratio was nine to one. I intentionally took a seat as close to the parent as possible. What made the meeting memorable was what happened when the speech report was summarized.

The speech clinician reported that the student, Terrance, had articulation problems, specifically in formulating consonant blends. The two blends I remember were "STR" and "SKR." People around the table started to comment on the conclusions by the clinician. The supervisor for the speech clinician took offense when asked by one of the educators about the assessment tools used to determine whether or not Terrance, an African American male, required speech and language services. When asked if assessment instruments or tools were used that were normed for a diverse group and were culturally sensitive, he simply lost it! He lost his cool at a full team meeting with the parent present to determine speech service for this child. The exact moment he lost his cool was when he was asked, "Did you interview any family members during your assessment process?"

The question was intended to get a sense of how the clinician included the perceptions of family members in his report, including whether or not the family perceived a problem with the child's speech. Reporting the perceptions of family members and asking for clarification in their presence is an expected practice at team meetings to make certain all areas of the child's home and school environment are included in the final report.

The reaction from the speech clinician did not promote such a discussion or indicate that he saw the importance of such an exercise. Emphatically he replied, " What is your point? How does that influence the observations in school? Why would I need to gather data from non-clinicians? I have been at this a long time, and I have never needed to go into the home or do family interviews. I don't need to know how they talk at home, I am trying to get him ready for the real world. Do you want people laughing at him?"

Given Terrance's background, the question was appropriate and should have generated a rich dialogue about the student. It should be noted that the child we were discussing was a nine-year-old, fourth-grade-male of African descent who was from a family of fourteen that had moved to Minnesota from the South. The family had a history of being transient but with an extensive extended family connection.

In my experience, many of these experts go into meetings like this to confirm what they already think they know. The speech supervisor knew a lot about articulation as a disability, but he knew nothing about how cultural speech patterns may render his knowledge base useless. He did not understand how the environment influenced the child's ability to perform in school. The specifics, in this case the geographical dialect differences, were relevant.

Educators know a lot about their field, but they often don't know a lot about the increasingly diverse student population they work with. The interviewing of family members is essential to the diagnostic process because it allows the clinician to assess the dynamics of speech patterns found within the child's environment, especially when working with students from traditionally marginalized groups.

Students of color in special education, from assessment to service delivery to exiting the system, are placed in double jeopardy: the jeopardy of the culture of special education and the jeopardy due to a lack of understanding of the cultural backgrounds students bring to the table. When professionals do not acknowledge that students of color bring with them diverse experiences, the opportunity to provide appropriate services may be lost.

There is a fog surrounding many educators' frame of reference, a fog filled with a lack of knowledge as they approach the special needs of a child of color. There is a complexity in the assessment process for all students referred for services, but this is especially true for students of color due to the diversity of their experiences. Professionals participating in this critical moment in this child's life, the IEP conference, frequently make decisions without any understanding of what defines that child and her/his environment.

The refusal to use or acknowledge the interview with parents as an additional source of data is an example of this fog. Educators have not been trained in, nor have taken the time to learn about, the cultural subtleties that operate during the data gathering process of the interview. They are often not familiar with how some families communicate: circle talk—responding to questions in what appears to be disconnected and random ways—or storytelling—answering questions through the telling of events rather than giving yes or no answers. Another common pattern of communication I have observed in some families from the South is speaking in the third person plural, non-gender specific language when others are around and they don't want them to know who is being discussed.

The individuals involved in the data gathering process expect to establish a trusting relationship with the parent in a few minutes in a brief encounter. Such an assumption is negated by a long history of distrust by disenfranchised groups in our country. Some educators assume that these families will open up to share the "family business," understand the purpose of their questions, and concur with their assessment of their child!

I listen intensely when sitting around the due process table, listening for comments from the people there that may provide information about the child, listening for words that alert me to bias. My seventeen years in the field of special education make me wonder: "Is the fog really a fog or a clever cloak to deny students of color their individuality, to minimize the impact of the student's experiences on educational performance? Can some experts acknowledge that students of color have relevant experiences outside of their own realm of experience and reality? Is the behavior of some experts/practitioners based on bias stemming from social paradigms and their own discomfort related to providing services for students of color? If so, how can the process of delivering IEP services be a vehicle for lifting the fog?

In the particular case of Terrance, the family history would have provided clues for the speech clinician. The non-verbal messages Terrance's mom sent me throughout the meeting gave me grave concerns. What was happening here? After the mother left the meeting, I felt a strong need to say, "What happened here? How can we eliminate the fog regarding students of color needing special education services? How do we start addressing this fog complex in a constructive, student-centered, systematically accountable way?" I suggest that we do the following:

- Acknowledge that there is a fog, and that it is a barrier to process.

- Recognize the fog for what it is—a lack of knowledge about cultural differences.

- Be intentional when assessing all students, including seeking input from family members. Purpose should drive the assessment.

- Learn how diversity issues manifest themselves in special education.

- Realize that there are unknown factors that can cloud the data gathering process.

- Acknowledge that children bring with them a history that may not fit your paradigm.

I closely watched Terrance's mother during this IEP conference. I did not speak to her, nor she to me. But the non-verbal messages between us were clear and intentional. At no point did she interrupt the exchanges among the professionals. She simply waited for the meeting to end.

At the end of the meeting she asked to have her son removed from his current program. One of the team asked, "Why do you want him removed? We are just now getting what we need." The mother looked in my direction, smiled, and left the meeting. She collected her son from his classroom and they both left the school for the last time.

ABOUT THE AUTHOR

Who am I? By training I am a teacher of special education students. My vocation of the heart is children's lives. I have worked in K-12 for seventeen years. I am now an assistant professor and director of disability services. Who listens to me? Most of the time I feel no one does. I hope you listen, and I hope you understand my concerns after reading the "Fog" piece. What was this parent thinking about all of us? I am a widow and a mother. I am the fourth child, fourth girl, from a family of ten born in Tennessee. I grew up in the "STR" & "SKR" environment. I wrote this piece because I got angry. Hopefully, the energy from the experience will lead to constructive ways of addressing the issues presented.

Words on My Tongue

David Mura

for Li-Young Lee

I am nine, sitting in a circle with our teacher.
I am to read out loud. Though I know these words
—*ball, the, I, throw, boy, girl* —they lodge
in my throat, dry as cotton balls, a cough that won't leave.
My teacher wears a look of concern or impatience,
it doesn't matter. My classmates giggle or shift
in boredom, it doesn't matter. The words
lie like ammunition on the page. I will not fire them.
(The gun aims at the center of my chest.)
The minutes pass, the day is long. Finally,
the teacher asks the next student to read on.

Deep at night, that first winter,
I lay in the cupola
of my sheets and rubbed
my hands together, half
in prayer, half
like two sticks, praying for fire.
Like those who took us in
as sponsors on Sunday,
I was asking for the Holy Spirit
to enter me, to speak in tongues of flame.

We were Chinese, from Sadec, just outside Saigon.
There the river flooded through the delta,
a miracle of mud and substances abounding
in the current—crates, chairs, water buffalo, branches
and sometimes bodies, the drowned
ones, eyes turned towards some other world.
My brother almost drowned there once.

This poem was previously published in *Another Way to Dance: Contemporary Voices of Asian American/Asian Canadian Poetry,* TSAR Publication, 1996, Canada.

My mother slapped me for taking him down.
That sting still rings in my ear like a gong.

I knew I spoke with this accent.
It was visible as a hump
or the limp my sister walks with,
the metal braces that reverberate her steps.
The noise that emptied from my mouth
contained a color I could not eradicate,
a grating sing song
like horsehair of a violin, a Chinese violin,
and even as I opened my mouth
I could see, in the eyes of a listener,
if they were white, spreading in every direction
across their face, a judgment
as inevitable as at evening
comes the descending night.

Uncomely noise, ugly noise, ching-chong
Chinamen noise, cavity ridden
and sounding of brown gums, yellowed teeth,
contorted lips struggling like some ape to speak,
and unlike the splinter
father drew with delicacy from my palm,
removing a pain I'd lived with all day,
down the streets of the city, the graffiti and traffic,
there was nothing he could do,
nor my mother. The words sat
on my tongue, like the questions
that sat inside my ear—*What did you say? What did he say?*

·And yet,
· even then, I was moving away,
coming to the time
when I would stand with father, mother,
before my teacher
and translate to them
both the praise, which I embellished,
and the checks, which I altered, fights　　.
on the asphalt schoolyard of broken glass
and a rumbling in my stomach

that spoke incessantly of fear.
Deep in the magical jungle,
in some country we traveled
to, my parents were wandering,
and I had to lead them, word by word,
in the grocer's, before the lawyer, my teacher,
to meaning, sweet land of comprehension
rising like an island from the chaos of oceans
back in the beginning when God made the word and the world.

You children, you who take your foreign parents
into these unfamiliar streets
know this trembling, this fear;
and even though you speak *for* them,
you cannot speak your fear.

So what is it I do now in the corporation?
I open my eyes to numbers, their possible blossoming,
beauty comprehensible to my tongue,
and only those occasional afternoons,
speaking under fluorescence,
like a prisoner confessing sins of the previous regime,
does it come back in the faces before me—

The smirk in their smiles, the sliver on my tongue.

And I know then
I have bitten
a ceiling of glass
which will never shatter
with the words I speak to you now
so like the words I spoke as a child
once upon a time, long ago: *Boy, ball, throw, me.*

ABOUT THE AUTHOR

This poem is in the voice of a young Chinese Vietnamese American who comes to this country at around seven and begins with his experiences learning the language in school and his refusal to read in front of his class. Later he has to translate for his parents before certain authority, an experience several of my friends have described as particularly unsettling. At the end of the poem he's working in a corporation dealing with the glass ceiling. In writing the poem I had in mind Jonothan Kozol's writings about the refusal of some children to learn or participate in school when they perceive that process is meant to exclude them or part of their humanity. I also had in mind Mitsuye Yamada's essay on the hierarchy of power in relationship to accent and the speaking of English.

AUTOBIOGRAPHY

Offer your experience as your truth.

—Pauline Oliveros

Teaching Students to Read the World

Willa Cofield

WHEN A SMALL GROUP OF INBORDEN HIGH SCHOOL STUDENTS left the school grounds in the spring of 1963 and walked in a body to the "whites-only" public library, we could no longer deny the obvious: our North Carolina community had joined the social revolution of the '60s. Earlier that day I had invited the students in the group to an evening meeting in my home to plan ways they could help in a voter registration campaign.

The student action was not the first act of defiance. I think it began when my husband, Reed Johnson, shocked the town when he announced his intention to run for a seat on Enfield's town council. This rash and impetuous act upset everyone, including me. No Black person in our town had ever had such gall.

We soon realized that Reed Johnson was serious about running for the council because he and schoolteacher Lillie Cousins Smith began taking carloads of Black people downtown to register to vote. In desperation, the local registrar closed her door and left word that the office was closed. Instead of dropping their heads and returning to their homes, several disappointed applicants went to the registrar's house and sat on her porch and lawn. In deference to this unprecedented militancy, the town officials opened the registrar's office but subjected all prospective registrants to a grueling and lengthy literacy test. The campaign resulted in the registration of several hundred Black people, not enough to elect my husband, but seriously shaking the previously un-challenged local white hegemony.

Near the end of the campaign, anonymous telephone callers threat-ened to burn down our house. One night we looked from the window of the bedroom and saw fire shooting from a flaming cross on our back lawn. A cross hadn't been burned in our town since local white people forced Dr. Dubisset, the town's one Black doctor, to abandon a small hospital and leave town in the early 1930s. When I was growing up, people shook their heads and spoke of him in hushed voices if they talked about him at all.

After the election, the town resumed its former somnolence and tried to return to its peaceful ways, with a small knot of white men sit-ting on the wooden bench in front of the police station and young white wives breaking the tedium of the morning with a coke at White-head's Drugstore.

But soon the Inborden High School kids created a new crisis. A few days before school closed, the students heard Floyd McKissick speak at Twilight Baptist Church. He told the biblical story of young Joshua, who ignored the old heads and successfully brought down the walls of Jericho. The next day the students immediately applied the parable to their own situation and decided that, despite the adults' reluctance to challenge the segregation at the local theater, they should confront the owner. When I advised them to move cautiously, they told me that they had their foot in the door. There was no turning around.

Inborden High School enrolled only Black students. A relatively young school, it was built on the grounds of the former Enfield Col-ored Graded School which I had attended until I was eleven. On land stingily carved from a huge farm and surrounded by fields and ditches, the school stood just inside the town boundary, separate and apart from the modest frame houses of the Black community.

For a decade before the school was built, the county transported its Black high school students to Edgecombe County to attend Brick Tri-County High School. When that school burned down, Halifax County built a short string of classrooms and called it Inborden High School. During the interim, Black students attended high school in churches, in other counties, or wherever they could. The Board of Education built Inborden High School only after it built a fine, gleaming struc-ture to replace the somewhat dated white high school. Inborden High School served Black youth who lived in Enfield and on farms within a radius of fifteen miles.

I began teaching at Inborden High School when it opened its doors in 1952. In the language arts and literature classes that I taught, I tried to make parallels between the lives of my students and the stories we read. When the Supreme Court announced its decision in the *Brown v. Topeka* case (which established that "separate but equal" is inherently unequal), we talked about the implications of that decision on our lives. None of us could imagine Blacks ever attending the local white school.

During the 1962-63 school year, however, few class discussions did not refer to the limited resources at our school, the segregated local theater, the town's exclusive swimming pool, or some indignity which a Black person had experienced in the downtown stores. We followed the activities of the militant young college students but from afar.

In those days neither my students nor I knew much about the political system. What we knew for sure, however, was that Black and White people in our small Southern town lived in separate worlds and that the resources of the White world were far superior to ours. We lived on unpaved streets without sidewalks and curbing while the Department of Public Works had paved some streets in the White section so many times that the surface was almost even with the curbing. When we went to see a local doctor, we sat in a separate waiting room. If we went to see a movie at the local theater, we purchased a ticket at the box office, then climbed outside steps to sit in the balcony. If we rode the Carolina Trailways bus, we took seats in the back.

Enfield's mayor, who administered many of his duties from behind the counter of a local hardware store, was White and so were the members of the town council, the county school board, the school district committee, and the local police force. Although we comprised at least half of the town's population, we had no representation on any of the governing bodies, and we held none of the jobs in the town government. In the downtown stores Black employees might sweep the floor or deliver groceries to well-to-do families, but they never rang the cash register or waited on customers.

As students in our all-Black school challenged some of the overt manifestations of this oppressive system, my classroom became a dynamic and exciting place. Instead of reading of distant people and events, we read about ourselves in the columns of the regional and state newspapers. To expand our consciousness of the outside world, the adult leaders of the local civil rights movement took carloads of students to hear the great civil rights orators. We heard Floyd

McKissick, the fiery, young lawyer from Durham who became director of the Congress of Racial Equality; Fred Shuttlesworth, leader of the Birmingham Movement; C. T. Vivian of the Southern Christian Leadership Conference (SCLC); Parren Mitchell, a young congressman from Maryland; and A. I. Dunlap, who held the reputation of being able to turn a church out more swiftly than any other speaker in the movement. Many of these leaders spoke at large rallies in our community.

One memorable night in the nearby town of Weldon, Inborden students filled the balcony of the First Baptist Church and began singing the freedom song, "We Shall Not Be Moved." At the end of each chorus, someone shouted, "One more time! Sing it over now." Before the students finally took their seats, everyone in the church stood and joined the clapping and singing of those passionate, young voices.

Students also helped in our campaign to get Blacks on the voter registration rolls. I remember using the language arts period to teach students how to pass the voter registration test, a ploy that had kept many Black people from voting. The students were too young to register, but I asked them to tutor their parents and neighbors and encourage these adults to go to the registrar's office.

In the summer of 1963, students made up a large part of the delegation from our town to the March on Washington, which focused national attention on the civil rights movement. They returned fired up to break the back of segregation in the local community. The massive demonstration in Washington gave them new spirit, and their conversations with youth from other communities gave them new ideas. Together we decided that they would defy the local ordinance which banned anyone under eighteen from picketing. Those who were arrested would go limp and force the police officers to carry them. Everyone wanted to volunteer for this direct action strategy, including the young elementary students who had joined our group.

The mass arrests that followed led to an all-out battle with the local police, who called in state troopers to clear the streets of Black people who had filled the downtown sidewalks. When the crowds did not respond to the fire whistle, which at nine o'clock on Saturday nights ordered Blacks to go home, the police officers brought in fire trucks with high-pressure hoses to force people from the area.

The powerful force of the water injured several students. This attack upon our community led us to organize a four-month economic boycott during which we would not shop at the White-owned downtown stores. This campaign forced the town to hire a Black police officer and the downtown merchants to hire Black clerks and cashiers.

In late fall that same year we invited John Salter, a young professor originally from Arizona, to join our struggle.* After heading the Strategy Committee in the Jackson, Mississippi Movement, he worked as a community organizer for the Southern Conference Education Fund. He was intense, smart, and completely committed to social justice. With his assistance, we organized the Halifax County Voter's Movement and ran a slate of Black men for offices in the local and state government. Because of his non-Black background, he was deeply hated by local Whites. The Halifax County Voter's Movement registered thousands of Black people and successfully challenged the racist literacy test, helping pave the way for the Voting Rights Act of 1965.

Through Salter's efforts, the staff of the Southern Christian Leadership Conference, led by Septima Clark and Dorothy Cotton, gave Enfield students and adults basic political education at Franklinton Center on the grounds of the former Brick School the following summer. The SCLC had taken over an experiment in basic adult education pioneered at the Highlander School, an outstanding center of political education in Tennessee, and begun to spread it throughout the South. For the first time, we heard about the power structure and began to draw lines between the local political system and the rich, White, landholding families in Halifax County.

Dorothy Cotton described the specific steps we should follow to build a program of nonviolent, direct action. She told us to gather the facts, educate the community, negotiate if possible, purify ourselves through spiritual preparation, and then undertake action. After the action, we were to be open to reconciliation. Septima Clark, supervisor of teacher training, showed us how to teach unlettered people to read and write using role plays and vocabulary which helped prepare them for active citizenship.

The week after the disappearance and suspected murder of James Chaney, Andrew Goodman, and Michael Schwerner, fifteen students and I traveled by bus to Dorchester, Georgia, to participate in the citizenship training offered at that site. We were tense and jumpy as we

---

*While teaching at Tougaloo College during the early 1960s, John Salter chaired the Strategy Committee of the Jackson, Mississippi Movement. Part Indian, he grew up in Flagstaff, Arizona. He is now known as John Hunter Gray.

changed buses in Charleston, South Carolina, and Savannah, Georgia, knowing that our backpacks and jeans and the youthfulness of everyone except me marked us as a bunch of civil rights workers.

Rooms in the Dorchester facility were stark and bare, and students voiced more than a few misgivings about the thin mattresses, curtainless windows, and archaic bathrooms. We soon forgot our poor accommodations in the presence of the strong members of the SCLC staff and the commitment of other young people from throughout the Deep South. We talked and sang about freedom. We heard the names of Black martyrs in the civil rights struggle that we had never known, people like Herbert Lee, an Amitie County, Mississippi, farmer who had worked in the voter registration campaign until assailants killed him with a bullet to the head. We sang a song, "I Will Never Turn Back No More," dedicated to his memory.

Hosea Williams of the SCLC gave chilling reports of the demonstrations that had been held in St. Augustine, Florida, and the brutal beating of some of the workers. We learned about the laws that supported our struggle, the Fourteenth and Fifteenth Amendments. We discussed the Bill of Rights and especially the First Amendment. We learned legal concepts such as *habeas corpus,* which could help us in our battle with the entrenched wielders of power. We learned how to behave if we were the targets of violence and what to do if we were arrested.

The SCLC staff told us that when we got home, we should find a civil rights organization and become a part of it. The same students who had joked about the rundown building when they arrived said good-bye to their new friends, their eyes brimming with tears as they boarded the bus.

After our trip to Georgia, I became a teacher in Martin Luther King's program to teach illiterate Blacks to read and write, pass the voting literacy test, and become active, engaged members of their community. We were actively participating in a process of liberating ourselves from a system of privilege and oppression. By challenging that system, we learned how the system entrapped us. For example, we had not understood very well how the mainstream media supports the *status quo,* but after sending a long press release to the local papers about the police attack upon our people, we got it. The front page story only included statements made by the police chief. We gained a new insight into the collaboration that goes on at many levels to maintain the *status quo.* It was a valuable lesson.

I saw clearly how school could take on a new significance when it addresses the problems of the community. As the saying went in the 1960s: "You can't be neutral; you're either working for change or you are a part of the problem." I made a conscious decision to join my husband and my students and work for change. I consider the work I did during this phase of my teaching career the most important teaching that I have ever done.

I could sense my own growth. My family's history of self-employment and business enterprise had protected me from some of the most brutal aspects of racial discrimination, but participation in the movement changed my life. I opened my home and my heart to people that I had not known very well, gaining a new respect for people inside and outside our community. Our house became the center of the movement, providing shelter for young Student Nonviolent Coordinating Committee (SNCC) workers, food for adult and student organizers, a resting place for volunteers from all over the state, a meeting place for out-of-town lawyers and local leaders, and a fortress when our friends and neighbors believed we were about to be attacked.

Learning transcended the classroom and became a part of the community. The teaching place became the funeral home chapel, my living room, or the downtown streets. We found the curriculum in the racial tension and poverty that pervaded our community. My students and I learned together on the picket line, in backwoods churches, in an isolated training institution in Georgia.

In a book co-authored with Ira Schor, Paulo Freire (1987) speaks of the tendency to separate the school from the world. Calling it a dichotomy between reading words and reading the world, he explained:

> My impression is that the world of American education, the school, is increasing the separation of the words we read and the world we live in. In such a dichotomy, the world of reading is only the world of the schooling process, a closed world, cut off from the world where we have experiences but do not read about those experiences. This schooling world where we read words that relate less and less to our concrete experiences outside has become more and more specialized in the bad sense of this word. In reading words, school becomes a special place that teaches us to read only school-words, not reality-words. The *other* world, the world of *facts*, the world of *life*, the world in which events are very alive, the world of struggles, the world of discrimination and economic crisis (all these things are there!) do not make contact with students in school through the words that schools ask students to read. You can think of this dichotomy as one

kind of "culture of silence" imposed on students. School reading is silent about the world of experience and the world of experience is silenced, without its own critical texts. (p. 135)

Then and now I believe it is of critical importance that teachers break through this dichotomy by using the experiences of their students as the basis for their education. I believe that students can benefit from understanding systems of oppression: racism, sexism, classism, ageism, ableism, heterosexism, and religious oppression. As teachers, we have more access to the young than any other group of adults besides parents. I think that we must use this opportunity to help erase the dichotomy between the school words and the words of reality.

Speaking to teachers at Montclair State University, Chandra Mohanty (1993) pointed to the myths that students bring into the classroom and reminded us of our opportunity to debunk those myths. Mohanty said that most students hold the following dangerous misconceptions about our society:

1. The United States is a meritocracy.

2. All who want to work can do so.

3. All who are not lazy can become entrepreneurs.

4. Freedom relates to free markets.

5. Equal opportunity and access are substitutes for justice.

6. The good life can be defined as access to consumer goods, being able to own what you like.

7. Myth of democracy: the state that does not interfere in the lives of its citizens is justified in taking no responsibility for its citizens.

8. Efficiency is a mark of social progress.

We pay a terrible price for the fact that many students leave our classes without having these beliefs challenged, knowing only school words, unfamiliar with the words of reality. One young New Jersey teacher told me that everyone she knows believes the myths that Mohanty listed. Sonia Nieto (1994) writes that we need to make certain that students are "encouraged to be critical of every book, newspaper, curriculum or piece of information by asking questions such as: Who wrote the book? Who's missing in the story? Why?" (p. 37).

I see a need not only to help students understand hierarchical systems, but to realize that these unjust structures can be changed. Such knowledge can lead to individual as well as group empowerment. Many of the students in that class of Inborden High School have gone on to achieve high personal and professional goals. The lesson they learned by addressing segregation in their local community taught them that change is possible.

As a teacher who is committed to social change, I believe that I can help students adopt a more inquisitive attitude toward the world they live in. It is no longer the sixties, but the social injustices and inequities persist. The stories of some groups remain omitted from the history book. Is it because they have no history? In telling the history of Halifax County, school Superintendent W. C. Allen (1918) wrote that during the period of Reconstruction, the district was represented by "ignorant" Blacks. It wasn't until the late 1980s that Black people in Halifax County discovered the story of James O'Hara, a local Black man who represented the district in Congress a hundred years earlier. Everyone thought that Reed Johnson was the first local Black person to seek political office when in fact the Second Congressional District had elected so many Black men that for the last quarter of the nineteenth century it was known as the Black Second.

O'Hara was a well-educated, accomplished lawyer. He founded the *Enfield Progress*, which had by then become a White-owned, racist newspaper. A Washington paper described Libby, O'Hara's wife, as "one of the loveliest ladies in Washington, a highly educated woman who speaks French, plays Beethoven, and understands art and literature to a degree that would make some of her White sisters blush for envy" (Anderson, 1981, 131). People whose lives were circumscribed by the dusty corn rows and cotton fields of eastern North Carolina would have been astonished to know that local Black people had ever boasted of such accomplishments.

I recently returned to my undergraduate college for the fiftieth reunion of my 1948 graduating class, in itself a mind-boggling experience. When we sang the alma mater, I remembered singing the words loudly and spiritedly as an undergraduate. Written by Sarah Collins Fernandez of the class of 1882, the words that we sang proclaimed that we would leave that institution and *serve* both God and our nation. Never once did any of us young Black women and men question that pledge and suggest that perhaps our first priority should be to *change* rather than serve the *status quo*.

Important to my own education as a teacher was the recognition of the inherently political nature of the school and classroom and the critical role these institutions play in continuing the cycle of oppression. We teachers are entrusted with educating the young, in many cases helping shape their lives. If we can see ourselves in this light, we can become agents of change, enabling our youth to see our society with all of its boils and warts, but also helping them envision and work toward a better, fairer, and more just society to the ultimate advantage of themselves, their community, and the planet.

REFERENCES

Allen, W. C. (1918). *History of Halifax County.* Boston: Cornhill.

Anderson, E. (1981). *Race and politics in North Carolina, 1872-1901.* Baton Rouge: Louisiana State University Press.

Mohanty, C. (1993, October). Notes from lecture by Chandra Mohanty at Montclair State University, sponsored by the New Jersey Project, October 15, 1993.

Nieto, S. (1994). Moving beyond tolerance in multicultural education. *Multicultural Education, 2,* 1:9-12, 35-37.

Shor, I. & Freire, P. (1987). *A pedagogy for liberation.* New York: Bergin & Garvey.

ABOUT THE AUTHOR

The experiences in Enfield, North Carolina, which I describe in this article, were life-changing and provided the foundation for all my work since that time. Though a truly fair and just society has yet to emerge, through retelling this story I realize anew that I have seen some changes. I continue to believe that it is possible for ordinary people to do extraordinary things. Currently I am enjoying my recent retirement from the New Jersey Department of Education, where I worked as a teacher trainer in the Office of Bilingual Education and Equity Issues.

You Say I Have What?

Gwendolyn L. Walker, Ph.D.

YOU SAY I HAVE WHAT? HE REPEATED IT SLOWLY. MULTIPLE sclerosis.

SPRING 1970

I was a senior at La Crosse State University, enrolled in the physical education program. During Easter break I drove to Madison, Wisconsin, and spent the break with my older sister and family. I loved to play ping-pong with my brother-in-law, so we went to the basement for our competitive series.

My brother-in-law loved to tease me, especially when he was winning. The more victorious, the more expansive his teasing. He would hit several hard, smashing shots and I kept missing them. I was surprised because I usually handled his shots with ease. I kept missing them and suddenly frustration became my focus. I couldn't see the whole ball as it crossed the net. What was wrong with my sight?

Whatever the problem, I knew I could overcome it because I was a physical educator: strong, healthy and determined. I later discovered the problem was not so easy to overcome.

After spring vacation I returned to La Crosse and began preparations for final examinations. At that time I was one of seven women living in a four-bedroom home. There was only one bathroom for all to share so it was necessary to develop a specific schedule.

It was my turn to be the first in the shower. When the alarm sounded I hopped from my bed and lost my balance to my left side. I fell into the pile of boxes stacked along the wall. I felt tingling and numbness on the left side of my body. Not to worry, I thought. I just slept wrong. For a brief moment I was worried so I took a cigarette, lit it, and tried to take a puff. Where was that cigarette? It had fallen to the floor between my legs. I didn't care about the cigarette on the floor but focused only on the time and my turn for a shower. Once in the bathroom I picked up my toothbrush, dabbed on some toothpaste and attempted to brush. I couldn't. The brush had fallen from my hand.

Something was wrong. I was frightened. I ran to the bedroom and woke my roommate. Nervously I explained the lack of feeling on the left side of my body and that I had fallen into the boxes.

Something was definitely wrong. My roommate told me not to worry, that I had slept funny. Nothing could be wrong. The tingling and numbness continued. I began to cry and convinced my roommate that my body was not working properly. We both were somewhat concerned, so we headed to the college infirmary which was not well-respected. Students only visited for "real" emergencies like the flu or a cold.

Inside the infirmary I anxiously sat and waited my turn. My name was called and I went into a small examination room. A nurse greeted me. The doctor was seated on a rolling stool, wore a white coat and glasses, and looked exhausted. I stared at this strange man and hoped that I could trust his advice. I explained the episode with my numbness and tingling while he closely listened without comment. When finished, I expected him to say that I had a new virus or something equally insignificant.

Instead he said he needed more information and wanted to do a spinal tap that very afternoon. What was a spinal tap and why did I need one? He explained that a needle would be inserted into my spinal column and spinal fluid would be removed for analysis. Didn't sound like a painless process to me. What on earth would that reveal? How could I avoid this procedure?

At first I refused the spinal exam because I was scared to death. I imagined a huge needle going into my spine to remove gooey fluid. The doctor continued to tell me that the procedure was necessary and that it wouldn't be painful. After several scared minutes I agreed to the spinal tap.

I was also anxious because my roommate and I were missing our classes. Math would have been a more pleasant alternative. I dressed in a white gown and climbed on a table, lying on my left side in the fetal position. My imagination went wild, thinking of a huge needle with a tip a yard long. Lots of sticky, brown fluid, slowly being sucked from my spine. Enough to fill a gallon jar.

The procedure was underway and I began to pray. The nurse placed her fist on my stomach and pushed hard to put pressure on the spine and allow space for the needle. Suddenly the doctor yelled, "Push harder, nurse!" Next the doctor yelled, "Get the book, nurse! Get the book!" The doctor took the medical book from the nurse and was frantically rustling pages. I closed my eyes and thought I should grab my clothes and get my butt off that table before anything could go wrong.

When the procedure was finished, I was curious and wanted to see the spinal fluid. The doctor showed me a test tube with clear liquid, not sticky, brown fluid. I thought to myself, "Just get me off that table and send me home to recover from my tingling and numbness." I knew everything would be back to normal following some rest. This was just related to stress, common during final exam periods.

Two hours later I was told to go home and lie flat for 24 hours. I needed time for the fluid to replace itself. I stayed flat on the couch for 24 hours. Something must be wrong. Something unknown is happening to me. But it would eventually pass because I was a healthy, tough athlete. I continued to tell myself not to worry.

Days passed and I tried to ignore the limp on my left side as well as the increased numbness and tingling. I had to prepare for final exams, pack all my junk from the house, and, most importantly, to graduate. I called the infirmary. They wouldn't give me the results. Well, I would deal with any challenge, any unknown. After all, this situation was only temporary.

MAY 1970

Graduation day was sunny and warm, a day filled with family cheer and joy. I sat proudly among other graduates in the auditorium and finally heard my name called from the podium, "Gwendolyn Lee Walker." I heard my family yelling words of encouragement, screaming at the tops of their lungs. I climbed the stairs to accept my diploma and was quickly reminded of my medical concerns. I limped across the stage with my left arm numbly hanging at my side. But I didn't care about the limp because the excitement was too great and the screams from my family too joyous. I was living for the moment, perhaps one of my last moments of joy without complication.

Still no results from my tests. What was the delay? What was the secret? Surely some results had come back by now!

JUNE 1970

I was hired to teach physical education in Madison, Wisconsin.

I finally got a message from the college infirmary to go directly to a rehabilitation clinic in Madison for further testing. They wanted me as an inpatient. Why? Why weren't they providing justification for becoming an inpatient? Why the secrets? Was this serious? I was concerned but not overly worried. I was going to my first teaching position no matter what! I couldn't worry about my body now because I had responsibilities and commitments to fulfill. I also had a summer recreational job waiting in Madison and it felt like my beginning as a responsible adult.

I arrived in Madison and registered as an inpatient at the rehabilitation center. For one week I was given a battery of tests to determine the cause of my numbness and tingling. I still prayed it was just some bug. At the end of the week I was summoned by a black medical doctor. Wow, a black neurologist! My mouth dropped to the floor because I had never met a black doctor. Not in my whole life. He had my test results and I was ready to move on with life. He gently told me that I had multiple sclerosis.

You say I have what? He repeated it slowly. Multiple sclerosis.

I hadn't heard of the illness and couldn't even pronounce it. It wasn't anything that was talked about around the neighborhood, in church or school. Must be serious because the doctor looked intent and sad. The neurologist explained some facts about multiple sclerosis, but those facts didn't pertain to me. How could they? My numbness and tingling were only "temporary." I was a strong and conditioned athlete and all athletes were healthy. I had graduated with honors and worked hard to reach my dream of teaching. I wasn't going to believe any of it.

He explained as much as he could about the disease and briefly shared his thoughts about my future. He defined multiple sclerosis as the crippler of young adults. I was only twenty-five years old. Multiple sclerosis. The brain and spinal cord are involved, the central nervous system. There is degeneration of myelin,[*] a material which serves as an insulation for the nerves.

Mama, Ora, had polio as a child. She would talk proudly of her athleticism and wouldn't dwell on her polio. All along she maintained a positive attitude and led a normal life. She walked with a limp and her right leg was smaller than the left. We couldn't afford trips to clinics to purchase a proper fitting shoe so she would put newspaper in her right shoe to build a better fit.

I never thought of Mama as a woman with a disability. She was strong and capable, and I thought polio was simply a condition that made one leg smaller. It didn't make her less of a woman, less of an athlete, less of a mama in any way. She was the greatest!

I politely thanked the neurologist for the information and my test results. Multiple who? What the hell was this disease? I was trying to tell myself not to worry. He gave some parting advice: always protect your eyes, your body will dictate its capabilities each day, and change your profession. Not be in physical education? I felt cool and blasé and knew those messages weren't for me. This guy was crazy!

Mama taught me to think about messages from other folks, to take their word with a grain of salt. I was taught to think about decisions and not to believe everything coming from someone's mouth. On the other hand, doctors were always right.

I was discharged from the rehabilitation center. His advice was still ringing in my head, none of which made any sense. I got behind the wheel of my car, started the engine, and burst into tears. Only for a

---

* Myelin surrounding the nerves is akin to the covering of an electric wire. This fatty insulation allows the nerve to transmit impulses at a rapid speed, enabling a person to move almost without much thought. The loss of myelin insulation causes, in effect, a short circuiting so that a person loses the ability to make smooth, rapid, coordinated movements. Multiple sclerosis is a demyelinating disease. This loss of myelin appears as a hardened sclerotic (scar) area. These areas are multiple within the central nervous system; thus the term multiple sclerosis.

The cause of multiple sclerosis has not been determined but several theories exist. It is now known that the immune system does not operate as it should. The immune system reacts strongly to some stimuli and produces large amounts of antibodies to protect itself. This may result in a turning against itself and the development of what is called an autoimmune reaction.

In two-thirds of the cases of multiple sclerosis, an elevated gamma globulin is noted in the spinal fluid. Special proteins called oligoclonal bands are found in the spinal fluid of 80 percent of people with multiple sclerosis.

quick moment, because I was tough! Why was I crying? I didn't understand the test results and really didn't believe any of them. Multiple sclerosis. You say I have what?

Mama didn't understand multiple sclerosis and would carefully watch as I walked. Sometimes she would say, "Oh, honey, I know you don't feel well but I know you feel better than I do. " Many times I didn't feel well but didn't argue the point. Maybe it was true that I had more energy but my body wouldn't allow me to use my energy. My mind wanted to do any and everything, but my body said, "I don't think so." I wondered if Mama ever felt responsible for my disease?

Following the hospital stint I went to work at my summer job with Madison Parks and Recreation. Among other things, I was responsible for organizing playground activities. One day the local newspaper came to take an action photo of the new staff. I ran after a large ball while the photographer took several shots. Why was it so hard to run? Why was I still limping and dragging my left leg? Why isn't this illness fading?

AUGUST 1970

I began teaching at my new physical education position at a large high school in Madison, Wisconsin. My job included a full day of teaching followed by year-round coaching of girls' team sports: volleyball, basketball and softball. In addition I coached golf and track and field. I loved teaching and coaching. I felt competent and confident and wanted to make a difference in the lives of young people. I had worked long and hard to achieve this honor! Nothing would stop me now.

Due to my rigorous teaching and coaching schedule, the days were long and tiring. I pushed myself hard. By the end of each day I was totally exhausted, but I blamed my exhaustion on any number of things other than "that illness." I convinced myself that it was only natural to work hard and to be tired at the end of each day.

My exhaustion carried over into my coaching. I would enter the gym and immediately look for a place to sit: a chair, the floor, anything to rest my tired limbs. I usually coached from a chair which was uncommon for any coach of worth. I felt I couldn't let my MS interfere with my job. I had to work harder, longer and be the super teacher, the super coach. I needed to keep it a secret and keep my job.

To keep it hidden, I had to find ways to get more energy, to get my legs and the rest of my body in working order before students and the public put two-and-two together. I would be exposed. They will figure out that I had a disability and think less of me. How could I be competent and have a disability? How could I be knowledgeable about coaching techniques and strategies and be able to coach these teams? Will I be dismissed by my school district and my teams?

Mama was often silent and didn't ask many questions about my illness. Once during a family reunion Mama asked that I not tell the relatives about my disease. I sat confused and wondered why I needed to keep this a secret. I hated secrets. I wondered about the magnitude of her fears. After all, multiple sclerosis was only a small part of my persona, not the total "me." Did she feel ashamed for me? Did she feel that I would be judged as less capable, less of a person? I'll never know. Mama died in September, 1985.

Being an outstanding teacher and coach was important to me. I was bothered when I had to teach and coach from a chair. I wanted to run and play with my students but my body had other plans.

During one basketball practice some team players asked me to show my stuff and to demonstrate my basketball talents. They wondered if I could make a basket from any spot on the floor. I knew I had to look exceptional. I knew I had to prove myself to keep their trust and respect.

I got up from my chair, strolled to the side line and took a deep breath. I placed the basketball in my left hand and pushed it forward. Swish. I moved to a different spot on the floor and let go of the ball. Nothing but net. I continued shooting for three minutes. I hit some incredible shots. I did it. I had gained some additional time to coach from my chair.

During my first three years of coaching, I felt I had to keep the secret from my players. The secret weighed heavier and heavier upon my heart. The players asked more questions about my lack of participation. Finally, I couldn't continue to carry the burden so I told my basketball team about my MS. They were shocked and saddened. They cried and asked questions about the disease, some of which I couldn't answer. Each practice they tried to show understanding, caring, and support. They created an opportunity for me to accept my disease and maintain my dignity.

It seemed that my days of teaching and coaching grew longer. I was more tired. My body was becoming more and more affected by fatigue, and I began to understand the advice from the neurologist: on a daily basis my body would dictate what I would and would not be able to do.

My gait was changing, pace was slower, balance was unstable, speech was slurred, vision was blurred, and coordination was challenged. What was happening to me? I thought I could win this race, this challenge. As an athlete I learned to push myself and give my best. I was used to winning and succeeding. Why can't I whip this damned illness into shape? Perhaps I could practice harder until I got it right or work harder at my job. I'll just get more rest and it will be better in a week or two.

FALL 1973

Weeks went by and my body gradually worsened. Advice from my neurologist rang in my ears: change your profession. Now it seemed that he was right. A life change was unfolding before me and at such a young age. Leaving my profession meant that I was losing my fight against MS. I tried to work in spite of my illness and to function as though I didn't have it. I tried to keep the illness hidden from everyone, but I couldn't continue the facade. I tried everything from my bag of tricks to win the battle. I wouldn't give up the fight. I would find another profession, one that was less of a challenge to my body.

I learned at an early age the lonely feelings of being devalued. Racism was evident early in my life, and I learned ways to deal with most of the scars left by its ugliness. Young kids would call out racial epithets from their houses, but Mama taught me to ignore their ignorance and to feel proud of my race.

Now I was faced with another dilemma—disability. How was I going to deal with one more problem? How was I going to deal with one more added societal discriminatory construct? Given the reality, how can I handle going between acceptance and denial of my illness?

It was disconcerting to make major life changes at twenty-nine. Because of the multiple sclerosis I tried to adjust and compromise my life while planning for another life. I had to keep a positive attitude about life and appreciate my many passions. At age twenty-five I could play a full set of tennis, play a complete game of softball, jog, read, even stay up until early morning. I couldn't give in to the disease. I had to find ways to compromise and still get the most out of my life. I couldn't compete like before so I had to find activities that would bring a smile to my heart. As my gait changed, I couldn't take long strides, so I had to adjust to a limp. My sight was deteriorating so I had to adjust to vision challenges. I thought it would be easier to relocate and to start a new career, a new identity.

FEBRUARY 1974

I went to the University of Minnesota to get a master's degree in educational administration. I knew my intellectual capabilities and wanted to continue my educational journey. I enjoyed the role of a student. I felt like I was on a mission. Time would run short. I needed to grab my learning and my dreams while I had the opportunity.

I was experiencing a lot of tingling and numbness in my arms and legs, and my vision was blurred. The doctors would call these episodes flare-ups or exacerbations. I was given different kinds of cortisone to reduce the inflammation from these flare-ups and to hope for physical improvements.

During an eye exam the doctor placed an eye chart in front of me and told me to read the letters. I waited for him to place the letters on the chart. And I waited. He wanted to know why I didn't respond. I replied that there weren't any letters located on the chart. Whoooops. Wrong. There were letters on the chart, but I was only able to detect the black border of the chart. Why me? Would I eventually become blind? I needed to hurry to see more before I lost my sight. I would stare long and hard at flowers, trees, and friends to fix their images in my brain. Another challenge, another compensation, another survival lesson.

1975

After I completed the master's degree in educational administration, I decided to get a doctorate. I thought that degree would help my self-image. Press on girl, because time is short.

1976

I was still in college doing a lot of reading. My sight was unpredictable—some days clear, some days blurred. Portions of words would be missing from the text and I would rely on past associations for meaning. It was a slow process and I was certainly frustrated. I used to love to read but now reading wasn't one of my favorite activities. Friends would discuss their favorite books from reading lists and tease me because my list was short. I could take the teasing or I could explain. I didn't explain.

As a doctoral candidate I needed to complete a practicum in my field. I was hired as an administrative assistant at a suburban high school. Being an administrator was stressful and I felt I had to absorb the stress and excel, always beyond the norm. I was determined to be

an exceptional administrator and wasn't going to let my illness interfere with my responsibilities. I had several MS flare-ups during that
year. Still, I felt I had to do my job, no matter what. I was not going to
give in to this disease.

*Don't give people another reason to judge and put you in another
irrelevant category. Our society places black people in the lowest of categories, so don't reveal your disability and give people another reason to
judge.*

One day I was tediously completing a written assignment at school,
concentrating on every movement of the pen. I tried to ignore the
numbness and lack of coordination in my hand. A student walked into
my office. After I talked to the student about the misbehavior that
brought him there, I had to write a pass to allow him admission into
his next class. I tried to ignore what was happening, but it was clear
that I was having yet another exacerbation. My coordination was totally gone. I couldn't write the student pass. How will I handle this
one? I told the student to complete the top portion of the form and I
simply signed the bottom with a ragged signature, something that only
I could recognize.

1977

I completed my practicum and continued my doctoral courses. School
life had drained my funds, leaving me with only $6.35 to my name. I
needed a job.

There was an administrative position available at another suburban
school and I applied. While I was completing the application, I suddenly became numb and terrified. A question on the form asked if I had
any physical disabilities. My heart sank. Answering the question honestly would be the end of all my dreams. I had worked hard for the
administrative degree and now that would be worthless. If I'm honest,
they won't hire me because they will think I'm incompetent. If I'm dis-
honest, I couldn't live with myself. I was taught that lies would always
catch up to you and bite you in the butt. What do I do? Time stood still.

That was one of the hardest decisions of my life. After what seemed
like an eternity, I checked the "yes" box and admitted to myself and to
them that I had multiple sclerosis. When I put down my pen, I prayed
that the employer would overlook that section of the application form.

My prayer was answered. I got the job and worked for the
Burnsville School District for seventeen years. Seventeen years as an
associate principal, seventeen years as a disciplinarian, and seventeen
years of flare-ups. Despite that hateful disease, I was determined to

excel in my job. Over those years I had episodes where my vision was blurred and my arms and legs lacked coordination.

I would arrive home after work, enter my house without turning on lights. I knew my sight was failing but I was determined to survive independently. With my eyes closed I would rehearse the location of my furniture, count off the distance between pieces and rely on my sense of touch. Don't give up. Maintain the fight. Hurry and appreciate the beauty! I received cortisone to correct my vision.

1980

You say I have what? Diabetes?

It wasn't just problems with my vision and coordination that I faced during those years. I was also told that I was diabetic. I wasn't totally surprised by the news because diabetes was a part of my family history. I was bummed. Why was I blessed with all these illnesses?

1994

Symptoms from multiple sclerosis and diabetes have become a way of life. Seventeen years of stress from my job and spiraling symptoms brought me face to face with another stage in my life. Once again I was being advised to leave my profession. What was I to do for employment now? What would happen to my identity? What would I do in life and who would I become? I would no longer be an educational administrator. That was devastating news! But deep down inside I knew it was good advice. The time had come to let go and to enjoy life as it presented itself. To let go of my life as an educator, an administrator, and establish a new identity.

Religion was important in our family. We attended church services every Sunday and sometimes three services on any given Sunday. Mama taught me to believe in the Lord and He would keep me strong. When times were rough, Mama taught me to pray and hope for a better situation.

I have given myself permission to read more literature by authors with disabilities to gain a clearer understanding of the social and moral views about people with disabilities. I must move forward and continue to define and refine my disability.

Those of us who live with disabilities understand the notion of change and facing unknowns. I'm often asked how I keep a smile and positive attitude when living with MS. What's my alternative? I must continue to define and redefine my purpose in life and build joys from unpleasant circumstances. I believe life is all about compromise. Life is filled with uncertainties and we are constantly challenged to find ways to survive.

I often think about the sources of my oppression from being black, a woman, and a person with several disabilities. I know it only takes a second to alter the course of someone's life. Those of us who live with disabilities are often treated in unwelcome ways and we serve as reminders of the mortality that is the fate of us all.

I want to explore my connection with the athlete I left behind, who could throw a ball with the speed of a freight train and was the team's designated batter; the teacher I left behind, who was prepared, competent, and concerned about students and their success; the coach I left behind, who developed outstanding teams and upstanding young women; the school administrator I left behind, who turned administration into teaching. I want to explore my connection with other people, my connection with my body, and my connection with Me.

ABOUT THE AUTHOR

I wrote this piece because I needed to tell my story about my disabilities. Recently I've read several books by authors with disabilities and appreciated and learned from some of their experiences. I kept trying to place myself and to find myself within their writings. I finally realized that the authors told of their experiences, not mine. I would find my experiences in print only if I provided it. I learned a lot from the process of writing my story. It was an enjoyable journey but at the same time sad. I uncovered a lot of loss and a lot of joy. This experience will make me stronger. I taught physical education and coached team sports for four years and was an educational administrator for seventeen years. Currently, I am an educational consultant and Director of the Administrators' SEED Institute. I have lived in Minnesota for twenty-four years.

The Wall

Ka Vue

A S A HIGH SCHOOL SOPHOMORE, I PARTICIPATED IN AN
Upward Bound camping trip in 1990 with my summer school
program at Michigan State University. Before going on this camping
trip, I thought that everyone in my group was really friendly, but when
we got to the campsite it seemed people's attitudes changed. Maybe it
was because everyone was having a hard time at the camp, but I wasn't
sure at the time.

Arriving at Camp Break Through in the early afternoon, my group
and I moved our belongings into the cabins and took the rest of the
evening to explore the camp area. I had a chance to listen and talk to
some other students who were in a different program and had already
gone through all the obstacle courses. They said the most challenging
activity was the forty-foot wall, an obstacle that replicated a mountain
climbing experience.

That night I went to bed early, expecting to have a long, exhausting
day ahead of me. As I quietly lay on the hard mattress I felt the rough-
ness on my body. I spent the night twisting and turning. As I gazed at
the moon, memories rushed in and tears filled my eyes.

∾ ∾ ∾

I could remember that same full moon, with crickets chirping all
over the thick, dark, deep Laotian forest. From the ground I could see

the reflection of the moon in a puddle of restless ripples left by the rain. Then the rain came again.

Oh, I wished I were home. My bed is not soft but it is comfy. I wish it were all a dream. I wish I were dreaming away in my mother's bosom. Her arms cuddling me, holding me tight. I am safe. I'm protected from harm. I could hear my five-year-old heart beating, pounding in my chest, pumping in and out each breath of air, as the night's thickness crept into my body like slimy worms crawling all over me. "It's going to be a very long night," I thought to myself.

I had no shoes, though I'm on a flight with my family from Laos to Thailand. Moving quickly, holding on tight to my older brother's hand, I feel sweat moisten my palm. Swiftly we moved, crossing the dirt road. From the look of the road, a group of men had passed by earlier, trudging in the rain with heavy machinery. As soon as we had crossed the road, my brother went to the end of the long, long line of people and counted each individual to see if anyone was left behind.

He came back and slowly and quietly we all moved forward again, hoping that we would not get lost or accidentally left behind. This land was strange and we did not know what would happen if we were caught in the light of day. Yet swiftly and quietly, like the wind, we moved into the darkness of the deep forest. Again I heard crickets chirping and drops of rain dripping from the leaves onto the undisturbed ground. In a drop of rain I saw water giving life. I hoped my life would also nourish life.

Once in a while as we trudged through the deep forest, I heard loud crashing and saw thundering light flashing, lighting up the quiet, dark forest. I heard cracking dry leaves and twigs breaking on the damp ground. I heard babies crying, screaming, terrified in the dark.

"I'm scared," I whispered in my brother's ear. He had me on his back along with the family's food supplies. For many nights and days my brother has been carrying me on his back. At times I felt it wouldn't be long before he decided to leave me along with the children I had seen sleeping alone on the road. I had seen children being put to sleep forever because they were hungry and crying. I had seen children crying, looking for their parents. I began to wonder, "Where are my parents?"

And then I knew my parents were watching over me. They were watching me through the spirit of my heart. They have been watching me, every little step that I took. They have been watching my brothers and their families, giving each and every one of us the strength to continue our journey.

That night we all moved from the mountain through the valley and when the sun rose, we stopped to rest. We took all of our belongings and quickly hid in a nearby cave. The day was still; not a word was heard or spoken. Everyone was tired and fell fast asleep, except for a couple of men sitting and watching for signs of trouble. We were all scared.

The next morning the mists were lifting moisture from the ground, leaving the restless land and hills, chasing after one another into the blue sky like a group of children playing tag on a hot weekend afternoon. The horizon was peaceful as I looked far past the hills. I asked my brother, "When are we going to get home?" He slowly turned to me with tears running down his bony cheeks. Then he pointed far beyond the mountain ridges to Thailand and said, "Over there. That will be our new home."

By midday everyone was hungry and digging through their baskets looking for food. All we had was rice. We were afraid to set up a campfire for fear of attracting attention. Running in the night, hiding in the day, we needed to be invisible. We ate our lunch cold. The rice was delicious. It was better than anything I had eaten since we left our home many weeks and a lifetime ago. I ate mine slowly, chewing little by little, swallowing piece by piece. I could feel every grain of rice dropping, sinking slowly, making its way down my throat. I could even hear the echo when the grain of rice fell onto the bottom of my stomach and slowly began to fill up the empty space, relieving my hunger.

As soon as night fell we moved out again, swiftly, quietly. Not a candle or a light was lit as we walked through the forest. Suddenly we stopped to listen to the peacefulness of the dark night and waited for further news before continuing on our journey. We checked our group and family by whispering each one's name. Everyone was safe.

After a while my brother came back to us from the long line of people and told the other men in the group that by midnight we should reach the Mekong River. Once there we should be on our way to Freedom. What a relief! Tears of joy rushed down everyone's faces. Some were happy, some were sad. But we were all thankful that we were still alive. That night I wept.

∿ ∿ ∿

It was morning at Camp Break Through. Slowly I slid down to the cold wooden floor. As the rising sun shone through the window, the birds sang beautiful songs all around the quiet forest. I wandered around, looking for my towel in an unfamiliar room. The room looked so empty except for one bed, a closet and a dresser. To me it seemed lifeless except for the wind blowing through the window shutter. I found my towel and headed for the shower.

I hadn't gotten much sleep. Maybe it was because the mattress was too rough, but it did not matter. The day that I was waiting for had come, and I was looking forward to it. "What's going to happen today?" I asked myself while I showered. "Will the task be as simple as what some people have said or will it be difficult?" It worried me because I had never failed anything. But this obstacle that I was about to face was different. I had never had any mountain climbing experience. But still, I was thrilled.

Throughout that morning I wandered from cabin to cabin, asking other people to tell me how they felt about climbing the big wall. I thought that it would be a good idea to get an overview of the task. I asked someone I thought was a good friend of mine how he felt about climbing. He told me that it would be impossible for me to get to the top because I was too short and heavy. I hadn't realized it until then, but I started to notice that other people were also discouraging me.

I almost believed them. But the more they discouraged me, the more determined I was to do well. Climbing the wall was important to me because I looked at the blocks on the wall as if they were stepping stones in life. The blocks were choices that I needed to make that would determine my future. I could succeed by choosing a different path of blocks than my classmates. If I was willing to stay on track and put in time and effort, I would reach the top. I would overcome my fear of heights. They would see that what they said to me didn't discourage me.

By midday the sun was really hot and it started warming the big wall. I watched other people in my group climb. The different colored blocks were placed in patterns of ascending difficulty. Climbers could choose to use the red and black blocks or the yellow and green blocks or, easiest of all, all the colors together. The fewer colors you chose to use, the harder the climb. It seemed like it was going to be an easy job, but some of the people didn't make it to the top. Some people chose the easier path. I decided to take the harder path.

Not knowing how tricky climbing the wall would be, I first took each step carefully and slowly as I decided where to go next. Everything seemed to be going well until I got to the middle part of the wall. I was tired and my fingers were sore. It seemed as if I couldn't move upward anymore. My desire to climb this wall was gone. So I turned to the people in my group below and asked for help to continue my journey. I didn't hear an answer. It seemed as if everyone was busy doing other things. But I held on tight, grabbing on to the blocks and hoping not to slip off. I knew if I fell off, it would have been harder than ever to get to the same place again.

Sweat started to run down my face, and my arms were beginning to feel sore. Trying to figure out how I could continue, I turned once more and asked the people below for help. No one seemed to hear me. I looked around and I felt my difference. Asian. Hmong. Short. No one would help me. I felt angry.

The motivation to achieve something that I wanted for myself had given me the courage to move on slowly to another block without worrying about what was going on below. I was determined to reach the top of the wall. From that point on I felt no pain. Depression and discouragement were replaced by joy. I accomplished what I had set out to do. I remember finally putting my right hand on the top of the wall, pulling myself up to take a deep breath of air, and seeing amazed faces looking at me.

∾ ∾ ∾

Every now and then I relate my life to this experience. Coming to America meant leaving friends and relatives in another country, learning a new language and culture, working with people of different ethnicities and cultures. I have learned to set my own goals and find my own way.

This experience also showed me how I should treat other people. I listen to them and encourage people who are having tough times. I've also learned not to discourage students, friends, or other people working with me when they are trying hard to succeed in whatever they may be pursuing. Many times people don't see the importance of one person's actions.

Letting go, learning to accept new things and new places, or facing obstacles can feel like scaling walls. Walls exist because of families, genetics, ethnicity, or loss. It's important to maintain unity in the face of walls that threaten to divide us. We must build walls that support and tear down walls that divide. The choices are ours.

I can help students climb walls and see what is on the other side. I can help them believe they can get there. I can nourish life.

ABOUT THE AUTHOR

Arriving in the United States in the summer of 1980 with my oldest brother was a memorable experience. I'm currently a student at Metro State University (Minnesota) and have a lot to learn from anyone willing to teach me. I see myself as a listener, listening for ways to teach that acknowledge the richness of cultures. I work with children, hoping to help them understand other cultures as well as their own. I believe that they, too, can be successful if we have the time and patience to work with them.

I'll Never Be a White Middle-Class Teacher

Emma Buffington Duren

I'VE BEEN TEACHING FOR ALMOST THIRTY YEARS, AND FOR most of those years I was never in my classroom. That might sound strange to you, but it's an easy feat to accomplish. Don't think I'm lazy or lacking in understanding of the fundamentals of teaching, or that I am not a committed and dedicated teacher. I am committed, dedicated, creative, and I understand the fundamentals of teaching. Yet for the majority of my teaching career, I was absent from my classroom. I just taught children and left myself at home.

I am an African American teacher in a predominately White school district. Most of the staff in this district is White. I am the only visible person of color on staff. There are few students of color in my school, but that's changing. While their number is increasing, the hiring of staff of color is not.

I grew up in a small town in southwestern Arkansas during the late '50s and early '60s. Both my parents were educators. My father was the school principal, my mother and several aunts were teachers. How could I *not* know the importance of education? Topics related to education were frequently discussed at the dinner table and family gatherings. My understanding of what the classroom climate should be was formed, in part, from listening to those conversations. I also began to discern that there was something different about the education of White and Black students.

In this visualization I saw White students as being much smarter than Black students. The schools that Whites attended had newer books, more supplies and equipment, and the teachers were better prepared. Black students had to work much harder to be as good as the average White student.

My first teaching job was at Central Elementary School in my hometown of Magnolia, Arkansas. In the fall of 1967, I was one of the two Black teachers first placed in the "White" schools. Most of my students, who were White, had never had any contact with a Black person other than their maids. During the first few weeks of school, I was frequently asked if I knew their maids. I could truthfully answer, "No."

There were three Black children in the three fifth grades. We knew each other but did little to acknowledge each other at school. They were there on open enrollment. Me? I was there because my parents were not about to give me their consent to accept a teaching position anywhere else. The Black students and I never talked about why I was there or our unique situation. I never shared any of my hopes and dreams with them, nor they with me. The issue of race was never mentioned. I was told not to bring it up and perhaps my students were told the same. Besides, it didn't seem to be an issue with us.

My understanding of the classroom was based on my perception of a middle-class, Eurocentric value system. All students were the same. They should all be taught in the same manner and with the same expectations. You don't see color, you just teach children. You teach about the European Americans who "made this country great" and their beliefs and values.

As the social studies teacher for three fifth-grade classes, I made sure that the students were aware of current events. We talked a lot about the Vietnam War, but I never asked what personal connections they had to it. Students met me at the door to ask if I had heard that Lyndon Johnson had announced that he would not run for President. They learned about the states and capitols. We never shared our adventures visiting other states. I didn't see color. I just taught children and left myself at home. I wasn't a Black teacher teaching White students. I was just a teacher. They were just students.

It was during my year of teaching at Central that Martin Luther King Jr. was assassinated. The schools were not closed. I was not allowed to miss school. The children were unusually quiet and well-behaved. Not one person, not even the teachers, mentioned the assassination. Nor did I. This was strange because as a class we talked about what was happening in the news. When rioting broke out across the county, it was never mentioned by the students. Nor by me. The last day of school one child told me that he was sorry about what had happened to Dr. King.

I only worked at Central Elementary for a year. I have since found it interesting that not more than ten years earlier the governor of our fair state barred nine Black students from entering Central High School in Little Rock, and there I was teaching little White boys and girls. Of course, we never mentioned the other Central. But then it wasn't in the textbooks.

In the fall of 1968 I decided to attend graduate school at the University of Minnesota. This was my way of running away from home. When you live in a small town, everybody knows everybody else's business. I wanted to go someplace where I didn't know anyone and no one could report my comings and goings. After a year of graduate school I decided to stay, and that meant getting a job.

I proceeded to send out numerous applications. I didn't know that very few Blacks were hired to teach in the school systems in the late '60s. I was interviewed and offered a job in a suburb of St. Paul, Minnesota. Not wanting to go home, I accepted. This was something of a coup because teaching in the suburbs was, for many, a dream job. For me it was just a temporary job, and I didn't have to go back home.

I was offered a fifth-grade position. After a year at Central and a year at the University of Minnesota, I was accustomed to being the only African American in the group. I had been trained to work in an all-White school. You see, in the late '60s I (along with many other prospective Black teachers mostly from historically Black southern colleges) was sent to a workshop in Baton Rouge, Louisiana, that focused on preparing us to work in all-White schools. At this time, school districts across the South were placing Black teachers in White schools. I guess we were the chosen ones. I was taught how to talk, walk, dress, look people in the eye, and blend in. I was ready. I needed to remember that I taught children and not color. But most of all I needed to remember that I was being a credit to my race. I was a teacher, not a Black teacher.

I worked diligently to be the best teacher I could, a teacher who just happened to be Black. I worked to adhere to the Eurocentric, middle-class values I perceived as essential to the ideal classroom. I put up beautiful bulletin boards that were adorned with White faces. The students sat in perfectly straight rows. My desk was in front of the class where I assumed a position of control. I knew people were watching me and I had to be better than the best teacher. I could not afford even the smallest mistake. I understood that there were families that did not want me as their child's teacher. I worked hard at being White and middle class so that I would be accepted. Many White families were moving into the suburbs because the Twin Cities were becoming increasingly Black. Guess who they ran into? ME! What a surprise.

I was determined to be seen as a good teacher, if not counted among the best, actively involving students in the learning process. While studying a unit on nutrition, we created a grocery store. Students brought in containers of various food items and we practiced shopping for balanced meals. A store manager came and talked to students about how and why foods are displayed a certain way in the store. Representatives from General Mills came and talked to students about the development and marketing of a new cereal. The person in charge of the school lunch program came and explained how the menu was developed.

In the mid-seventies the state of Minnesota required teachers to take a human relations course. Curriculum was also developed to teach students about our likenesses and differences, about stereotypes, and about the contributions people of various racial, ethnic and religious backgrounds have made to this country. There was one lesson on skin color. We talked about why people have different skin color. I compared my skin color to those of my students. Some of my White students' skin was darker than mine.

We talked about how each of us is unique. Students brought in pictures of their families and talked about their likes and dislikes, what they were good at, and about their favorite foods and books. I brought in pictures of my family. My father is very fair with a red skin tone and my mother is fair. One student asked me if I was adopted. I was embarrassed and angered by the question. Memories of childhood taunts about my skin color came rushing back and once again I didn't fit in. I was different. I have never again shared pictures of my family.

To address the issue of diversity, our district began to observe Brotherhood Week rather than Black History Week. During this time we focused on how we might look different and come from different backgrounds but we were basically all the same. I remember this as being both an exciting and embarrassing time for me. I have always been proud of my African American heritage. But when you're the only person of color in an ocean of mostly White faces, conflicting emotions surface. I was somewhat fearful, angry and confused. Someone may actually notice that I'm not like them and I would cease to fit in.

Being somewhat passive-aggressive, my way of saying "I am Black" was to wear my hair in a "natural." I have naturally curly hair so this was not an easy undertaking, especially when several White colleagues' "naturals" looked better than mine. It was fun to watch people talk to my hair instead of to me.

If you have ever pretended to be someone that you're not, you know the fear of being found out. In my case the masquerade was not because I was ashamed of who I was. It had to do with the fact that I wanted desperately to fit in. By trying to be White and middle-class, I missed a lot of opportunities to be an ally for many students and families. We were all living in a state of self-denial.

There was only one Black family in our attendance area in the 1970s. One year the son was in my fifth-grade class. I don't remember any unusual bonding that took place between us. He was just a student and I was just his teacher who happened to be Black. Had I not been so desperate to fit in, too busy not noticing differences, perhaps my memory of him would be more vivid. I didn't understand that all the students, White and otherwise, were just as confused as I was. I didn't understand that by working to create a classroom community where we could discuss differences openly and honestly, we could all have a sense of belonging.

During that same time period, the district experienced a decline in student enrollment and the school I was working in closed. I was transferred to a school on the other side of town. This school was considered to be "not as middle class" as the previous school. There were more students of color and children who lived in apartments.

Once again I needed to prove that I was just as good as the other teachers. I needed to be better than the best. I was a teacher who just happened to be Black.

Good teachers have control over their classroom. I was considered a strict teacher.

Good teachers have high expectations. I expected and demanded quality work.

Good teachers are resourceful. I organized a group of parents to assist in a book writing project that included writing by each student.

Good teachers are creative. One year I choreographed the battle be-tween the Mouse King and the soldiers in the *Nutcracker Suite* for a holiday concert.

I guess I would still be trying to be White and middle class, better then the best, who just happens to be Black, had I not participated in the Minnesota S.E.E.D. (Seeking Educational Equity and Diversity) Leaders' Workshop in 1993. This experience forever changed me as a person and as a teacher. The process gave me the opportunity to look at the real me. The me who had for many years tried so hard to be just like everybody else. I discovered the courage within myself to face the truth that I had always known. No amount of trying was going to make me White and middle class.

I realized that I have a lot of wonderful talents to share with my students just the way I am. I have found the courage to put me in my classroom. I could work on becoming the teacher I wanted to be, cre-ate the kind of learning environment that was comfortable for me and my students.

I completely rearranged my room. For years I had kept my blinds and the door closed. I opened them both. I rearranged the seats. In-stead of rows, I placed the students' desks in a semicircle. I moved my desk to the side of the room and removed the small bookcases that were on top of it. There are now large overstuffed chairs so that stu-dents can sit and read. There is now a private area tucked into a corner for a student who wants or needs to be alone for a while. There are pic-tures representing all kinds of people displayed around the room. There are pictures of students in the hallways and around the room. There are now computers, Lego blocks, jigsaw puzzles, Scrabble, mag-netic poetry strips and lots and lots of books to engage students in the learning process. I am no longer the focus of the room. The students are. I want students to know that this is not my classroom but our classroom. They can no longer hide. Neither can I.

I love my room. It's the most multicultural place in our building. There are pictures of people who look like me and people who don't. Parents tell me how comfortable they feel in my classroom, and stu-dents seem to enjoy being there. I know it makes a difference.

Recently, many Southeast Asians began moving into our atten-dance area. Occasionally, because of language differences, we have trouble understanding one another. At a parent-teacher conference, a father of one of my Southeast Asian students looked around the room and saw a picture of his son. The most wonderful smile spread across his face. Language was no longer a problem.

I began to collect and read books to students that reflected various cultural backgrounds. One such book was *White Socks Only* by Evenly Coleman, which is about a little Black girl who misinterprets the sign on a water fountain that says "Whites Only." During Book Week the students selected this book as their favorite. As part of that week, students decorated our door to represent this book. A Vietnamese student, who was not proficient in English, reading or math, created a fantastic picture for our door. The students were amazed at his artistic ability. Though we often had trouble understanding what he was saying, we had no trouble understanding the wonderful pictures he continued to draw throughout the year.

I believe that a person's name and its correct pronunciation are very important. My name is a source of pride to me, as I am named after my mother and grandmother. Many of my students also have names that are important family names.

Each morning we start our day in what has become known as our opening circle. In the circle each student has the opportunity to share something. The only rule is that whatever is shared must be "appropriate" material for the classroom. Students are free to talk about their feelings and experiences. Listeners may ask questions or make appropriate comments. You really learn a lot about students by listening to them. Students have shared what it's like to live in a trailer park during a tornado, the illness and death of a family member, the pain and uncertainty of divorce.

In our sharing circle, students learn a lot about me as a person and as their teacher. Most of my students know that I don't drive on the freeway and that I am afraid of dogs. They have even offered suggestions to help me overcome my fears. We use our circle to discuss and make decisions about events and concerns related to our classroom. I'll always remember a student sharing what it's like to sit in front of the pencil sharpener. I had no idea what a distraction it could be, so I had it moved. We resolve conflicts, plan classroom projects and celebrations, agree on classroom procedures and schedule changes.

In spite of my efforts to build a classroom community, there is the occasional student who appears to resist all opportunities to become part of that community. I have spent hours trying to understand and devise a plan to help that student. Then I had an experience that helped me understand why some students appear to refuse to be productive in the classroom.

Our school had a tradition of having a yearly staff retreat. I never go and am quite willing to engage in an alternative activity. One year the retreat was held during the month of January. It was going to be held on Martin Luther King Jr.'s birthday. When I mentioned this, no one said a word. Everyone looked down at their feet. The discussion continued and I learned that those of us not attending the retreat would have to attend a workshop on multiple intelligences. I could not be excused from the workshop, nor could it be taped for later viewing. I was very angry.

The materials presented at the workshop were meaningless to me. I simply shut down and refused to learn. My White colleagues did not appear to have a problem being at the workshop. They seemed happy and eager to be there. Their attitude made me even angrier. Why didn't they understand my anger? I felt like an invisible and non-valued person. When I walked out of that building, I hated everybody in it. I wanted to scream, destroy something, hurt someone. Had I been a student, I would never have entered that school again voluntarily. But I am an adult with bills to pay, and so I returned the next day. Once I felt like I belonged. I have not been able to feel that way since.

The hurt from that experience still lingers. This experience had a significant impact on me. If I, as an adult, could feel so shut out of the learning environment, many of my students may have similar feelings. I began to look for additional ways for students to assume ownership in our classroom.

At the beginning of the school year, students select a class name. Students can also create a button with the name and a representative drawing. Students have named themselves "The Smart Ones," "The Multi-Age Learners," "The Smart Stars," "The Awesome Eagles," and "The Crazy A's." Any class publications have that name and picture on them. Students also create a class rap that sums up the beliefs of the class. This rap is said every morning during our opening circle. My favorite is, "Knowledge is power. I know what I know. When you get an education, you'll be taking a step because knowledge is power. I know what I know."

Putting *me* in my classroom has given me the freedom and opportunity to grow in ways that I have only begun to explore. I don't have to be afraid of not being perfect or not fitting in. No matter how hard I try, I will never be perfect and I will always be different. I don't have to build a wall between me and my students because I see us all as unique and very special.

It has been a long journey for me, but I think that at last I'm on the right road. Remembering my own story helps me to understand why my students might respond in certain ways. I can understand their anger, frustration, and the need to be accepted for who they are and who they hope to become.

When an African American college student asked if she could do her student teaching with me, I knew that I was on the right road. She wanted to work with someone who would be supportive, truthful, and fair and who would understand her passion for teaching multi-culturally.

I've given up trying to be a White, middle-class teacher. My road is still under construction, and there is a long journey ahead of me. But I think that the teacher I have become is far more exciting and effective than the one I was trying to be. I hope the truth and honesty I bring to my students helps them to see the world in a broader context. I hope this gives them a foundation upon which to work for social justice and advocate for equality.

ABOUT THE AUTHOR

I wrote this story because I hope that it will be a "window and/or a mir-ror" for you, the reader. If this story is a mirror for you, I encourage you to be true to your heritage or your own unique "oneness." If this story is a window for you, I challenge you to seek to create an environment that is inclusive, welcoming, and supportive of everyone. I currently teach in a suburban school district north of St. Paul, Minnesota.

White Privilege:
Unpacking the Invisible Knapsack

Peggy McIntosh

THROUGH WORK TO BRING MATERIALS FROM WOMEN'S Studies into the rest of the curriculum, I have often noticed men's unwillingness to grant that they are over-privileged, even though they may grant that women are disadvantaged. They may say they will work to improve women's status in the society, the university, or the curriculum, but they can't or won't support the idea of lessening men's. Denials which amount to taboos surround the subject of advantages which men gain from women's disadvantages. These denials protect male privilege from being fully acknowledged, lessened or ended.

Thinking through unacknowledged male privilege as a phenomenon, I realized that since hierarchies in our society are interlocking, there was most likely a phenomenon of white privilege which was similarly denied and protected. As a white person, I realized I had been taught about racism as something which puts others at a disadvantage, but had been taught not to see one of its corollary aspects, white privilege, which puts me at an advantage.

I think whites are carefully taught not to recognize white privilege, as males are taught not to recognize male privilege. So I have begun in an untutored way to ask what it is like to have white privilege. I have come to see white privilege as an invisible package of unearned assets which I can count on cashing in each day, but about which I was "meant" to remain oblivious. White privilege is like an invisible weightless knapsack of special provisions, maps, passports, codebooks, visas, clothes, tools, and blank checks.

Describing white privilege makes one newly accountable. As we in Women's Studies work to reveal male privilege and ask men to give up some of their power, so I, in writing about having white privilege, now ask, "Having described it, what will I do to lessen or end it?"

After I realized the extent to which men work from a base of unacknowledged privilege, I understood that much of their oppressiveness was unconscious. Then I remembered the frequent charges from women of color that white women whom they encounter are oppressive. I began to understand why we are justly seen as oppressive, even when we don't see ourselves that way. I began to count the ways in which I enjoy unearned skin privilege and have been conditioned into oblivion about its existence.

My schooling gave me no training in seeing myself as an oppressor, as an unfairly advantaged person, or as a participant in a damaged culture. I was taught to see myself as an individual whose moral state depended on her individual moral will. My schooling followed the pattern my colleague Elizabeth Minnich has pointed out: whites are taught to think of their lives as morally neutral, normative, and average, and also ideal, so that when we work to benefit others, this is seen as work which will allow "them" to be more like "us."

I decided to try to work on myself at least by identifying some of the daily effects of white privilege in my life. I have chosen those conditions which I think in my case *attach somewhat more to skin-color privilege* than to class, religion, ethnic status, or geographical location, though of course all these other factors are intricately intertwined. As far as I can see, my African American co-workers, friends, and acquaintances with whom I come into daily or frequent contact in this particular time, place, and line of work cannot count on most of these conditions.

1. I can if I wish arrange to be in the company of people of my race most of the time.

2. If I should need to move, I can be pretty sure of renting or purchasing housing in an area which I can afford and in which I would want to live.

3. I can be pretty sure that my neighbors in such a location will be neutral or pleasant to me.

4. I can go shopping alone most of the time, pretty well assured that I will not be followed or harassed.

5. I can turn on the television or open to the front page of the paper and see people of my race widely represented.

6. When I am told about our national heritage or about "civilization," I am shown that people of my color made it what it is.

7. I can be sure that my children will be given curricular materials that testify to the existence of their race.

8. If I want to, I can be pretty sure of finding a publisher for this piece on white privilege.

9. I can go into a music shop and count on finding the music of my race represented, into a supermarket and find the staple foods which fit with my cultural traditions, into a hairdresser's shop and find someone who will cut my hair.

10. Whether I use checks, credit cards, or cash, I can count on my skin color not to work against the appearance of financial reliability.

11. I can arrange to protect my children most of the time from people who might not like them.

12. I can swear, or dress in second hand clothes, or not answer letters, without having people attribute these choices to the bad morals, the poverty, or the illiteracy of my race.

13. I can speak in public to a powerful male group without putting my race on trial.

14. I can do well in a challenging situation without being called a credit to my race.

15. I am never asked to speak for all the people of my racial group.

16. I can remain oblivious of the language and customs of persons of color who constitute the world's majority without feeling, in my culture, any penalty for such oblivion.

17. I can criticize our government and talk about how much I fear its policies and behavior without being seen as a cultural outsider.

18. I can be pretty sure that if I ask to talk to "the person in charge," I will be facing a person of my race.

19. If a traffic cop pulls me over or if the IRS audits my tax return, I can be sure I haven't been singled out because of my race.

20. I can easily buy posters, postcards, picture books, greeting cards, dolls, toys, and children's magazines featuring people of my race.

21. I can go home from most meetings of organizations I belong to feeling somewhat tied in, rather than isolated, out-of-place, out-numbered, unheard, held at a distance, or feared.

22. I can take a job with an affirmative action employer without having coworkers on the job suspect that I got it because of race.

23. I can choose public accommodation without fearing that people of my race cannot get in or will be mistreated in the places I have chosen.

24. I can be sure that if I need legal or medical help, my race will not work against me.

25. If my day, week, or year is going badly, I need not ask of each negative episode or situation whether it has racial overtones.

26. I can choose blemish cover or bandages in "flesh" color and have them more or less match my skin.

I repeatedly forgot each of the realizations on this list until I wrote it down. For me, white privilege has turned out to be an elusive and fugitive subject. The pressure to avoid it is great, for in facing it I must give up the myth of meritocracy. If these things are true, this is not such a free country; one's life is not what one makes it; many doors open for certain people through no virtues of their own.

In unpacking this invisible knapsack of white privilege, I have listed conditions of daily experience which I once took for granted. Nor did I think of any of these perquisites as bad for the holder. I now think that we need a more finely differentiated taxonomy of privilege, for some of these varieties are only what one would want for everyone in a just society, and others give license to be ignorant, oblivious, arrogant and destructive.

I see a pattern running through the matrix of white privilege, a pattern of assumptions which were passed on to me as a white person. There was one main piece of cultural turf; it was my own turf, and I was among those who could control the turf. *My skin color was an asset for any move I was educated to want to make.* I could think of myself as belonging in major ways, and of making social systems work for me. I could freely disparage, fear, neglect, or be oblivious to anything outside of the dominant cultural forms. Being of the main culture, I could also criticize it fairly freely.

In proportion as my racial group was being made confident, comfortable, and oblivious, other groups were likely being made inconfident, uncomfortable, and alienated. Whiteness protected me from many kinds of hostility, distress, and violence, which I was being subtly trained to visit in turn upon people of color.

For this reason, the word "privilege" now seems to me misleading. We usually think of privilege as being a favored state, whether earned or conferred by birth or luck. Yet some of the conditions I have described here work to systematically overempower certain groups. Such privilege simply *confers dominance* because of one's race or sex.

I want, then, to distinguish between earned strength and unearned power conferred systemically. Power from unearned privilege can look like strength when it is in fact permission to escape or to dominate. But not all of the privileges on my list are inevitably damaging. Some, like the expectation that neighbors will be decent to you, or that your race will not count against you in court, should be the norm in a just society. Others, like the privilege to ignore less powerful people, distort the humanity of the holders as well as the ignored groups.

We might at least start by distinguishing between positive advantages which we can work to spread, and negative types of advantages which unless rejected will always reinforce our present hierarchies. For example, the feeling that one belongs within the human circle, as some Native Americans say, should not be seen as privilege for a few. Ideally it is an *unearned entitlement.* At present, since only a few have it, it is an *unearned advantage* for them. This paper results from a process of coming to see that some of the power which I originally saw as attendant on being a human being in the U.S. consisted in *unearned advantage* and *conferred dominance.*

I have met very few men who are truly distressed about systemic, unearned male advantage and conferred dominance. And so one question for me and others like me is whether we will be like them, or whether we will get truly distressed, even outraged, about unearned race advantage and conferred dominance and if so, what we will do to lessen them. In any case, we need to do more work in identifying how they actually affect our daily lives. Many, perhaps most, of our white students in the U.S. think that racism doesn't affect them because they are not people of color; they do not see "whiteness" as a racial identity. In addition, since race and sex are not the only advantaging systems at work, we need similarly to examine the daily experience of having age advantage, or ethnic advantage, or advantage related to nationality, religion, sexual orientation, or physical ability.

Difficulties and dangers surrounding the task of finding parallels are many. Since racism, sexism, and heterosexism are not the same, the advantaging associated with them should not be seen as the same. In addition, it is hard to disentangle aspects of unearned advantage which rest more on social class, economic class, race, religion, sex and ethnic identity than on other factors. Still, all of the oppressions are interlocking, as the Combahee River Collective Statement of 1977 continues to remind us eloquently.

One factor seems clear about all of the interlocking oppressions. They take both active forms which we can see and embedded forms which as a member of the dominant group one is taught not to see. In my class and place, I did not see myself as a racist because I was taught to recognize racism only in individual acts of meanness by members of my group, never in invisible systems conferring unsought racial dominance on my group from birth.

Disapproving of the systems won't be enough to change them. I was taught to think that racism could end if white individuals changed their attitudes. But a "white" skin in the United States opens many doors for whites whether or not we approve of the way dominance has been conferred on us. Individual acts can palliate, but cannot end, these problems.

To redesign social systems we need first to acknowledge their colossal unseen dimensions. The silences and denials surrounding privilege are the key political tool here. They keep the thinking about equality or equity incomplete, protecting unearned advantage and conferred dominance by making these taboo subjects. Most talk by whites about equal opportunity seems to me now to be about equal opportunity to try to get into a position of dominance while denying that *systems* of dominance exist.

It seems to me that obliviousness about white advantage, like obliviousness about male advantage, is kept strongly inculturated in the United States so as to maintain the myth of meritocracy, the myth that democratic choice is equally available to all. Keeping most people unaware that freedom of confident action is there for just a small number of people props up those in power, and serves to keep power in the hands of the same groups that have most of it already.

Though systemic change takes many decades, there are pressing questions for me and I imagine for some others like me if we raise our daily consciousness on the perquisites of being light-skinned. What will we do with such knowledge? As we know from watching men, it is an open question whether we will choose to use unearned advantage to weaken hidden systems of advantage, and whether we will use any of our arbitrarily-awarded power to try to reconstruct power systems on a broader base.

ABOUT THE AUTHOR

I conceptualized white skin privilege in 1986 after leading faculty development seminars for seven years at Wellesley College Center for Research on Women and in other institutions. Starting with the autobiographical and testimonial mode which is my way of developing theory, I compared my circumstances only to those African American women in my building and line of work. Now I have done over one hundred co-presentations on privilege systems with colleagues of color sharing the podium time and speaking fees, which is one of my answers to my own question about how to use unearned privilege to weaken systems of unearned privilege. I am Associate Director of the Wellesley College Center for Research on Women. I founded and co-direct the National S.E.E.D.(Seeking Educational Equity and Diversity) Project on Inclusive Curriculum.

The Children's Ward

Lois Berg

WE ALWAYS LIVE our childhood again
Even then, we don't want it back.
                              —*Jaan Kaplinski*

It began with the cold insult of the bedpan,
and the precise syringe. The ritual of nine o'clock
quickly concluded by the metal slam of bars raised
to cage us in our iron beds. Then darkness.
Sobbing. Our eyes beseeching
the empty yellow light in the hall.

Monday night we cried for our mothers.
On Tuesday we sang little songs
to ourselves in our heads.
On Wednesday we sang to each other
until our nurse appeared and said "Hush,"
a curse in the light.

We never slept, only occasionally called forth
a brief shallow dream of a soft blanket.
Our eyes fixed on the jaundiced glow
empty of comfort, empty of hope.
And in Thursday's darkness we felt our longings,
our companions, leave us.

On Friday we thanked them for the teasingly
small cup of juice. We smiled in gratitude
at the needle's stab. "Yes," they said,
"Now look and see how brave you are."
Wisely, we embraced our kind nurse, our disease,
then slept for years in numb silence.

ABOUT THE AUTHOR

In 1992, the week of SEED Leadership Training provided a safe place where I spoke of my disability for the first time. Later I wrote this poem—forty years after hospitalizations for childhood polio—and it's become part of my litany of how silence, as a response to all the ways one is made to feel other, excluded, and inconsequential, is destructive to one's true, best self. I currently teach Language Arts in the Hopkins Alternative Program at Hopkins High School in Minnetonka, Minnesota, and strive to maintain another safe place for my students.

FRAMING MULTICULTURAL EDUCATION

Multicultural education is a process which enables all children, teachers, and parents to understand and analyze their own culture, thereby developing a strong self-concept, while learning to interact and relate with respect to other individuals and culture groups.

—David Abalos

Curriculum as Window & Mirror

Emily Style

CONSIDER HOW THE CURRICULUM FUNCTIONS, INSISTING with its disciplined structure that there are ways (plural) of seeing. Basic to a liberal arts education is the understanding that there is more than one way to see the world; hence, a balanced program insists that the student enter into the patterning of various disciplines, looking at reality through various "window" frames.

Years ago a Peanuts cartoon illustrated this vividly for me. Schultz's dog Snoopy was pictured sitting at his typewriter, writing the cultural truth "Beauty is only skin deep." When the dog looked in the mirror however, it made more sense (to the dog) to write "Beauty is only furdeep."

In the following day's comic strip, the bird Woodstock had apparently made a protest; Snoopy responded by shifting the definition to "featherdeep." Woodstock, too, had looked in the mirror and insisted on naming truth in a way that made the most sense to him.

Perhaps the only truth that remains, after such an exchange, is that "Beauty is," still no small truth to expound upon.

First published in *Listening for All Voices,* Oak Knoll School monograph, Summit, NJ, 1988.

For me, the beauty of the classroom gathering lies in its possibilities for seeing new varieties of Beauty. This multiplicity, in turn, enables both students and teachers to be engaged in conversation about an evolving definition of the beautiful. Such dialogue requires the practice of *both/and* thinking as participants acknowledge the varied experiences of reality which frame individual human perspective.

In considering how the curriculum functions, it is essential to note the connection between eyesight and insight. As the Peanuts cartoon illustrates, no student acquires knowledge in the abstract; learning is always personal. Furthermore, learning never takes place in a vacuum; it is always contextual.

This brief paper will explore the need for curriculum to function both as window and as mirror, in order to reflect and reveal most accurately both a multicultural world and the student herself or himself. If the student is understood as occupying a dwelling of self, education needs to enable the student to look through window frames in order to see the realities of others and into mirrors in order to see her/his own reality reflected. Knowledge of both types of framing is basic to a balanced education which is committed to affirming the essential dialectic between the self and the world. In other words, education engages us in "the great conversation" between various frames of reference.

Theologian Nelle Morton, who taught for years at Drew University in Madison, NJ, has made a significant contribution to balancing the Western educational emphasis on the importance of the Word, the logos of communication. She suggests that the opening lines to the gospel of John, "In the beginning was the Word," are often understood as the whole truth—when, in fact, they probably more accurately render only half the picture. She illustrates the other half of the dialectic when she insists, "In the beginning is the Hearing."

At this point, I would link hearing and seeing to emphasize a further aspect of shared framing. The delightful truth is that sometimes when we hear another out, glancing through the window of their humanity, we can see our own image reflected in the glass of their window. The window becomes a mirror! And it is the shared humanity of our conversation that most impresses us even as we attend to our different frames of reference.

In her commitment to inclusive seeing, Eudora Welty wrote,

The frame through which I viewed the world changed too, with time. Greater than scene, I came to see, is situation. Greater than situation is implication. Greater than all of these is a single, entire human being who will never be confined in any frame.

In acknowledging the fluidity of framing, however, it is essential that dialogue about differences not get lost. Sidney Jourard, in his commitment to education as dialogue, once put it this way:

> Another person's words are the windows to his or her world, through which I see what it is like to be that person. When another speaks to me in truth, he or she becomes a transparent self, and releases in me an imaginative experience of his or her existence. If he or she cannot speak, if I do not listen, or if I cannot understand then we must remain suspicious strangers to one another, uncognizant of our authentic similarities and differences.

Jourard's statement makes obvious that another person's words will not function as window—if no one hears them or if, for some reason, the words are not even voiced—which is exactly the case in the following narrative poem by New Jersey poet Lew Gardner.*

> My mother's uncle had a horse.
> The best time of a deadly relatives' Sunday
> was to walk with him to the stable
> and watch him feed the quiet animal,
> to give it sugar from my own hand
> and jump back away
> from the big warm tongue,
> to smell the hay and manure, to see
> the white horse in the next stall,
> with tail and mane like yellow silk
>
> If my mother and I ran into him
> as he and the horse were making their rounds,
> buying up the wonderful junk
> they heaped and hauled in the wagon,
> he'd lift me up to the seat
> and let me hold the reins and yell "Giddy-up!"
> In the spring of 4th grade,
> one afternoon of silent division
> we heard a clanking and looked outside.

---

*Copyright 1973, used with permission.

> My great-uncle! I could tell them all
> how I had held those reins!
> But everyone laughed at the hunched old man,
> the obsolete wagon and horse,
> the silly, clattering junk.
> I did not tell them.

While everyone in that fourth grade classroom looks out the same window, they do not all see the same old man. For all but one, their knowledge is "detached" and "objective." And all but one of them suffer (unaware) from the limitation of their detachment. The poem's narrator, on the other hand, is aware of his suffering as he acquires another view of the old man to whom he is intimately connected. Prior to the classroom window experience, the narrator's view had been purely provincial. Now he is forcefully educated during "one afternoon of silent division" to see more than he has before. He sees his great-uncle reduced to being a mere "Other" in the eyes of the others.

But there are more observations to be gleaned from this poetic incident. The child's (understandable) silence means that the others in the classroom remain trapped in their limited, "objective" view of the old man. His otherness, his alien nature, is all they can see. This is a particular shame in the light of the insight of the painter Van Gogh who once asked in a letter to his sister-in-law,

> Could it not be that by loving a thing one sees it better and more truly than by not loving it?

Recent scholarship (including Howard Gardner's *Frames of Mind*, Edward De Bono's *Six Thinking Hats*, and Belenky et al's *Women's Ways of Knowing*) distinguishes various kinds of knowing. Credit is due to Harvard scholar Carol Gilligan who pioneered attention to gendered dimensions of ways of knowing in her 1982 book *In a Different Voice*.

Scholar Peter Elbow has also done important work in naming how the dominance of the "doubting game" in the Western educational tradition obscures the equal, but different, benefits of taking an empathic approach to something or someone seen initially as Other, alien to one's own experience and frame of reference.

In *Women's Ways of Knowing* and other feminist scholarship, the terms "connected-knowing" and "detached-knowing" are used to clarify the differences between kinds of knowing which have frequently been aligned with traditional gender socialization. Females have been taught the importance of feeling *with* another in the "care perspective," while males have been taught the importance of thinking critically *(against)* another in order to protect their own "right(s)" perspective.

Recent scholarship not only increasingly delineates between kinds of knowing, however. It also returns again and again to the basic need for the whole spectrum of thinking/feeling competencies to be taught to all students, regardless of gender and other cultural variables.

To return to the central metaphor of this paper, the need for curriculum to function both as window and as mirror, we need to acknowledge that this perspective is in line with the ancient liberal arts tradition which pursues multiple perspectives (in insisting on a variety of disciplinary paradigms). Intrinsic to this classical perspective is the actuality and validity of differences.

Traditionally, American education has been more comfortable focusing on similarities. Despite our democratic rhetoric, differences have made us uncomfortable. In fact, there are still American educators who pride themselves on being "colorblind," thinking that ignoring "accidental" differences of race or gender or region or class creates the best classroom climate. Promoting such partial seeing is highly problematic for the creation of curriculum which will serve all students adequately.

Perhaps noting the wording of the traditional Golden Rule will clarify the importance of building both windows and mirrors into the educational process. To "do unto others as you would have them do unto you" takes one's own sensibilities and projects them through the window onto the other. Granted, at times when similarities abound, this Rule can lead to ethical decision-making of the highest order. Its strength comes from the knowledge of one's own humanity which we can liken to studying oneself closely in a mirror.

I would suggest, however, that there are times when to "do unto others as they would have you do unto them" is the more appropriate ethical guideline, one which frames a window into the humanity of another whose preference might be very different from one's own. One who is blind to the existence of such difference might, for instance, purchase a gift for another which she herself would like but which, in fact, is highly inappropriate, unwanted or even resented by the recipient of the gift.

Now, the common sense of needing to provide both windows and mirrors in the curriculum may seem unnecessary to emphasize, and yet recent scholarship on women and men of color attests abundantly to the copious blind spots of the traditional curriculum. White males find, in the house of curriculum, many mirrors to look in, and few windows which frame others' lives. Women and men of color, on the other hand, find almost no mirrors of themselves in the house of curriculum; for them it is often all windows. White males are thereby encouraged to be solipsistic, and the rest of us to feel uncertain that we truly exist. In Western education, the gendered perspective of the white male has presented itself as "universal" for so long that the limitations of this curriculum are often still invisible.

Linda Nochlin asked, in a 1972 essay, this question, "Why have there been no great woman artists?" Think about how the understanding of women's quilts as art has evolved in the last twenty years. Imagine the neglect of a curriculum which teaches a female student to look always through the window at the art done by others while ignoring the art of the quilt made by her own grandmother which is reflected in the mirror of her very own bedroom.

By now it should be obvious that some of the "missing" great women artists were making quilts. But, if what is close to home and reflected in your own mirror is excluded from the very definition of art, your gaze will only see "the windowed half" of art history. Such an education will be unbalanced, incomplete and inaccurate—though pretending to be otherwise.

Consider another example. In the summer of 1987, *Sports Illustrated* magazine published a photo essay in a special baseball issue which illustrated the poet Donald Hall's definition of the sport. In Hall's words, "Baseball is fathers and sons playing catch," and in twelve pages of father-son photos, the magazine pictured this relational (connected-knowing) definition of the sport by featuring some of the faces of the sixty-seven sons (and one grandson) of former major leaguers currently playing organized baseball in the United States.

Then, abruptly, but without any fanfare, the final page of the photo essay switched to the heading *Mother & Son*. The following words accompanied the essay's last two photos:

The All-American Girls Baseball League was big in the '40s, and one of its stars was 5'1" Helen Callaghan. One of Helen's five kids, Casey, grew up to be the Montreal Expos 5'9" second baseman. If someone tells Casey he throws like a girl, he won't mind.

Unless one's life experience is other-wise, one might never notice that Hall's poetic definition of the sport of baseball excludes half the population from participation by rendering them invisible at the basic definitional level. In other words, girls cannot see themselves mirrored in the line "Baseball is fathers and sons playing catch." It is only a window for them, to others' lives. Even the altered caption of *Mother & Son* still excludes girls' experience as daughters, sidelining the female-female connection central to their development.

The challenge of integrating women and minority studies into the traditional school curriculum comes at this very basic level. More than half of our culture's population (all girls, and boys from minority groups) are trained and expected to look through windows at others who are viewed as the valid participants in a sport; an exclusionary curriculum, often perpetuated by the unaware, holds no mirrors for the majority of the students. Females are taught their "proper role" as spectators on life's playing field. But that is only half the damage.

At the same time those whose (white male) experience is repeatedly mirrored are narrowly and provincially educated to see themselves (and their own kind) as the only real players on life's stage. Like the disadvantaged fourth-graders who see the old man only as Other, many white males miss half of what a balanced education should be for all of us:

- knowledge of both self and others,

- clarification of the known and illumination of the unknown.

All students deserve a curriculum which mirrors their own experience back to them, upon occasion—thus validating it in the public world of the school. But curriculum must also insist upon the fresh air of windows into the experience of others—who also need and deserve the public validation of the school curriculum.

Differences as well as similarities exist. The mathematician and the linguist see the world in different ways. One is not superior to the other; a balanced education encompasses both.

Differences exist. They never melted down into "the melting pot" and, now, in a nuclear age we have no choice but to educate youngsters (and ourselves) to handle them more realistically so as to avoid, at all costs, a foolish nuclear melt-down of all of us. One "sandlot" of encounters with difference is located in classroom curriculum and dynamics. Imagine how students' sense of historical perspective (on sandlot encounters) would shift if the academic subject of history were taught using the definition suggested by South African playwright Athol Fugard at the Georgetown University commencement in June 1984:

> I am talking about the living of life at the most mundane level, and what I am saying is that at that level—at the level of our daily lives—one man or woman meeting with another man or woman is finally the central arena of history.

Of course, students' educational diet is not balanced if they see themselves in the mirror all the time. Likewise, democracy's school curriculum is unbalanced if a black student sits in school, year after year, forced to look through the window upon the (validated) experiences of white others while seldom, if ever, having the central mirror held up to the particularities of her or his own experience. Such racial imbalance is harmful as well to white students whose seeing of humanity's different realities is also profoundly obscured.

Such inaccuracy and imbalance diminish the education of all our children. Some students, like the narrator in Gardner's poem, remain subordinated and silent, though their vision is actually wider, while others strut their stuff on the life stage insensitive to other points of view. All of us lose when education is framed this way.

It is limiting and inaccurate to only educate our children provincially when they must live their lives in a global context, facing vast differences and awesome similarities. They must learn early and often about the valid framing of both windows and mirrors for a balanced, ecological sense of their place(s) in the world.

ABOUT THE AUTHOR

As a high school English teacher in Madison, New Jersey, I needed to figure out a way other than "coverage" to take up my classroom task with a sense of integrity. I first talked about my commitment to balance using the metaphor of "curriculum as window & mirror" in a seminar during the 1986-87 school year sponsored by the Geraldine R. Dodge Foundation, Morristown, New Jersey. In the course of that seminar, directed by Peggy McIntosh, colleague Margaret Crocco of the Oak Knoll School urged me to write about this metaphorical concept, thereby serving as a midwife to its coming into print.

Transforming the
Mainstream Curriculum

James A. Banks

S CHOOLS TODAY ARE RICH IN STUDENT DIVERSITY. A GROWING number of American classrooms and schools contain a complex mix of races, cultures, languages, and religious affiliations.

Two other sources of diversity are becoming increasingly prominent as well. The widening gap between rich and poor students is creating more social class diversity, and an increasing number of gay students and teachers are publicly proclaiming their sexual orientations.

ᦉ Toward an Authentic Unum ᦉ

The increasing recognition of diversity within American society poses a significant challenge: how to create a cohesive and democratic society while at the same time allowing citizens to maintain their ethnic, cultural, socioeconomic, and primordial identities.

This article was originally published in *Educational Leadership* 51, 8: 4-8. Reprinted with permission of the Association for Supervision and Curriculum Development.

Our ideal as a nation has been and continues to be *e pluribus unum*—out of many, one. In the past, Americans have tried to reach this goal by eradicating diversity and forcing all citizens into a white Anglo-Saxon Protestant culture (Higham, 1972).

This coerced assimilation does not work very well. An imposed *unum* is not authentic, is not perceived as legitimate by nonmainstream populations, does not have moral authority, and is inconsistent with democratic ideals. To create an authentic, democratic *unum* with moral authority and perceived legitimacy, the *pluribus* (diverse peoples) must negotiate and share power.

Even with its shortcomings, the United States has done better in this regard than most nations. Still, citizen expectations for a just *unum* are far outpacing the nation's progress toward its ideal. Many citizens of color, people with low incomes, or speakers of languages other than English feel alienated, left out, abandoned, and forgotten.

Our society has a lot to gain by restructuring institutions in ways that incorporate all citizens. People who now feel disenfranchised will become more effective and productive citizens, and new perspectives will be added to the nation's mainstream institutions. The institutions themselves will then be transformed and enriched.

In the past two decades, multicultural education has emerged as a vehicle for including diverse groups and transforming the nation's educational institutions (Banks, 1994a; Banks & Banks, 1992). Multicultural education tries to create equal educational opportunities for all students by ensuring that the total school environment reflects the diversity of groups in classrooms, schools, and the society as a whole.

Considering the Dimensions
∾ of Multicultural Education ∾

The following five dimensions of multicultural education can help educators implement and assess programs that respond to student diversity (Banks, 1993, 1994b).

1. The first dimension, *content integration*, deals with the extent to which teachers illuminate key points of instruction with content reflecting diversity. Typically, teachers integrate such content into curriculum in several different ways (Banks, 1991b). One common approach is the recognition of contributions—that is, teachers work into the curriculum various isolated facts about heroes from diverse

groups. Otherwise, lesson plans and units are unchanged. With the additive approach, on the other hand, the curriculum remains unchanged, but teachers add special units on topics like the Women's Rights Movement, African Americans in the West, and Famous Americans with Disabilities. While an improvement over the passing mention of contributions, the additive approach still relegates groups like women, African Americans, and disabled people to the periphery of the curriculum.

2. A second dimension of multicultural education is *knowledge construction*, or the extent to which teachers help students understand how perspectives of people within a discipline influence the conclusions reached within that discipline. This dimension is also concerned with whether students learn to form knowledge for themselves.

3. The *prejudice reduction* dimension has to do with efforts to help students to develop positive attitudes about different groups. Research has revealed a need for this kind of education and the efficacy of it. For example, researchers have shown that while children enter school with many negative attitudes and misconceptions about different racial and ethnic groups (Phinney & Rotheram, 1987), education can help students develop more positive intergroup attitudes, provided that certain conditions exist. Two such conditions are instructional materials with positive images of diverse groups and the use of such materials in consistent and sustained ways (Banks, 1991a).

4. The *equitable pedagogy* dimension concerns ways to modify teaching so as to facilitate academic achievement among students from diverse groups. Research indicates, for example, that the academic achievement of African American and Mexican American students improves when teachers use cooperative (rather that competitive) teaching activities and strategies (Aronson & Gonzalez, 1988).

5. The *empowering school culture and social structure* dimension concerns the extent to which a school's culture and organization ensure educational equality and cultural empowerment for students from diverse groups. Some of the variables considered are grouping practices, social climate, assessment practices, participation in extracurricular activities, and staff expectations and responses to diversity.

∽ Knowledge Construction and Transformation ∽

I would like to suggest an alternative to the contributions and additive approaches that are used in the content integration dimension. This alternative, the *transformation approach*, changes the structure, assumptions, and perspectives of the curriculum so that subject matter is viewed from the perspectives and experiences of a range of groups. The transformation approach changes instructional materials, teaching techniques, and student learning.

This approach can be used to teach about our differences as well as our similarities. Teachers can help students understand that, while Americans have a variety of viewpoints, we share many cultural traditions, values, and political ideals that cement us together as a nation.

The transformation approach has several advantages. It brings content about currently marginalized groups to the center of the curriculum. It helps students understand that how people construct knowledge depends on their experiences, values, and perspectives. It helps students learn to construct knowledge themselves. And it helps students grasp the complex group interactions that have produced the American culture and civilization.

༄ Reinterpreting the Montgomery Bus Boycott ༄

The history of the Montgomery (Alabama) bus boycott, which began on December 5, 1955, can be used to illustrate how the transformation approach works. Viewing this event from different perspectives shows how historians construct interpretations, how central figures can be omitted from historical records, how history can be rewritten, and how students can create their own interpretations.

Textbook accounts of the Montgomery bus boycott generally conclude that: (1) when a bus driver asked Rosa Parks to give up her seat to a white person, she refused because she was tired from working hard all day, and (2) the arrest of Rosa Parks triggered the planning and execution of the boycott.

Two important accounts by women who played key roles in the boycott contradict important aspects of the textbook conclusions. The two memoirs are those of Rosa Parks (with Haskins, 1992) and Jo Ann Gibson Robinson (Garrow, 1987). Robinson was an Alabama State College English professor and president of the Women's Political Council.

Students can compare mainstream accounts of the events (such as those in textbooks) with transformative accounts (such as those by Robinson and Parks). This activity presents an excellent opportunity both to learn content about diverse groups and to gain insights about the construction of knowledge.

According to Robinson, professional African American women in Montgomery founded the Women's Political Council in 1946 to provide leadership, support, and improvement in the black community and to work for voting rights for African Americans. Many council members were Alabama State College professors. Others were black public school teachers.

In 1953, the council received more than 30 complaints concerning bus driver offenses against African Americans. For instance, black people (even when seated in the "Negro" section of the bus) were asked to give up their seats to whites. Further, blacks often had to pay their fares in the front of the bus, exit, and reenter through the back door—and sometimes when they stepped off the bus, the driver left them.

Robinson and other council members worked with city leaders to improve the treatment of black bus riders, but to no avail. African Americans continued to experience intimidating, demeaning, and hostile encounters with bus drivers.

As the negative pattern of incidents persisted, the council concluded that only a boycott against the bus system would end the abuse of black bus riders and bus segregation. A boycott was thought to have good potential for success because about 70 percent of Montgomery's bus riders were African American. The council planned the boycott and then waited for the right time to launch it.

The year 1955 presented three choices for the "right time." On March 2, 1955, Claudette Colvin, a 15-year-old high school student seated in the "Negro" section of a bus, was arrested after refusing to give up her seat to a white rider. Next, Robinson said:

> They dragged her, kicking and screaming hysterically, off the bus. Still half-dragging, half-pushing, they forced her into a patrol car that had been summoned, put handcuffs on her wrists so she would do no physical harm to the arresting police, and drove her to jail. There she was charged with misconduct, resisting arrest, and violating the city segregation laws (Garrow, 1987).

Claudette Colvin was later found guilty and released on probation. The conviction enraged the African American community. Six months after the Colvin incident, Mary Louise Smith, 18, was arrested on a similar charge. Smith was fined. Then, on December 1, Rosa Parks was arrested for refusing to give up her seat. She gives quite a different reason for her intransigence than has commonly been reported:

> People always say that I didn't give up my seat because I was tired, but that
> isn't true. I was not tired physically, or no more tired than I usually was at
> the end of a working day. I was not old, although some people have an
> image of me being old then. I was 42. No, the only tired I was, was tired of
> giving in.
>
> The driver of the bus saw me still sitting there, and he asked was I
> going to stand up. I said, "No." He said, "Well, I'm going to have you ar
> rested." Then I said, "You may do that." These were the only words we said
> to each other.
>
> . . . People have asked me if it occurred to me that I could be the test
> case the NAACP had been looking for. I did not think about that at all. In
> fact if I had let myself think too deeply about what might happen to me, I
> might have gotten off the bus. But I chose to remain.

Fed up with mistreatment, the African American women of Montgomery, led by their council, called for a boycott of city buses. Robinson described the preparations for the boycott:

> I sat down and quickly drafted a message and then called a good friend
> and colleague, John Cannon, chairman of the business department of the
> college, who had access to the college's mimeograph equipment. When I
> told him that the WPC was staging a boycott and needed to run off the
> notices, he told me that he too had suffered embarrassment on the city
> buses. Like myself, he had been hurt and angry. He said that he would
> happily assist me.
>
> Along with two of my most trusted students, we quickly agreed to
> meet almost immediately, in the middle of the night, at the college's du
> plicating room. We were able to get three messages to a page, greatly re
> ducing the number of pages that had to be mimeographed in order to
> produce the tens of thousands of leaflets we knew would be needed. By 4
> a.m. on Friday, the sheets had been duplicated, cut in thirds, and bundled
> (Garrow, 1987).

Part of Robinson's leaflets read:

> Another Negro woman has been arrested and thrown in jail because she
> refused to get up out of her seat on the bus for a white person to sit down.
> . . . This has to be stopped. Negroes have rights, too, for if Negroes did not
> ride the buses, they could not operate. Three-fourths of the riders are Ne-

groes, yet we are arrested, or have to stand over empty seats. If we do not do something to stop the arrests, they will continue. The next time it may be you, your daughter, or mother. This woman's case will come up on Monday. We are, therefore, asking every Negro to stay off the buses Monday in protest of the arrest and trial. Don't ride the buses to work, to town, to school, or anywhere else on Monday (Garrow, 1987).

⟋⟍ Reinterpreting the Past ⟋⟍

Robinson's and Parks' accounts of the Montgomery bus boycott reveal that significant players in historical events can be virtually ignored in written history. For instance, most textbook accounts of the Montgomery bus boycott emphasize the work of men (like Martin Luther King Jr. and Ralph D. Abernathy) or organizations headed by men. The work of women like Robinson and her female colleagues in the Women's Political Council simply cannot be found in most textbooks.

Further, Rosa Parks' stated reason for refusing to give up her seat helps students understand that recorded history can be wrong. Students can also see that when people who have been excluded from the construction of historical knowledge begin to play active roles in interpreting history, the resulting accounts can be strikingly different and much more accurate. As Robert Merton (1972) observed, insiders and outsiders often have different perspectives on the same events, and both perspectives are needed to give the total picture of social and historical reality.

⟋⟍ Incorporating New Scholarship ⟋⟍

Since the 1970s, people of color—who have historically been outsiders and transformative scholars—have produced a prodigious amount of scholarship on multicultural education. Their thoughtful and informative works include Ronald Takaki's *A Different Mirror: A History of Multicultural America* (1993); John Hope Franklin's *The Color Line: Legacy for the Twenty-First Century* (1993); Gloria Anzaldua's *Borderlands: La Frontera* (1987); Patricia Hill Collins's *Black Feminist Thought: Knowledge, Consciousness, and the Politics of Empowerment* (1991); and Paula Gunn Allen's *The Sacred Hoop* (1986).

Because men of color have often been as silent on women's issues as white men have been (hooks [sic] & West, 1991), a special effort should be made to include works by women (such as those by Anzaldua,

Collins, and Allen). Two important new books edited by women are Carol Dubois and Vicki Ruiz's *Unequal Sisters: A Multicultural Reader in U.S. Women's History* (1990) and Darlene Clark Hine and her colleagues' *Black Women in America: An Historical Encyclopedia* (1993).

∾ Teaching Civic Action ∾

One of multicultural education's important goals is to help students acquire the knowledge and commitment needed to think, decide, and take personal, social, and civic action. Activism helps students apply what they have learned and develop a sense of personal and civic efficacy (Banks with Clegg, 1990).

Action activities and projects should be practical, feasible, and attuned to the developmental levels of students. For instance, students in the primary grades can take action by refusing to laugh at ethnic jokes. Students in the early and middle grades can read about and make friends with people from other racial, ethnic, and cultural groups. Upper-grade students can participate in community projects that help people with special needs. Lewis (1991) has written a helpful guide that describes ways to plan and initiate social action activities and projects for students.

When content, concepts, and events are studied from many points of view, all of our students will be ready to play their roles in the life of the nation. They can help to transform the United States from what it is to what it could and should be—many groups working together to build a strong nation that celebrates its diversity.

REFERENCES

Aronson, E., & Gonzalez, A. (1988). Desegregation, jigsaw, and the Mexican-American experience. In P. A. Katz & D. A. Taylor (Eds.), *Eliminating racism: Profiles in controversy.* New York: Plenum Press.

Banks, J. A. (1991a). Multicultural education: Its effects on students' racial and gender role attitudes. In J. P. Shaver (Ed.), *Handbook of research on social teaching and learning.* New York: Macmillian.

Banks, J. A. (1991b). *Teaching strategies for ethnic studies* (5th ed.) Boston: Allyn & Bacon.

Banks, J. A. (1993). Multicultural education: Historical development, dimensions and practice. In L. Darling-Hammond (Ed.), *Review of Research in*

Education, Vol. 19. Washington, D. C.: American Educational Research Association.

Banks, J. A. (1994b). *Multiethnic education: Theory and practice* (3rd ed.). Boston: Allyn & Bacon.

Banks, J. A., with Clegg Jr., A. A. (1990). *Teaching strategies for the social studies: Inquiry, valuing, and decision-making* (4th ed.). New York: Longman.

Banks, J. A., & Banks, C. A. M. (1992). *Multicultural education: Issues and perspectives* (2nd ed.). Boston: Allyn & Bacon.

Garrow, D. J. (1987). (Ed.) *The Montgomery bus boycott and the women who started it: The memoir of Jo Ann Gibson Robinson*. Knoxville: The University of Tennessee Press.

Higham, J. (1972). *Strangers in the land: Patterns of American nativism 1860-1925*. New York: Atheneum.

hooks, b., & West, C. (1991). *Breaking bread: Insurgent Black intellectual life*. Boston: South End Press.

Lewis, B. A. (1991). *The kid's guide to social action*. Minneapolis: Free Spirit Publishing.

Merton, R. K. (1972). Insiders and outsiders: A chapter in the sociology of knowledge. *The American Journal of Sociology*. 78 (1). 9-47.

Parks, R., with J. Haskins. (1992). *Rosa Parks: My story*. New York: Dial Books.

Phinney, J. S., & Rotheram, M. J. (1987). (Eds.) *Children's ethnic socialization: Pluralism and development*. Beverly Hills, Calif.: Sage Publications.

ABOUT THE AUTHOR

I am Professor of Education and Director of the Center for Multicultural Education at the University of Washington, Seattle. I began my career as a fifth-grade teacher. I entered graduate school and became a writer and teacher educator because I wanted to have more influence on the school curriculum and the way in which teachers were educated than I could as a classroom teacher. However, I loved teaching fifth grade. One of the most painful days of my life was when I decided to leave fifth grade teaching and enter graduate school at Michigan State in 1966. Both my students and I were in tears that day. I edited the *Handbook of Research on Multicultural Education* with Cherry A. McGee Banks. Last year I served as President of the American Educational Research Association (AERA), the largest educational research organization in the world. While serving as President of AERA, I had the opportunity to share my ideas with 12,000 educators who are located in all parts of the world, a highlight of my career as a teacher educator and scholar.

Interactive Phases of Curricular and Personal Re-Vision with Regard to Race

Peggy McIntosh

NEARLY 20 YEARS AGO, ONE AFTERNOON IN 1972, A FRIEND on the faculty of the University of Denver was standing in the door of my office. We were talking about some aspect of race relations. My colleague said, with gentle offhandedness, "I wouldn't want to be white if you paid me five million dollars." I was startled to hear that she would not want to trade her racial identity for mine. In the previous three years, I had seen this friend survive many problems caused by systemic and personal racism. My dim awareness of, and paltry education in, just about everything pertaining to our lives made me think that hers was a racial identity not to be desired. Now I learned that I had a racial identity that she wouldn't think of wanting.*

My friend's candor was a gift. Her comment opened doors into areas whose distinctness I had been taught not to see: her culture and my culture. Like many people of my race and economic class, I had been taught that there was only one culture, and that we were both in

---

* My colleague is Gwendolyn Thomas, who in 1972 was Assistant Professor of English at the University of Denver. She is now a member of the English Department at Metropolitan State College in Denver.

it. Looking toward hers for the first time, I began to see what I had missed. I learned that my colleague would want to change her circumstances in a racist society, but not her cultural identity. I had been led to assume that her circumstances relative to mine *were* her cultural identity, which I thought must consist mostly of burdens. Her strong words made things more complicated, pluralized the picture, and started me doing what felt and still feels like essential Ethnic Studies homework on the elements of my friend's culture that sustained her and the elements in mine which made the idea of being "white" anathema to her.

I tell this story as a description of an awakening from what I now see as a generic state of mind trained into middle-class "white" Americans: monoculturalism or single-system seeing. Racial or ethnic monoculturalism is the assumption that we are all in the same cultural system together, and that its outlines are those which have been recognized by people who have the most ethnic and racial power.

Single-system seeing with regard to gender takes a related form. I see it especially when men, and many women, assume that we who work in feminist movements toward alternative ways of organizing life and using power must want to do what men have done. I know a number of men who think that when we women get together, we must talk about them, or plot against them. But if one listens plurally instead of monoculturally, one will hear that women want to survive with dignity, and agency, but in general do not want to do what white Western men have done, or been asked to do.

Monoculturalism, like all forms of single-system seeing, is blind to its own cultural specificity. It cannot see itself. It mistakes its "givens" for neutral, preconceptual ground rather than for distinctive cultural grounding. People who have been granted the most public or economic power, when thinking monoculturally about "others," often imagine that these others' lives must be constituted of "issues," "problems," and deficits relative to their own lives. But in fact, the politically "lesser" are, or can be, culturally central to themselves. Most will see much that is positive about their lives, through strength inherited with their traditions. Most will have learned despite and through the conditions of their lives how to behave in ways that sustain and stabilize themselves and the cultural fabrics of the world.

I write about monoculturalism and single-system seeing both as a financially secure white person in the United States who has been, within those dimensions of my identity, seen as fitting a monocultural norm, and as a woman who has been, in my gender identity, seen as culturally lesser, in Anglo-European male terms. I now know that with regard to my sex I do not simply have a deficit identity, i.e., a defective variant of male identity. Moreover, though my chosen place of work is located at the very edge of a College, we who work here call this marginal place devoted to research on women the Center. So it is with people in all cultures, I now think; we can be culturally real or central to ourselves, knowing that no one center is entitled to arbitrary dominance. And if we do not challenge the single-system seeing which projects deficit identities onto us, we will continue to be seen only as defective variants of ideal types within ruling but unacknowledged monoculture.

One great gift of my colleague's comment nearly 20 years ago was that she located herself in a position of strength and made it clear that she saw my racial group as something she would under no circumstances want to join. Within white monoculture, her position was unfamiliar; she was locating herself outside what I imagined was her status within the "one system." Her words made me begin to see my own culture as ethno-particular, ethno-specific, and in fact ethno-peculiar.

It took me some years to revise my understanding to the point at which my colleague's words came to bear very directly on the ways I taught. For like most traditionally trained "white" teachers, I needed a long time to reconceive myself before I could ground teaching in cultural pluralism. While coming around to seeing both my culture and hers in their distinctness and their interrelations, I experienced with regard to race the same slow interactive processes of re-vision which I have traced with regard to teaching about women. It is the process I described in my 1983 paper "Interactive Phases of Curricular Re-Vision: A Feminist Perspective."*

I review here that typology of Interactive Phases of Curricular Re-Vision, this time with a focus on race, and on processes of making curricula and personal perception more multicultural. Once again, a group of hypothetical 17-year-old students appears at the end of the paper, and in this case, I write about the various kinds of understanding the "Little Women" are given with regard to Native American women and men.

---

*McIntosh, Peggy (1983). "Interactive Phases of Curricular Re-Vision: A Feminist Perspective." Working Paper #124, Wellesley, MA, Wellesley College Center for Research on Women.

In working on this account, I was reminded again that typologies are rather blunt instruments, which can be misused and misunderstood. It is important in the case of this typology of Interactive Phases to keep in mind the key adjective "interactive." Interactive ways of seeing coexist in dynamic interrelation. Varieties of awareness are within us; we are not fixed within them. For this reason, it is a mistake to use the typology of Interactive Phases to label, type, or critique individual persons, as though they were fixed forever in one or another form of awareness, or as though we could pass from one to another form of awareness forever. Plural ways of seeing contextualize but do not simply erase single-system understandings. When we widen our ways of knowing, we cannot simply leave previous ways of knowing behind, nor the understandings they gave us. We can become aware of the cultural particularity and the societal consequences of various ways of knowing, seeing, or being.

At their best, typologies create frameworks within which we can understand frequently observed phenomena which at first were not seen to be in coherent relation to each other. The theory of Interactive Phases of Curricular and Personal Re-Vision has spoken to some readers about their own and others' efforts to put academic understandings on a broader and more humane base. For some readers, the phase theory illuminates the evolution of a discipline, a department, an idea, or an institution. For some it has been a tool for evaluation or assessment of curriculum in general, individual course syllabi, or assignments. For many it has been useful in describing, inspiring, and justifying shifts in teaching methods. It has been applied by me and others to analysis of patterns in management, leadership, government, science, social and economic policy, education and interpersonal behavior. It has illuminated for many individuals their own changing thoughts and practices in educational settings and beyond.

At the outset of this discussion of interactive phase theory in terms of race, I want to mention three matters which often need to be clarified in faculty development discussions of curriculum change along lines of race. First, to repeat what I have already said, all people have racial and ethnic identities. Each "white" person has a racial and an ethnic background; there is no culturally unmarked person. Second, each person brings to his or her life the influences of a particular complex of circumstances. For example, my academic writing, including this piece, bears the marks of my own experience as a Caucasian woman who has worked in several private and wealthy sectors of

American society, and who has both resisted some of their norms and at the same time internalized and benefited from their powers. Third, as I have suggested, when "whites" look at "race" only under the rubric of "others" and "issues," this is a sign of monocultural and single-system seeing, which is culturally controlling. All people have racial identities, and people in all racial groups have more to their lives than their "issues" relative to dominant groups. Academic work in broadening racial or ethnic understanding is ineffectual if it doesn't result in shifts of sensibility such as my colleague's comment produced for me, shifts into pluralized awareness. Ethnic Studies reinforces white dominance and Women's Studies reinforces male dominance if they measure by previous norms rather than recognizing distinct be-ing in people of all groups and all circumstances.

My discussion of phase theory and race needs one further prefatory comment: work in developing racial awareness ought to produce greater awareness of gender relations as well. As we begin to work on curricular and personal re-vision, however, "white" people often reflect previous miseducation by speaking as though race and sex are wholly separate factors of people's experience. In the monocultural, vertical worlds of either/or thinking one can't think of both *at once*. For in a white male monocultural frame of reference, whatever isn't the norm is cast as a separate and different form of anomaly. In discussing the first three interactive phases of curricular and personal re-vision here, I will keep sex and race "issues" separate as if it were indeed possible to focus on race without seeing intersecting conditions of experience which impinge on racial experience. But in Phase Four, one sees that sex and race are not separate "issues," and that the commonly used phrase "women and minorities" serves monocultural ends while having no more logic than the phrase "parents and men," or "Chinese and men," since "women" are comprised of people in every cultural group, and half of every racial and ethnic group is female. People of color and "white" women constitute a substantial majority in the U.S., while our present monoculture overentitles a "white" male minority. As long as monoculture's racial and gender outlines are unrecognized, it will be able to project separate problematical status by race and sex on those it does not entitle, and thus keep the actual majority conceptually divided against itself, not knowing in any politically usable way what is happening.

My 1983 typology of Interactive Phases of Curricular and Personal Re-vision derived from work with college faculty members to bring into the liberal arts curriculum new materials and perspectives from Women's Studies. I saw that in the early 1980's, traditionally trained white faculty members in History, for example, were likely to move from Phase One: Womanless History, to Phase Two: Women in History, on its terms. Both kinds of thinking are challenged by what I identified as Phase Three: Women as a Problem, Anomaly, or Absence in History. I meant "in History" in two senses: in the past, and in History's telling of the past. Phase Three involves and requires more anger and critique than either of the first two, but can get arrested in victim-studies. It can also lead constructively to a potent wordlessness and to a daring plunge into the moving, grounded, humble, and plural inquiry of Phase Four: Women's Lives *As* History, looking toward Phase Five: History Reconstructed and Redefined to Include Us All, which I said would take us 100 years to conceive.

After observing traditionally-trained faculty in all academic fields over the last eleven years, I think that the schema can be applied to the processes of faculty growth and development in all of them, even the so-called hard sciences. Teachers in any field are likely to begin teaching chiefly in what I termed Phase One: Womanless Scholarship or Science, with perhaps a little attention to Phase Two: Women in Scholarship or Science, but only on the existing terms. There may follow, if the faculty member has been keeping up with scholarship on women, and is not too defensive about what it reveals, some teaching along lines of Phase Three: Women as a Problem, Anomaly, Absence, or victim in and of the Scholarship or Science. Phase Four teaching and inquiry dares put what was neglected or marginal at the center, to see what new insight or theory can be developed from hitherto excluded or overlooked sources whose absence helped to determine the shape of each field. It can be called Experienced-based Scholarship and Science; it goes far beyond the exceptional achievements allowed in Phase Two and the discussion of "issues" allowed in Phase Three. Always the dynamic interactions among the phases suggest the making of new knowledge, the making of Phase Five: Scholarship and Science Redefined and Reconstructed to Include Us All.

As I have said, no one person or course exists in complete fixity in a given phase, and the phases I describe do not always occur in the chronological order given. Some of those who are born either within or outside of dominant groups may have been immersed since childhood in awareness of the "issues" of Phase Three, or in the relational alertness and the plural consciousness which I attribute to Phase Four.

Most traditionally trained white faculty members, however, started teaching within the framework of Phase One mono-culturalism, oblivious of the racial and gender elements they were immersed in. Some have moved on to think in rather predictable Phase Two ways about how to get more overlooked individuals (for at first it is seen only as a matter of overlooked individuals) into the essentially single-system version of reality which is handed on to students and is not, within monoculture, acknowledged as a version at all. One sees often in sequence the dawning realizations and syllabus changes which I identify as belonging to Phases Two, Three, and Four of consciousness.

When one considers Interactive Phase Theory with regard to race, an obvious curricular example to begin with is the U. S. History course required of all students in high school or college, or both. This course is not usually liked by students. Though it is required of all students at some point, it seems not to provide them with a sense that they are in History as voters-to-be or active makers of political policy. As it undergoes revision in the hands of teachers and textbook authors who hope to make it more representative and engaging, it usually follows predictable patterns with regard to race.

Phase One: All-White History is followed by Phase Two: Exceptional Minority Individuals in U.S. History, which leads to Phase Three: Minority Issues, or Minority Groups as Problems, Anomalies, Absences, or Victims in U.S. History. Then may come a rare and important conceptual shift to Phase Four: The Lives and Cultures of People of Color Everywhere *As* History. I think such courses, if they survive at all, will move toward an eventual Phase Five: History Redefined and Reconstructed to Include Us All.

A Phase One all-white course in U.S. History usually begins by describing the voyages of Europeans and this entry point does not bring any challenges from students. A Phase Two course will encourage students of color to emulate the most "ambitious" of their forbears, and overcome obstacles to advancement in American society. In the case of Native Americans, there may be an emphasis on those who are seen to have interacted well with the "settlers." Phase Three courses focus on, or at least give serious attention to, racism and other systemic oppressions. In the case of Native peoples, the late 19th century U. S. government policy of genocide is recognized. Phase Four is entirely different, imaginatively honoring a variety of cultures on their own terms, trying to see them through the testimony or actions of their people. For example, teaching in this mode goes far beyond Indian "issues" to Indian cultures; it suggests the wholeness and intricacy of Native cosmologies, and the Indians' particular relation to the land and consonance with the spirit in the land, before the Anglo-European ethos of land ownership was imposed. Phase Four recognizes Anglo-European ideas, actions, and standards as ethno-specific. Phase Five will require a vocabulary for perceiving, feeling, and analyzing which is both plural and coherent, and will put us in a new relation to ourselves and the world.

My original analysis of Interactive Phases Of Curricular Re-Vision was placed in context of, and diagrammatically overlaid upon, my theoretical model of double structures within both psyche and society in the industrialized West: overvalued, overdeveloped, "vertical," competitive functions at odds with undervalued, underrecognized, "lateral" collaborative functions. The shape of the whole is that of a faulted pyramid or mountain range with a vertical "grain" in the higher rocks and a horizontal "grain" in the rock of the substructure.

Phases One, Two, and Three, all on a vertical axis, focus respectively on the top, middle, and bottom of the pyramidally-shaped competitive functions of psyche and society. Phase One: Exclusive History focuses on the functions of controlling, ordering, subduing, or prevailing. It tends to emphasize laws, wars, contests, or management of systems, and to tell the stories of winners, at the tops of the ladders of so-called success, accomplishment, achievement, and excellence. A little lower on the ladders comes the Phase Two: the Exceptions History of "ambitious" Others. Then at the bottom of the win-lose vertical territory comes the Issues-oriented History of the losers, and struggling but often defeated fighters.

Phase Four gives us the lateral valleys and plains below the geological fault-line. This is the territory of the sustaining fields and the cyclical growing and harvesting of food. This is the territory of repetitive upkeep and maintenance, the daily making and mending of the social, material, intellectual, and spiritual fabrics, without which the climbing work within vertical structures of psyche and society is not possible. To observe the lateral world is to observe most of inner and outer life, quite beyond what the formal academy has sanctioned as worthy of study. I think the lateral world corresponds to what Paul Tillich has called "the ground of our being." Phase Four provides Experience-based History, which recognizes and strengthens fabrics and interconnections and knowledge of the multiplicities of self. Phase Five will give us Reconstructed Global and Biological History to Survive By.

The present histories of conflict which implicitly underlie all of the disciplines are not histories we can survive by, in an age when we must learn to connect or re-connect, for our survival.

Phases One, Two and Three teach monocultural modes of dominance and defense, and educate the wary and controlling self; Phase Four fosters the making of what I have proposed we should call *the contingent self,* and the responsive society. Phases One, Two and Three can only see in terms of the "top" and the "bottom;" Phase Four looks to the far vaster and sustaining lateral habitat, and to the mystery of how connections, communities, and vulnerable growing things are best fostered. The hidden ethos hanging over Phases One, Two, and Three is competitive and has an either/or axis: "You win lest you lose; kill or be killed." The hidden ethos of Phase Four is collaborative and has a both/and feel: "You work for the decent survival of all, for therein lies your own best chance for survival."

Phase One consciousness involves identification with publicly powerful "white" Western males. In this phase, "whites" neither study people of color nor notice that they have not. The obliviousness of single-system seeing is a hallmark of this phase. The Phase Two remedy admits a few "minorities" to History, but only on History's terms, still without any reflectiveness on the racial history of those traditional terms and definitions. Phase Three takes us into "race" issues. It identifies "race" monoculturally, ascribing race only to people of color, and sees people of color only in the category of Problem, identifying whole groups of people chiefly with losers' "issues" rather than with human life experienced fully. Doing work only in Phase Three can be inadvertently racist or sexist, for it is a cultural insult to any group to imply that its main feature is what I have called above a *deficit identity.* Phase Three never does a full analysis of the psyche or peculiarity of the "oppressor." The oppressed group is set up to look powerless and defective by contrast with the more powerful group, which is seen as the norm, and not examined for its cultural specificity, peculiarity, or pathology. Still, Phase Three at least encourages students to recognize the existence of invisible systems of power and disadvantage.

Phase Four comes out of and recognizes the lateral, connected, and diverse functions of psyche and society; it is about creativity, integrity, wholeness, ordinariness, and multiple forms of power and talent unrecognized in vertical systems of appraisal. It honors both/and thinking about who exists and what counts. Without it, we will not be able to make sense of the world nor policy for our survival. Phase Four reveals us, in LeRoy Moore's language, as "bodies in the body of the world," and as distinctly different from each other, not measurable against one standard, and indeed not hewing to one, any more than the biological forms of life on the planet belong to one type.

Phase Four can be healing. But Phase Four unattached to the is-sues-awareness of Phase Three can be sentimental. It may be a celebra-tion of diversity as if there were no politics which had prevented, and keeps working against, such celebration. If teachers lapse into Phase Four while forgetting about vertical power structures, they may be-come romantic, and not face the pain which systems of subjection in-flict. For example, while honoring the strengths of African American culture as Toni Morrison may describe them, I need to keep in mind the contexts that produced these strengths. My ancestors on one side were slave-owners. This fact bears on the conventions and particulari-ties of many aspects of Morrison's culture and of mine. Only it bears differently on each.

Though Phase Four without Phase Three awareness can be naive, Phase Four has potential reconstitutive power for all students and teachers. For an enormous shift in the consciousness occurs when the ordinary lives of people, including people of color as the world's ma-jority, are seen to constitute the main human story, and history is de-fined as all of those elements of the past in the multiplicities of our heritages which can make each of us feel *fully real* in the context of ed-ucation or life. In Phase Four, the question of "How was it for people?" opens the study of History to every kind of humble detail. All voices count. Pedagogy shifts so that the professor's forms of knowing are not necessarily superior to the students' forms of knowing. The elements of Phase One are not obliterated, but take a new place in the picture. Someone has said that if you study the experience of an escaped slave woman in Boston in the 1850's you will find Lincoln, but if you start with Lincoln, you will not necessarily get to the experience of any en-slaved person. Phase Four stays very close to the ground of daily human experience, and asks many questions of people about their lives, listening for many human voices, and examining the cultural and political specificity of frameworks for collecting and evaluating infor-mation. All experience is seen as a source of knowledge.

My previous paper provided brief examples of Phase Four teaching with regard to both race and gender in the disciplines of Literature, Psychology, Biology, and Art. I concluded by saying that I saw the work toward Phase Five as taking one hundred years because it involves a reconstruction of consciousness, perception and behavior. It will very likely attempt to create, and then maintain, public awareness that we must, locally and globally, value life more than conflict, and attend to the processes of maintaining life. I think we cannot at this time even imagine the categories within which we will collect information for balanced plural Phase Five understandings and reconstructions of education. Most "educated" minds seem terribly stuck in narrow frameworks leading to personal anxiety, and accepting of social repression, turmoil and global danger. But if our descendants work at Phase Five, they will probably find many fugitive precedents for their work in the perplexed and tentative legacies we leave now.

With regard to race in the undergraduate curriculum, most of our universities still feature Phase One introductory courses in virtually all departments. These courses feature the thought and research of Anglo-European-American scholars, i.e. "white" forefathers in the making of knowledge. The courses feature winners in law, war, or trade; the getting and holding of literal or conceptual territory; the making of frameworks for understanding; the wresting of "order" from "chaos"; the development of cultural traditions from nothingness or from "primitive" originals. In such courses, one may study people of color like Egyptians under the impression that they are really "white." In monocultural, single-system courses, students of all races are asked to imagine that the essential insights into human thought, labor, imagination, and care can all be found in the study of Caucasian people.

My generalizations may bring objections from some who say that the introductory level college curriculum is now overstretched through inclusion of new materials on "race and class." This is an illusion. The fact is that no works by people of color are seen as *central* to understanding any of the traditional liberal arts disciplines, and people of color are presented chiefly as disadvantaged, or as primitive forbears of real civilization, or as recent immigrants with cultural traditions that create problems for "America." Moreover, there is very little material of any kind by and about non-Western majorities in most college and school students' courses.

If readers doubt this, they should examine the introductory-level course reading lists of their own institutions. "White" teachers should imagine themselves as students of color, for example as Asian American students, trying to find their people reflected as valid in basic readings. Most courses are still monocultural, even Anthropology, in which teachers focus on the thinking of "white," mostly male, anthropologists. This gives "white" students the impression that there is one main piece of cultural turf and it is their turf. The students of color, like the "white" women, are implicitly shown they have not been necessary to knowledge, enterprise, and past culture-making, nor are they essential to future cultural invention or reclamation. In such courses, oral traditions are seen to count for nothing at all; argumentative written traditions, though very culture- and gender-specific in origin, inform most of the "objective" texts and all of the assignments. Historiography courses, much touted for their plural, comparative sophistication, focus on "white" men.

Phase Two courses bring in a few famous or notable people of color but do not challenge the traditional outlines and definitions of what is worth studying. Therefore the emphasis continues to be on "firsts," laws, wars, winners, talented individuals, fighters, and those who nearly matched what is taken to be "white" male achievement. People of color who succeeded in getting and holding onto some kinds of social, political, or artistic territory are seen as possibly worth studying. But often those who are noticed in Phase Two courses are represented as having gone far but not irrationally far in challenging existing "white," male, or colonial frameworks, and therefore are seen as being worth noticing; for example, Sacajawea, Sequoyah, Black Elk, Douglass, Baldwin, King, Walker, Morrison. Usually Latinos and Asian Americans do not get into Phase Two courses at all; recent and rare exceptions are Maxine Hong Kingston, Yoko Ono, and Cesar Chavez. Those who most strongly rebelled against "white" dominance are usually annihilated in the telling of history as they were in life. Those who accommodated or assimilated somewhat may become cultural heroes, especially in retrospect; they may come to be seen as almost within the "mainstream."

In Phase Two, teaching about people of color as exceptional and therefore worthy of notice, can create psychological problems. Many teachers think that in holding up "exceptions," they are providing role models for students of color, and demonstrating to "white" students that people of color should be taken seriously. The impulse can be genuine, and a fairly wealthy "white" person like myself should take care not to dismiss models of "success" for students who may be feeling desperate and continually put down. It is easy to critique prevailing definitions of success from a position of economic security. Still, the Phase Two-Famous Few curriculum can be damaging, as it may deliver to students of color the message that most of their people are not worth studying, and that if they become *unlike* their people, they may be worthy of notice. It may serve as a bribe: leave your people and you may rise up the "real life" ladders from the bottom to become an American hero. Phase Two can put students at psychological risk, encouraging them to make their way not as members of their ethnic group but as soloists.

Elizabeth Minnich has pointed out that this loner status makes a person from a nondominant group vulnerable to every setback. Once the loner goes through the gates alone, refusing to identify with her or his stigmatized group, then every setback must seem like something which has been caused by personal behavior or is at some level merited.

A second psychological danger to students of Phase Two-Famous Few teaching is the implication that if you are "really good," you will not be seen as African American, Latino, Asian American, or Native American, but only "as a person." We women are sometimes taught that we will be seen as persons, if we will just forget that we are women. No; we will be seen as having sex and race and ethnic identity, especially if we are female or dark-skinned, or have features identified with a cultural sub-group. It is mere illusion to imagine that American adults see anyone as "just a person"; our "educational" and media training in type-casting, hierarchical placing, and mistrust has been too strong. Phase Two success stories of "achievers" imply to students that all they need to do to get out of their debilitating circumstances is to work a little harder and "make it on their own," without complaint, and without ties to their (impaired) people.

One further problem with Phase Two teaching is that the singling out of cultural heroes misrepresents the values of cultures in which the making of the individual hero is not thought of as possible or desirable. Sojourner Truth and Harriet Tubman were working for and with their people, yet are featured as outstanding individuals. Often collaborative group work is not seen to exist. The chief poster for the UN Decade for Women 1985 conference in Nairobi features a single woman weaving a basket. Women weave baskets together in Kenya; it is a group activity. In order to create the poster the designer had to misrepresent the culture. Phase Two courses featuring a famous few who stand out "above the crowd" can grossly misrepresent Asian American, Native American, and Latino cultures in which the star system is not the norm. American baseball players in Japan today have said, "The Japanese play for ties; no team and no player should get too far ahead." Asian American youngsters who do very well in the American school system may be doing so not for stardom but as a reflection of other cultural values, for example duty, obedience, or honor, a cultural ideal poorly understood by North Americans who do not have Asian ancestry.

The shift to Phase Three usually comes when teachers realize that Phase Two is politically naive: it features a few who survived in society but gives little attention to the structures of power in society. An important emotional shift occurs when teachers look past individual lives and experiences to invisible hierarchical systems which have very strong predictive power for the general outlines of any given life. Most teachers in the United States were not educated in school to see these systems at work, but were taught that the individual is the main unit of society and that the U.S. system is a meritocracy. It is a sign of personal growth when teachers begin to pass on to students systemic awareness of social inequities in resources, opportunities, and access to public power.

Phase Three, then, focuses on racism, classism, sexism, struggle, overt violence, persecution, persistence, protest, and work toward new policies and laws. Especially in the field of social history, the emphasis is on those who fought for change which would benefit oppressed people. Phase Three usefully focuses on interlocking oppressions, and at its best it links the study of power within the United States to power world-wide, so that students can see how patterns of colonialism, imperialism, and genocide outside of the U.S. match patterns of domination, militarism and genocide at home. All teachers and students in the United States need this experience of asking who has the most power, and why, and how it is used, and what is going on.

But Phase Three has its weaknesses. Many white social historians think they are studying multiculturally when in fact they are merely studying protest movements monoculturally. All the protesters look more or less the same. Phase Three scholarship never asks "ordinary" people about their lives, never takes children, women, or servants as authorities, never listens to voices which the academic world has not yet respected.

Phase Three, then, like Phase Two, opens some doors and keeps others shut. Its main conceptual fault is that it keeps the powers of definition and evaluation in the hands of the present "authorities," within a single system of meaning and value defined monoculturally. We will never make most people's experience seem either real or valid if our teaching and research still rest on the kinds of credentialing and vertical appraisal derived from the experience of those who have had the most power. Just as Phase Two analyses of "Black achievement" rarely encompass one chief achievement of African Americans, which is to have survived and endured with dignity, Phase Three tends to focus on visible political deficits without acknowledging any political dimension in focusing on "deficits" to begin with. The analysis of others' "issues" does not prepare Caucasian people to look at their own psyches, or to learn from "others."

I have noticed that many or most of us in the "white" academic world are more comfortable discussing issues of disempowerment than taking seriously those lives which do not center on, depend on, or resist "white" male governance, and which embody alternative forms of power. As I have said, Phase Three attributes to whole groups *deficit identities*, while denying their *cultural identities*, and in doing so it maintains control for the dominant group. It sets up a dominant paradigm in the mind of the student and then allows the underdog to be seen only as challenging it. It says to students of color, "You can be a fighter," not "You are a maker of culture and of life." It says to "white" students, "You are high; others are low." Such monocultural teaching about racism may ironically increase arrogance or ignorance in "white" students. It may teach them to sympathize with, or even admire the struggles of people of color but it will not teach that "winners" have anything to learn from "losers," except perhaps how to fight. Its lenses are useless for clarifying my colleague's comment that she would not want to be white.

Phase Four, on the other hand, illuminates her comment. For Phase Four makes a crucial shift to a lateral, plural frame of reference beyond winning and losing. It produces courses in which we are all seen to be in it together, all having ethnic and racial identity, all having cultures, all placed by birth in particular social and political circumstances, all with some power to say no, and yes, and "This I create"; all with voices to be heard, all damaged, and all in need of healing, all real, very distinctively ourselves, potential makers of new theories and new understandings of life. When I say "all damaged," I am thinking of the fact that my slave-holding ancestors were damaged. They were not damaged in the same ways that their slaves were, but they were made cruel and sick by their roles. Phase Four, being a frame of mind that goes beyond monoculturalism to cultural pluralism, allows me to see this. It opens the doors that my friend opened for me, onto my own culture newly realized by me *as* a culture, and onto hers, formed on a different base of experience. Phase Four suggests multiple worlds, or in the words of Pueblo Indian Gregory Cajete, it suggests *Multiversal Realities*, rather than a single *Universe.*

Phase Four reading lists in any discipline often contain multiple short works or kinds of material, including work by students, and provide multiple insights on any situation, in several media, with a de-emphasis on "issues" of disempowerment and a more unusual emphasis on cultural detail, and voices from daily life. Phase Four classes can be wondrous in their energy, interest, and healing power. Students feel co-ownership of them, and sometimes experience such courses as life-lines. It is true that competitiveness, anxiety, and vertical stereotyping from the conventional types of teaching carry over into the work of Phase Four classes, but teachers creating laterally expanded and culturally explicit syllabi usually try to redistribute power more evenly than usual in a classroom, and to weaken privilege systems which interfere with listening to many voices, and respecting testimony from many sources.

Whereas Phase Three emphasizes differences from an assumed but unexamined norm, and Phase Four recognizes distinctiveness without accepting any norm; it recognizes in experience the equivalent of what Gerard Manley Hopkins named as the "inscape" of created things—particular and vivid internal distinctness.

Some time ago I wrote a paper which lists 46 ways in which I daily experience having "white" skin privilege relative to my African American colleagues in the same building.* This is a Phase Four analysis. The paper rests on my sense of ethno-particularity, ethno-specificity, and ethno-peculiarity with regard to unearned advantage in my workplace. "White" skin privilege is invisible in the Phase Three monocultural focus on "others'" issues and deficits. I could see the cultural circumstance of having unearned *over*-advantage and its attendant cultural deformities only within the multi-cultural framework of Phase Four, in which my racial group is not assumed to embody a neutral or desirable norm.

Phase Four understandings take some blame out of the description of dominant groups; all people are seen as born into circumstances

---

*McIntosh, Peggy (1988). "White Privilege and Male Privilege: A Personal Account of Coming to Understand Correspondences Through Work in Women's Studies." Working Paper #189, Wellesley, MA, Wellesley College Center for Research on Women.

they did not ask for and systems they did not invent. The processes at work in Phase Four include listening, observing, making connections, respecting many kinds of life, power, and thought, including one's own, and imagining how to institutionalize the protection of diverse forms of life including distinct forms of human community.

Phase Five is needed to help us to an as-yet-unthinkable reconciliation between the biologically based competitive, hierarchical propensities and the biologically based contingent and relational propensities in each individual. Phase Four education helps to develop and reward the capacity for being in relation to others; Phase Five will need to help us also to rethink organizational structures in complex worlds where distribution of resources, services, and basic supports requires balanced uses of the vertical and lateral abilities which are in each person.

For this reason, as I imagine Phase Five, my diagrammatic model of psychic and societal structures turns into a large, three-dimensional globe. The faulted pyramids, with their bedrock lateral functions underlying the vertical functions, become simply one element in the topology of each continent, in a world like our own in which mountain ranges are one of the forms of geography. Each continent, each person or group of cultures, has its ranges, its "peaks," its dynasties, but mountain climbing is understood to be one particular human activity, not the only human activity. Sending expeditions to climb very high mountains requires preparation, equipment, freeze-dried food, support systems, base camps, porters, sponsorship, and people who can bow out of other life-sustaining activities or responsibilities. Certain maps can be drawn from high summits only. Many useful maps can never be drawn from summits at all. In any case, high summits do not support most forms of life. They are deoxygenated, and it is well known that people on too little oxygen do not make very wise decisions about the welfare of themselves or others.

It is the foothills, valleys, and alluvial plains which support life best, with rainfall, fertile soil, and concentrations of human knowledge about growing and harvesting. And at the edge of the water as we can learn to farm the sea as well. For the last 40 years, we in the U.S. have, figuratively speaking, taught that mountain climbing is the worthiest activity, the mark of ambition and of success. To shift to more metaphors of making and mending the fabrics of culture and environment seems to me to make more sense now. We can also usefully teach metaphors of journeying. Many of our students in the U.S. are free to travel, metaphorically speaking, to many sites in the topology, to experience many varieties of life, on many figurative continents, inner and outer. Some will stay in single locations throughout a lifetime. But we will continue to suffer if educators keep teaching that mountain climbing and peak experience are the best activities, and that the resources of the society are well spent operating base camps which help a few people or nations to stand briefly on summits and feel they have prevailed over life or each other.

The metaphysical shift from a faulted pyramid to a globe in which peaks and valleys are parts of cultural topology is accompanied by a further conceptual shift. The multicultural globe is interior as well as exterior; the multicultural worlds are in us as well as around us. Early cultural conditioning trained each of us as children to shut off awareness of certain groups, voices, abilities, and inclinations, including the inclination to be with many kinds of children. Continents we might have known were closed off or subordinated within us. The domains of personality that remain can and do fill the conceptual space like colonizing powers. But a potential for pluralized understanding remains in us; the moves toward reflective consciousness come in part from almost-silenced continents within ourselves. Greater diversity of curriculum reflects not just the exterior multicultural world but the interior self which in early childhood was aware of, and attuned to, many varieties of experience.

Readers of my 1983 paper on phase theory will know that I matched the phases with the sensibilities of hypothetical first-year college students called Meg, Amy, Jo, and Jo's twin daughters, Maya and Angela, and their younger sister Adrienne. I wished to indicate that what and how we teach in each of these frames of reference actually has life outcomes for students. This is true for the various ways we teach Ethnic Studies. I cannot guess about the effects on students of color of Phases One, Two, and Three, but I will sketch some portraits of the ways in which I have seen instruction in these phases affect the development of Anglo-European-American students, and then suggest the consonance between Maya and Angela's lives and Phase Four curriculum. My focus here is on the various kinds of understanding which the "Little Women" are given with regard to Native American culture.

Meg, who is a casualty of a Phase One curriculum, is a white girl who tries very hard to be good. She wants to be "sugar and spice," and also to be kind. When she is growing up, her brother plays Cowboys and Indians every afternoon with his friends in the neighborhood. She watches shows on cowboys and Indians. She learns in elementary school that the "settlers" had to contend with many "dangers of the wilderness," which included Indians and wild animals. She learns in high school that the settlers had to protect their families from Indians, who took scalps. In four years of college, she reads one chapter on "The North American Indian," which cites 12 white male anthropologists, refers to nearly 300 tribes and hundreds of language groups, yet does not make Indians seem the slightest bit real to her. This is Phase One Ethnic Studies in which "white" people neither study people of color nor notice that they haven't. Meg has studied "white" anthropologists. During her years in college, Meg will never start a conversation with a student of color. The way they "band together" makes her nervous. She seeks her friends, for safety. Meg will marry young, feeling a need of protection from many perceived dangers. She will marry a "white" man who turns out later to be neither a settler nor a protector. Many years later, as a Continuing Education student, Meg will find herself in another college course, reading for the very first time the words of a Native American. She reads *Black Elk Speaks*, and she is in tears. The sacred hoop is broken. Meg is devastated to discover the wholeness of Indian worlds just at the same time that she learns of their near destruction.

Amy, the ambitious art student schooled in Phase Two, appraises Indian work casually, as well as competitively. She knows it is only "craft," not Art, but feels the need to find grounds for putting it down. She finds it repetitive, primitive, inexpressive, and of course merely functional. Amy thinks some of the rugs and pots are handsome, and she is sure that she would recognize the work of a first-rate Indian artist, if only these people would put away their talk about broken treaties, and transcend their "cause." Amy cannot understand why they keep repeating old stories of their traditions, instead of joining what she thinks of as the cultural mainstream. She feels no curiosity about Indians, but gives a silent cheer when she hears that Wilma Mankiller has become Principal Chief of the Cherokee Nation. "That's the way it should be done," she thinks. "Just go for it and don't let anything get in your way." The idea that Wilma Mankiller was chosen because of her consonance with, rather than her competition against, others in her nation does not occur to Amy, who has been deeply dyed in the tradition of "the individual versus society." Amy takes a passing interest in Curtis's photographs of Indians, for their strong and striking faces. She feels, however, that if these people were "really good," they would have prevailed. She cannot imagine a culture in which the aim is not to prevail. As a gallery owner in middle age, Amy is criticized for her failure to show works by artists of color. She says that she would show some if she could find a truly outstanding artist. Her mind is as open as the "exceptions" curriculum of Phase Two can make it.

Jo, the older "white" woman who comes to college out of a failed marriage at the age of 40, is appalled by what she learns in her course on Gender, Race, and Class in American society. She had never understood why the Indians disappeared; she had known nothing of the slaughter of the buffalo, which took away the Plains Indians' means of existence, the Trail of Tears which killed tens of thousands of Cherokees and deprived most of the Nation of its native habitat, or the outlawing of Indian languages, laws and rituals. She sees in the silencing and crippling and betrayal of the Indians the same kinds of systemic oppression she has felt as a woman, silenced, dispossessed, beaten and battered in a marriage which now feels to her like a broken treaty. She is outraged that the books in which "white" anthropologists speak about Indian demographics do not make Indians' sufferings come alive. She writes a history paper on the way in which "whites" have named as "great" Indians only those who met Europeans halfway, but she does not know what to say about the corrective except that the American historians should recognize the fiercest fighters more honestly, and make the betrayals by European Americans clearer. Jo is distressed by this paper as she hands it in; something is missing, but she does not know what.

After the class ends, Jo starts a correspondence with an Indian woman in prison whose name she has found in an anthology of writing by North American Indians. As this correspondence goes on, she begins a support group for imprisoned Indian women, in order to raise money for their legal expenses and their families, and to provide them with reading and writing materials. Jo feels that she is at the edge of a vast territory about which she is wholly ignorant, and is angered to see in retrospect that the book she read on United States Women's History in a Women's Studies course did not contain a single mention of Native American women. She wonders whether she shouldn't have majored in Ethnic Studies rather than having to find out about Indians in this roundabout way. She can't seem to get people in her field, Women's Studies, interested in Native Americans. She persuades the Student Union Committee to show the film "Broken Treaty at Battle Mountain." She thinks of her work for Indians as being *for them*, but not for herself.

Maya and Angela, Jo's twin children, are attached both through schooling and through life outside of school to both their Anglo-American and their African American cultural roots. Whereas the "white" feminists they meet often talk about inventing new forms beyond patriarchy, they think of their "black" culture as both prepatriarchal and nonpatriarchal, and assume that it is these cultural traditions which need to be reclaimed in order to make the world a saner place. They own a cassette of the television interview in which Bill Moyers asks Louise Erdrich how Indian values can survive in this world of individuality, competition, and technology. Erdrich asks how the world can possibly survive *without* Indian values, saying that it has come to the brink of ecological crisis without them. The twins also like Michael Dorris's account of the mailman who came to his door asking him how to run an all-Iroquois week for a group of Cub Scouts in the woods. Dorris laughs and says that the most important thing was to take these boys' mothers, because Iroquois boys wouldn't possibly know how to get along in the woods without their mothers to teach them.

Maya and Angela are of course aware of Indian persecution, but they share Beth Brant's feeling that they are not victims; they are "organizers, freedom fighters, feminists, healers, and ... none of this is new; it has been true for centuries." They like their own laughter, their powers of spirit, *their identities*. They would not like to trade their identities for anyone else's. They feel affinities with Native Americans, with many other men and women of color, and with the few "white" feminist women and men who have made common cause with them. Their mother wants to talk about Indian Issues with the Cherokee friend whom they bring home for a meal. Maya and Angela have to explain why their friend did not make eye contact and did not respond warmly to this subject. They explain that her lack of eye contact is a mark of respect, and that her manner reflects Tsalagi cultural values of patience, respect for age, personal caution, listening and observing, making criticism indirectly, and keeping the emphasis on the whole group.

Maya and Angela see themselves as coming from different Nations than Indians, with heritages of different stories, but feel that they are similarly guided by spirits, and they have deep attachments to the "black" community. In their identification with darkness, they find nurturance. They do not study Indians so much as to derive strength from them; Carol Lee Sanchez, Joy Harjo, Beth Brant, Marilou Awiakta, Bea Medicine, Brenda Collins, Linda Hogan. They feel connected to their ancestors, to the invisible world, and to birds, trees, earth and sky.

Maya and Angela write on Native American cultures in college term papers; Maya writes on Mother Earth and Grandmother Earth, describing the distinction between Mother Earth, who is embodied in trees and corn, and Grandmother Earth, who appears in some Indian cosmologies as the soil itself. She contrasts Plato's view of the defects of the accidental or merely actual, as against the pureness of pure Form, with the Indian view that Mother Earth's products are not defective reductions of any purer principle. Angela, in a Phase Four Education course, writes a primer for grade school children, explaining that the Indians were the settlers, and illustrating elements of the wholeness and integrity of their lives, before the European invaders arrived. It is no surprise when several years after their leaving college, these women are adopted into one of the clans of the Cherokee Nation, and continue various forms of teaching and learning on the Cherokee theme that we are all part of the human circle.

Adrienne, their younger sister, is trying to help work on the curriculum toward survival. She dreams of balance between the creatures of the earth and their habitats, and she dreams of balance among nations and individuals so that all may survive with dignity. She is rather abstracted and preoccupied, and is working toward metaphors for the new texts which might sustain us.

Maya, Angela, and Adrienne have refused to accept the projections onto them of deficit identity by the dominant culture. Though my description of them may sound simple and even halcyon, they are doing heroic work in refusing monocultural messages about what they are. Their affirmation of their wholeness and their will to connect rather than sever themselves from others is a hard-won sanity which could cost them very heavily. They may be seen as unnatural, neurotic, unambitious, devious, secretive, out of touch with the "realities" of modern civilization, non-professional, unable to "progress." They may be seen as enemies of the government, and vilified both subtly and obviously by those who have the most cultural power. Ethnic Studies and Women's Studies can strengthen their hand if taught not only with a focus on aspiration (Phase Two) or understanding of systemic oppressions (Phase Three), but also with respect for and reinforcement for their personal and cultural integrity. Mending the sacred hoop is dangerous political work, but it is work toward survival. When Women's

Studies makes common cause with the Ethnic Studies to put human dignity and integrity at the center, then both will be doing their most dangerous and healing work.

It is significant that Meg, Amy, and Jo never receive a version of curriculum that goes much beyond the boundaries of the United States. Maya and Angela, on the other hand, have been supported to think beyond national boundaries, recognizing people everywhere, and seeing the earth and the sky as more basic organizers of human life than local governments. They have cross-cultural curiosity and commitment, trusting their own daily experience to lead to questions about larger world patterns. It is as though they have mentally signed a treaty of peace with others across national boundaries, regardless of what national leaders allow or want. They think of people in cultures other than their own as having cultural complexity and integrity, and as being unknown to them, but potentially in conversation with them. They feel a strong need to find common bonds and make some common policy amidst the diversities. Differences in governing bodies and strategies are not to them any indicator of final separateness; instead, they feel they belong in contingent affiliation with life everywhere. To citizens like this, we could entrust policy-making. Our choices about education will determine whether we will have such citizens.

ABOUT THE AUTHOR

My work in faculty development began in the 1970s at the University of Denver and has continued at the Wellesley College Center for Research on Women where I have been Associate Director since 1979. My Interactive Phase Theory was my solution to the problem of arguing mentally with Freud's and Jung's models of personality. I decided to devise my own model, and in conceiving of my interior life as mountain and valley terrains, I saw that these psychological structures corresponded to the sociological and institutional structures within which I had been raised, and that this model tied together many social and historical dynamics for me. As a maker of theory, I start testimonially and use as plain a language as I can, a matter of political principle for me. If readers can fill my model with data from their lives, fine; if not, fine; my aim is coherence without coercion.

Challenging the Myths
About Multicultural Education

Carl A. Grant

MULTICULTURALISM IS BECOMING PERVASIVE IN MOST aspects of our lives because of a significant shift in the sociological paradigm of the United States. This shift has been created by three major forces.

The foremost of these forces is the changing population demographics of our nation. The population of the United States has increased more than 10 percent since 1980: there are now nearly 250 million people living in this country. Forty percent of the increase is due to immigration, mainly from Asia, the Caribbean, and Latin America. In addition, the birth rate of women of color is on the rise. The Population Reference Bureau has projected that by the year 2080 the United States may well be 24 percent Latino, 15 percent African American, and 12 percent Asian American. In other words, within the next 90 years, the white population may become a "minority."

The face of the workforce is also changing. The ethnic breakdown of the workforce in 1988 was: 41 percent native white males; 33 percent

This article originally appeared in *Multicultural Education* 2, No. 2 (Winter 1994). Reprinted with permission of National Association for Multicultural Education. Copyright © 1994 by NAME. All rights reserved.

native white females; 10 percent native males of color; 9 percent native females of color; 4 percent immigrant males; and 3 percent immigrant females. The projections for workers entering the workforce between 1989 and 2000 are: 28 percent native white females; 21 percent native females of color; 21 percent native males of color; 12 percent immigrant males; 9 percent immigrant females; and 9 percent native white males (National Association of State Boards of Education, 1993).

Finally, our national ethic is changing from "individual" centeredness to the acceptance and affirmation of both groups and individuals. The rugged hard-working individual since colonial times has been portrayed as the hero and the contributor to this country. The 1960s witnessed the rise and identification with groups—e.g., ethnic/racial, women, lesbian and gay, physically challenged, and the poor. All of these groups demanded fairness and justice within and throughout all of society's formal and informal structures.

With the increasing pervasiveness of multicultural education have come myths, especially about what it is and what it isn't. These myths often serve to impede or halt the progress of multicultural education. Consequently, important to challenging and correcting these myths is first providing a definition of multicultural education that can frame and provide a context for espousing these myths.

⮜ Definition of Multicultural Education ⮞

Multicultural education is a philosophical concept and an educational process. It is a concept built upon the philosophical ideals of freedom, justice, equality, equity, and human dignity that are contained in United States documents such as the Constitution and the Declaration of Independence. It recognizes, however, that equality and equity are not the same thing: equal access does not necessarily guarantee fairness.

Multicultural education is a process that takes place in schools and other educational institutions and informs all academic disciplines and other aspects of the curriculum. It prepares all students to work actively toward structural equality in the organizations and institutions of the United States. It helps students to develop positive self-concepts and to discover who they are, particularly in terms of their multiple group memberships. Multicultural education does this by providing knowledge about the history, culture, and contributions of the diverse groups that have shaped the history, politics, and culture of the United States.

Multicultural education acknowledges that the strength and richness of the United States lies in its human diversity. It demands a school staff that is multiracial and multiculturally literate, and that includes staff members who are fluent in more than one language. It demands a curriculum that organizes concepts and content around the contributions, perspectives, and experiences of the myriad of groups that are part of United States society. It confronts and seeks to bring about change of current social issues involving race, ethnicity, socioeconomic class, gender, and disability. It accomplishes this by providing instruction in a context that students are familiar with, and builds upon students' diverse learning styles. It teaches critical-thinking skills, as well as democratic decision making, social action, and empowerment skills. Finally, multicultural education is a total process; it cannot be truncated: all components of its definition must be in place in order for multicultural education to be genuine and viable.

This definition, I believe, encapsulates the articulated and published ideas and beliefs of many multicultural scholars, and is not far removed from what many other multiculturalists believe multicultural education to be.

◠ Six Myths About Multicultural Education ◠

There are numerous myths about multicultural education. The ones that are most frequently voiced are:

1. It is both divisive and so conceptually weak that it does little to eliminate structural inequalities;

2. It is unnecessary because the United States is a melting pot;

3. Multiculturalism—and by extension multicultural education—and political correctness are the same thing;

4. Multicultural education rejects the notion of a common culture;

5. Multicultural education is a "minority thing;" and

6. Multicultural education will impede learning the basic skills.

These six myths will be the focus of my discussion.

Myth 1: Multicultural education is divisive, and/or multicultural education is a weak educational concept that does not attempt to eliminate structural inequalities.

As multicultural education has grown as a philosophy and a practice, critics representing both radical and conservative ideologies have opposed it.

Radical critics argue that multicultural education emphasizes individual choice over collective solidarity (Olneck, 1990); that it neglects to critique systems of oppression like race or class (Mattai, 1992) and structural inequalities; that it emphasizes "culture" over "race" (Jan-Mohamed & Lloyd, 1987). Radical critics also argue that multicultural education's major purpose is to advocate prejudice reduction as a solution to inequality. Therefore, they argue, its purpose is naive and misdirected.

Conservative critics of multicultural education argue that the United States has always been "multicultural" so there is, in fact, no controversy. Ravitch (1990) writes, "The real issue on campus and in the classroom is not whether there will be multiculturalism, but what kind of multiculturalism will there be" (p. A44). Ravitch is against "particularism," i. e., multicultural education that is defined as African American-centric, Arab American-centric, Latino-centric, and/or gender-centric.

Similarly, E. D. Hirsh (1987) believes that there is value in multicultural education because it "inoculates tolerance and provides a perspective on our own traditions and values." However, he adds, "It should not be allowed to supplant or interfere with our schools' responsibility to insure our children's mastery of American literate culture" (p. 18).

Although these conservative critics believe in multicultural education, their vision of multicultural education is one that adheres to traditional Western thought and ideology and seeks to perpetuate institutions as they presently exist.

Also, since many conservative critics believe that there is already adequate attention given to race, class, and gender in American life, they have harsh criticisms for proponents of multicultural education. They argue that multicultural education is a movement by a "cult" (Siegel, 1991), or it is ideas from former radical protesters of the 1960s (D'Souza, 1991). Further, these conservative critics argue that multicultural education is divisive (Balch, 1992; D'Souza, 1991), and that too much attention is given to race and ethnicity. The multicultural education now being proposed, they argue, will "disunite America"

(Schlesinger, 1991) and lead to "balkanization" or "tribalism."

Both radical and conservative critics of multicultural education often leave their research skills, scholarship, and willingness to conduct a thorough review of the educational literature at the academy door. Most radical critiques of multicultural education seem to be written after reading (not studying) a few limited selections from the multicultural literature. For example, some (e.g., Olneck, 1990) claim that dominant versions of multicultural education are divorced from sociopolitical interests, and that multicultural scholars see ethnic conflict as the result of negative attitudes and ignorance about manifestations of difference, which can be resolved by cultivating empathy, appreciation, and understanding.

It is for certain that these critics have not examined the work of Nieto (1992), Banks (1991), Banks and Banks (1989), Gay (1986), Gollnick and Chinn (1994), Grant (1988), Sleeter and Grant (1988) and Sleeter (1993). These authors point out that people of color, women, the disabled, and the poor are oppressed by racism, sexism, and classism, and that one goal of multicultural education is to empower students so that they may have the courage, knowledge, and wisdom to control their life circumstances and transform society.

Some of the radical scholars (e.g. McCarthy, 1990a) mainly quote from earlier publications on multicultural education, ignoring the context of time in which these publications were written, ignoring the conceptual evolution of multicultural education, and ignoring the more recent essays on multicultural education. Also, these critics seem to read what they wish into the writings on multicultural education. For example, McCarthy (1990b) compares the argument put forth in Sleeter and Grant's (1989) "Education That Is Multicultural and Social Reconstructionist" approach to one of crosscultural competence for enhancing minority negotiation with mainstream society (p. 49). This is difficult to understand, because a good deal of this approach is concerned with providing students with strategies for social action and developing self-empowerment (Sleeter & Grant, 1988, p. 201).

These misinterpretations of multicultural education by radical and conservative critics lead to continuous controversy, and undercut the influence that multicultural education can have on society. Paul Robeson Jr. (1993) tells us:

> The controversy over multiculturalism is not, as many claim, merely a manifestation of the politics of race and gender; rather, it is at the heart of a profound ideological struggle over the values of American culture and

the nature of U. S. civilization. Above all it is a debate about whether the melting-pot culture, which is the foundation of the American way of life and imposes its Anglo-Saxon Protestant values on our society, should be replaced by a mosaic culture incorporating the values of the diverse groups that make up America's population. (p. 1)

This statement by Robeson provides an excellent response to the conservative critics, but I believe the radical critics have somewhat of a different problem. Their problem is one of a need to understand that many multicultural educators are not simply interested in an education that will lead to the assimilation of students into society as it presently exists. Many multicultural educators are interested in changing the knowledge and power equation so that race, class, and gender groups that have previously been marginalized have equity and equality in all the structures of society.

Myth 2: The United States is a Melting Pot for all U.S. citizens.

An increasing number of people are coming to the realization that the United States never was a melting pot. The argument they put forth is that people of color have not been able to "melt," and other groups, such as women, the physically challenged, lesbians and gay men, and the poor, have not been fully accepted into the mainstream of American society. Many realities—the glass ceiling in corporate America that prevents women and people of color from reaching top leadership positions; inequities in pay between men and women and between people of color and white people; the lockout of women, people of color, and the poor from much of the political system; and the increasing slide of the United States into a two-class society of "haves and have nots"—invalidate the melting pot thesis.

Robeson explains that the melting pot is based upon the denial of group rights and a one-sided emphasis on "radical individualism," whereas the mosaic culture affirms group rights along with individual rights and emphasizes a balance between individual liberty and individual responsibility to the community. Robeson further adds:

This difference underlies the conflicts between the melting pot and the mosaic over the issue of race, ethnicity, gender, and class, since the melting pot has traditionally used the denial of group rights to subordinate non Anglo-Saxon White ethnic groups, non-White, White women, and those who do not own property (i.e., people who do not belong to the middle or upper class). (p. 3)

Myth 3: Multicultural Education and Political Correctness are the same thing.

Multicultural education is not a synonym for "political correctness." Many educators and other members of society unknowingly connect Political Correctness to multicultural education. Hughes (1993) states:

> Much mud has been stirred up by the linkage of multiculturalism with political correctness. This has turned what ought to be a generous recognition of cultural diversity into a worthless symbolic program, clogged with lumped-radical jargon. Its offshoot is the rhetoric of cultural separatism. (p. 83)

Political correctness, it is argued, is about doing the proper thing. Hughes (1993) also says it is "political etiquette." Some conservative critics argue that political correctness is about speech repression. For example, penalizing students for using certain words on campus, that they would not be penalized for if they used these same words off campus. Cortes (1991), an observer of social history, explains:

> . . . some campuses have instituted ill-conceived speech codes that have reached ludicrous extremes of attempting to micro-manage the "unacceptable." Such actions have had the unfortunate side effect of trivializing the critical issue of continuing campus bigotry, while at the same time casting a pall on the entire higher educational struggle against prejudice and for multicultural understanding . . . . (p. 13)

Repressing the use of speech, or limiting the books that make up the "canon," leads many—especially those who are opposed to multicultural education, or who are unsure about its meaning—to view multicultural education and political correctness as one in the same. An example may help to illuminate this point.

I was recently told that many P. C. advocates would probably ban or discourage the reading of *Huckleberry Finn*. I was then asked what would I, an advocate of multicultural education, do about the use of this American classic in schools. My reply was that *Huckleberry Finn*, or *Tom Sawyer*, can be read but in so doing needs to be read in a "context." By context, I mean the teacher leading the discussion should have experience teaching from a multicultural perspective. This would include having introduced the students (before the reading of *Huckleberry Finn*) to a variety of literature, some of which features African Americans as heroes and heroines; some of which has explained the historical meaning of words and terms; some of which included a rounded view of other ethnic groups, including whites. I would also add that the sequencing of *Huckleberry Finn* is important. It may not be wise to have it as the first book the class reads. It should be read after a positive climate is established, and students have developed an attitude of sensitivity and respect for each other within groups and across groups.

Garcia and Pugh (1992) claim that "political correctness" serves the purpose of defining a political and intellectual perspective as an aberrant ideology and then attacking it as indoctrination (p. 216). When multicultural education is reduced to P. C., Garcia and Pugh (1992) argue,"[it] undercuts the validity of pluralism as a universally shared experience," and I would add it minimizes the importance of women, the poor, the physically challenged, and lesbians and gay men.

Myth 4: Multicultural education rejects a common culture.

Multicultural education offers a way to achieve the *common* culture that doesn't presently exist. We all are aware that the United States is a land of many people, most of whose foreparents came from other countries, bringing different languages, customs, and religious beliefs. We are also aware that the United States' strength and humanity come from its diverse people. Additionally, we are aware that from this "diversity" it is important that we create a "oneness" or a common culture. Peter Erickson, using the canon as the context for his argument, offers four reasons why multiculturalism is not fraying America, and why it can help us achieve a common culture.

First, Erickson (1991) argues that traditionalists view the canon as made up of diverse, inconsistent elements, but whole in the sense of being conceived as a single entity. He states, "The basic unit of organization is single authors, however diverse; their diversity is expressed through the framework of a single literary tradition" (p. B2). Multicultural education, on the other hand, supports the acceptance and affirmation of multiple traditions. Erickson writes,

> In a multicultural approach, the basic organizational component is not individual authors, but multiple traditions. Diversity is thus placed on a different conceptual foundation. This foundation implies that each mi-

nority tradition is a distinct cultural entity that cannot be dissolved into an overarching common tradition through the catalytic action of adding one or two minority authors to the established canon. (p. B2)

Second, multicultural education expands the idea of what constitutes "valid criticism." Criticism is not confined to the rules laid out by established classical authors. Erickson argues:

> Multicultural criticism . . . recognizes the possibility of a sharp criticism of Shakespeare that cuts through the mantle of his established position. Such criticism does not seek to eject Shakespeare from the canon, but proposes that Shakespeare no longer be viewed as an inviolable fixture. (p. B2)

Third, multiculturalists do not reject the idea of a common culture, as many opponents of multicultural education claim. Instead, "it [multiculturalism] opposes the traditionalist way of constructing a common culture through over-simplified appeals to a common heritage achieved by applying the principles of universalism and transcendence to peoples' differences" (p. B2). Erickson argues that for the multiculturalists, "common culture is not a given: it has to be created anew by engaging the cultural differences that are part of American Life" (p. B2).

Fourth, the common reader for the multiculturalist is shaped by "identity politics." In other words, the identity of the reader(s) needs to be taken into account if we are to understand the culture we hold in common. Similarly, race, class, and gender are active factors that must be acknowledged and deemed important to understanding and interpretations.

Myth 5: Multicultural education is a "minority thing."

Many teachers and teacher educators see multicultural education as a "minority thing." They see it as mainly related to the school experiences of people of color. It is seen as an educational plan to help enhance the self-concept of students of color, especially African American and Hispanic students, who many educators believe come to school with a negative self-image. Also, it is viewed as an educational plan to help manage the behavior of these same students. Additionally, it is regarded as a curriculum innovation that seeks to include the culture and history of under-represented groups in the American experience.

Conversely, multicultural education is not seen as important and necessary for whites. One reason for this is that many whites see the focus of multicultural education as mainly race, and "race" is perceived narrowly as a "black or brown" problem—a problem that black and brown people need to overcome (Omi & Howard, 1986). Often forgotten is the United States' history of slavery and discrimination and the need for whites to understand how they contribute to everyday racism (Essed, 1990). Although the social science literature is replete with arguments that "race" (and racism) is very much the white man's problem, and that its evilness works against *all* of United States' society (Myrdal, 1944; Report of the National Advisory Commission on Civil Disorders, 1968; Tocqueville, 1969), this point is too often ignored (Omi & Winant, 1986; Ringer & Lawless, 1989).

Also ignored when race is seen as the only foundational pillar of multicultural education is the attention scholars of multicultural education gave to discussing socioeconomic class issues (e.g., control of wealth in society, discussion of the causes of poverty and homelessness), gender (e.g., the gender-based glass ceiling in corporate America, treatment of girls in math and science class), disability (e.g., the isolation or absence of the physically challenged in the classroom and at school events).

Additionally, when multicultural education is seen as only a "minority thing" whites are mis-educated. They are inclined to develop ethnocentric and prejudicial attitudes toward people of color when they are deprived of the opportunity to learn about the sociocultural, economic, and psychological factors that produce conditions of ethnic polarization, racial unrest, and hate crimes. As a result, they do not understand their responsibility to participate in eliminating the "isms" (Miel, 1967; Suzuke, 1979).

Further, when multicultural education is seen as a minority thing, the importance of analyzing the impact of race, class, and gender interactions which are important to multicultural education research is ignored or understated. For example, Grant and Sleeter (1986) reported that studies of cooperative learning that mainly paid attention to one status group (race) oversimplified the behavior analysis, and this oversimplification could contribute to perpetuation of gender and class bias. Similarly, (Bossard, 1994) discusses the importance of studying the interaction effects of race, class, and gender over time in order to understand and break down the negative institutionalized patterns of social life in school.

Myth 6: Multicultural education will impede the teaching of the basics and preparation of students to live in a global technological society.

Learning the basics and being able to apply them to real life situations is essential to any quality educational program, and the purpose of multicultural education is to provide a high quality educational program for all students. Multicultural education includes curriculum and instructional approaches that place learning in a context that challenges students, while at the same time allowing them to have some familiarity with the learning context and the purpose for learning the content being taught (Gay, 1990; Trueba, 1991).

Much of the early multicultural curriculum in the 1970s and the early 1980s dealt with how to help teachers include or integrate multicultural education into the subject matter they teach daily. Reading and social studies especially received multicultural attention (Banks, 1979; Grant, 1977). More recently, beginning in the late 1980s, materials have been readily available to help teachers understand how to make their science and mathematics relate to their students' thinking and conceptual understanding (e.g., Grant & Sleeter, 1989; Fennema & Franke, 1992).

The integration of multicultural education throughout the entire curriculum and instructional process is advocated to encourage students to learn the basics, understand that mathematics and science are tools that they can command, and that what they learn should give them greater control of their destiny.

Also important to multicultural education is developing the ability to listen to, appreciate, and critique different voices and stories. Development of these abilities, along with gaining an appreciation for differences, is essential to being able to successfully live in the 21st century. Hughes (1993) reminds us:

> The future of America, in a globalized economy without a Cold War, will lie with people who can think and act with informed grace across ethnic, cultural, linguistic lines. (p. 26)

Finally, it is clear that multicultural education is being challenged, but we should not be dismayed or discouraged by this challenge. Just a few years ago, only a few people were seriously discussing multicultural education or paying attention to its potential and possibilities. Positive circumstances and events for multicultural education are happening all across the United States. For example, the State of Maryland has recently passed a law for education in the State entitled "Education That Is Multicultural."

Finally, it is important to remember the words of Frederick Douglass:

> If there is no struggle, there is no progress. Those who profess to favor freedom, and yet deprecate agitation, are men who want crops without plowing up the ground. They want rain without thunder and lighting. They want the ocean without the awful roar of its many waters. This struggle may be a moral one; or it may be both moral and physical; but it must be a struggle. Power concedes nothing without a demand.

REFERENCES

Balch, S. A. (1992, Winter). Political correctness or public choice? *Educational Record*, 21-24.

Banks, J. A. (1991). *Teaching strategies for ethnic studies* (5th ed.) Boston, MA: Allyn & Bacon.

Banks, J. A., & Banks, C. A. M. (1989). (Eds.) *Multicultural education: Issues and perspectives.* Boston: Allyn & Bacon.

Brossard, C. A. (1994, March). Why do we avoid class in this sig? Why do we fail to integrate two or more topics across race, class, and gender, in our paper? "Critical examination of race, ethnicity, class and gender in education." *AERA SIG Newsletter*, 9 (1).

Cortes, C. (1991, September/October). Pluribus & unum: The quest for community amid diversity. *Change: The Magazine of Higher Learning*, 8-13.

D'Souza, D. (1991). *Illiberal education: The politics of race and sex on campus.* New York: The Free Press.

Erickson, P. (June 26, 1991). Rather than reject a common culture, multiculturalism advocates a more complicated route by which to achieve it. *The Chronicle of Higher Education*, 37 (41). Bl-B3.

Essed, P. (1990). *Everyday racism.* Claremont, CA: Hunter House.

Fennema, E., & Franke, M. L. (1992). Teachers' knowledge and its impact. In D. A. Grouws (Ed.), *Handbook of research on mathematics teaching and learning.* New York: Macmillian.

Gay, G. (1986, Winter). Another side of the educational apocalypse: Educating for being. *Journal of Educational Equity and Leadership*, 6(4). 260-273.

Gay, G. (1990). Achieving educational equality through curriculum desegregation. *Phi Delta Kappan*, 72 (1).

Gollnick, D. M. & Chinn, P. C. (1994). *Multicultural education in a pluralistic society* (4th ed.) New York: Merrill/Macmillan.

Gracia, L., & Pugh, S. L. (1992). Multicultural education in teacher preparation programs: A political or an educational concept. *Phi Delta Kappan,* 75 (3). 214-219.

Grant, C. A., (1977). *Multicultural education: Commitments, issues, and applications.* Association for Supervision and Curriculum Development: Washington, D. C.

Grant, C. A. (1988). The persistent significance of race in schooling. *The Elementary School Journal,* 88 (5). 561-569.

Grant, C. A., & Sleeter, C. E. (1986). Race, class, and gender in education research: An argument for integrative analysis. *Review of Educational Research,* 56: 2, summer.

Hirsh, E. D. (1987). *Cultural literacy.* New York: Houghton Mifflin. p.18.

Hughes, R. (1993). *Culture of complaint the fraying of America.* New York: Oxford University Press.

JanMohamed, A., & Lloyd, D. (1987). Introduction: Toward a theory of minority discourse. *Cultural Critique,* 6. 5-12.

Mattai, P. R. (1992). Rethinking multicultural education: Has it lost its focus or is it being misused? *Journal of Negro Education ,* 61(1). 65-77.

McCarthy, C. (1990a). Race and education in the United States: The multicultural solution. *Interchange,* 21 (3). 45-55.

McCarthy, C. (1990b). *Race and curriculum.* London: Falmer.

National Association of State Boards of Education (1993). *The American tapestry educating a nation.* Alexandria, Va.: The National Association of State Boards of Education.

Miel, A. (1967). The shortchanged children of suburbia. Institute of Human Relations Press, The America Jewish Committee. New York: Institute of Human Relations Press.

Myrdal, G. (1944). *An American dilemma.* New York: Harper and Brothers.

Nieto, S. (1992). *Affirming diversity.* New York: Longman.

Olneck, M. (1990). The recurring dream: Symbolism and ideology in intercultural and multicultural education. *American Journal of Education,* 98 (2). 147-174.

Omi, M., & Winanat, H., (1986). *Racial formation in the United States: From the 1960s to the 1980s.* New York: Routledge.

Ravich, D. (1990). Multiculturalism yes, particularism no. *The Chronicle of Higher Education,* October 24, 1990. p. A44.

Ringer, B. B., & Lawless, E. R. (1989). *Race, ethnicity, and society.* London, England: Routledge.

Robeson, P., Jr. (1993). *Paul Robeson, Jr. speaks to America.* New Brunswick, NJ: Rutgers University Press.

Schlesinger, A. Jr. (1991). *The disuniting of America.* Whittle Direct Books

Siegel, F. (1991, Feb. 18). The cult of multiculturalism. *The New Republic.*

Sleeter, C. E. (1992). *Keepers of the American dream: A study of staff development and multicultural education.* London, England: The Falmer Press.

Sleeter, C. E. & Grant, C. A. (1988). *Making choices for multicultural education.* New York: Merrill.

Suzuki, B. (1979). Multicultural education: What's it all about? *Integrated Education.*

Tocqueville, A. de (1969). *Democracy in America.* Garden City, NY: Doubleday and Co.

Trueba, H. T. (1991). Learning needs of minority children: Contributions of ethnography to educational research. In L. M. Malave & G. Duquette (Eds.), *Language, culture & cognition.* Clevedon, England: Multilingual Matters Ltd.

U.S. National Advisory Commission on Civil Disorders Report (1968). New York: Bantam Books.

ABOUT THE AUTHOR

I wrote "Challenging the Myths about Multicultural Education" to correct or at least provide another perspective on several issues confronting multicultural education. Multicultural education is often the subject of unfair criticism based upon ethnocentric beliefs and/or beliefs that offer a narrow conception of multicultural education. My hope is that educators will approach discussions and reviews of multicultural education with an informed and a critical eye. I am a professor with the College of Education, University of Wisconsin, Madison, and President of the National Association for Multicultural Education.

Multicultural Leadership

Joyce Stephens Bell

"**I**WANT TO BE A TEACHER, BUT NOT A REGULAR ONE," I WROTE in my ninth grade autobiography. A "regular one," in retrospect, meant "teacher" in the traditional sense. I didn't want to be the kind of teacher who saw students as empty vessels waiting for me to fill their heads with "stuff;" who told students what they were supposed to think so they could reproduce it on the test. I had witnessed firsthand the destruction done by robotic teachers supporting a system which advocated a type of social justice which only rewarded those students and teachers who possessed talents deemed to be the most relevant to the needs of the institution.

This system tracked students, placing them in "groups of matched ability, or homogeneous groups, within classes (e.g., reading groups in self-contained classes), subject areas (e.g., a low-level math group in seventh grade), or even specific programs (e.g., academic or vocational programs) at the high school level" (Nieto, 1996, p. 87). Research is clear about what an inequitable practice tracking is and the fact that grouping decisions tend to be made on "tenuous grounds." Tracking negatively marked my schooling.

Looking back, my elementary school experience was more positive than negative. I can recall each of my teachers by name and face. Reading groups prevailed, but most instruction took place in a whole group. I read well and memorized my math facts. However, I did have a troublesome subject. My stretch area was handwriting. I will never forget the Palmer cursive writing method. I spent many recesses with a ball point pen, trying over and over again to present a writing sample that would meet my teacher's standards.

Junior high school really began my arduous educational journey. In seventh grade I was placed in the 7A section. Sections included X, A, B C, D, E and maybe there was an F, too. Except for homeroom, I can't recall any of my Black friends in any of my classes. I lived in an essentially *defacto* segregated neighborhood where a few blue collar whites lived in a predominantly African American section of our town. Lunch time revived me somewhat, giving me an opportunity to reconnect with the friends I walked with to and from school.

Eighth grade was different. Someone decided to shift my section A status to section D. Perhaps this change came about from not faring too well in seventh grade math, who knows? The good news was that I had other students in my classes who were also Black and from my neighborhood. I question how challenging eighth grade was, but I can still remember a connectedness I didn't experience the year before. Granted, taking remedial reading when I knew I could read felt humiliating. However, enjoyment and fun were high on my list of priorities.

The tracking system was tweaked for my ninth grade stint. Instead of using the letters from A to E to denote "high" to "low" sections, it changed to D to A. I gained entry, for some reason, to section D and became reacquainted with classmates from my seventh grade year. This was confusing because it left me wondering: Do I have the talent or not? Who was I supposed to believe?

How significant it is that at that point in my schooling, I wrote about wanting to be a different kind of teacher. I wanted my students to have more trust in the system and in the individuals entrusted with responsibility for educating them than I did. I wanted my students to see themselves as capable learners, building on their strengths. In retrospect, I believe my search for educational equity and diversity began then.

I was allowed to keep on the academic track during my entire high school career. I was delighted that I no longer had to take any more math courses following my sophomore year. This decision came back to haunt me when my SAT scores reflected this omission. My sense of self-esteem and knowing tumbled, especially after my guidance counselor informed me I ought not go on to college. She felt my scores reflected my unworthiness. Several rejection letters seemed to confirm her predictions. I could have easily been a casualty from an hegemonic school system. Family and friends who served as spiritual guides sustained my belief in myself and continue to do so as I work on my doctorate in education.

∾ Defining the Landscape ∾

Working toward equitable education and education that is multicultural reflects my personal commitment to be a different kind of educational leader. As a new interdisciplinary field of study, multicultural education takes from, reflects, and duplicates concerns in ethnic studies, multiethnic education, women's studies and (to a lesser degree) research and scholarship on exceptionality. An important concern in multicultural education theory and research is the interrelationships of variables such as race, class and gender. Also, multicultural education applies content from these connected fields and disciplines to teaching and learning development in educational settings (Banks & Banks, 1995).

hooks (1994) states,

Multiculturalism compels educators to recognize the narrow boundaries that have shaped the way knowledge is shared in the classroom. It forces us all to recognize our complicity in accepting and perpetuating biases of any kind. Students are eager to break through barriers to knowing. They are willing to surrender to the wonder of re-learning and learning ways of knowing that go against the grain. When we, as educators, allow our pedagogy to be radically changed by our recognition of a multicultural world, we can give students education they desire and deserve (p. 44).

This vision of multicultural education contrasts sharply with my own experience as a student. Multicultural education has reflected and validated my drive as a classroom teacher to meet the needs of all students.

Nieto (1996) frames multicultural education as education for social justice.

Multicultural education invites students and teachers to put their learning into action for social justice. Whether debating an issue, developing a community newspaper, starting a collaborative program at a local senior center, or beginning a petition for the removal of a potentially dangerous waste treatment plant in the neighborhood, students learn that they have power, collectively and individually, to make change. (p. 317)

My own values and beliefs about social justice are the result of my being part of a marginalized group and my response to this reality. Counter-hegemonic practices, i.e., institutionally cooperative and culturally relevant educational practices, acknowledge and create learning environments where ALL learners have a sense of well-being, knowing, and academic initiative. Every child not only can learn but will learn if given high expectations and opportunities to flourish.

ᴖ Bridging Theory and Practice ᴖ

People in leadership positions in school need to identify, develop, and implement strategies, policies, and standards with the explicitly stated goal of achieving high academic results among all students. This undertaking is more than a mere notion.

Baker's (1994) thoughts on multicultural leadership and advocacy are profound:

> The success of any effort depends on effective and committed leadership. Leadership, in this context, is not limited to the superintendent of the local school district or is it confined to the efforts of a building principal. The kind of leadership that is needed to ensure the successful implementation of education that is multicultural will require all who have the responsibility for making decisions to provide leadership. Leaders who are committed often will be able to provide the advocacy needed. However, the advocacy needed to promote multicultural education will also require the commitment of those who represent the full spectrum of the community. (p. 32)

As I find myself in transition from a classroom teacher into an administrative role, I'm amazed at the number of missed opportunities for schools to promote a social justice principle of democratic equality. These democratic principles would eliminate tracking, promote cooperative schools and schooling, encourage multi-age classes, interdisciplinary and inter-dependent team teaching, and eradicate the use of language describing "good kids/bad kids," "the best and the brightest," and "low ability students."

The school is a bridge to the larger community, and nurturing the learners within the school community in an inclusive, positive way serves the common good. Multicultural education creates the experiences and expectations within each classroom that each student is capable and that each student belongs to our community. Creating this learning environment does not come quickly nor easily. To be an effective multicultural educational leader requires unwavering commitment to all learners.

⌘ Concluding Remarks ⌘

I began by sharing the story of how I came to view myself as a multicultural leader. It ought not have been such an arduous journey. Mary McLeod Bethune, a feminist, educator, and social activist, left a legacy for me. Barnett (1996) writes about Bethune's basic principle "that what was good for one was good for all; the rights of one were the rights of all" (p. 141). Bethune's views of feminism, education, and social activism coincide with multicultural theories of today.

I feel compelled to continue on behalf of the least advantaged and for the common good. My resiliency and strength grows from my interactions with the spiritual guides, living and dead, I have encountered in my life's journey. Reflecting on my mother's, father's, grandfather's, and grandmother's childhood messages, reading stories about black women's lives, talking with those who accept my voice without hegemonic judging, or reading a copy of my great grandfather's bill of sale from enslavement have helped me develop a healthier sense of identity and resiliency.

It is this healthy sense of identity and resiliency that builds healthy schools and communities. It ought not have been such an arduous journey for me, and it ought not be such an arduous journey for our students today. What the times require is multicultural leadership.

REFERENCES

Baker, G. C. (1990). *Planning and organizing for multicultural instruction.* Menlo Park, CA: Addison-Wesley.

Banks, J. A., & Banks, C. A. M. (1995). (Eds.) *Handbook of research on multicultural education.* New York: Macmillan.

Barnett, E. F. (1996). Mary McLeod Bethune: Feminist, educator, and activist. In J. A. Banks (Ed.) *Multicultural education, transformative knowledge, and action.* 217-232. Columbia University, NY: Teachers College Press

hooks, b. (1994). *Teaching to transgress: Education as the practice of freedom.* New York: Routledge.

Nieto, S. (1996). *Affirming diversity: The sociopolitical context of multicultural education.* White Plains, NY: Longman.

ABOUT THE AUTHOR

I am a single parent whose greatest achievement has been to nurture my daughter and watch her graduate from an historically black college with a Masters of Business Administration. She has inspired me to achieve my goals. My career vision has been to be an educator who both personally and professionally facilitates learning while emphasizing educational equity and diversity. Since earning a Master of Elementary Education and now pursing an administrative license in concert with an education doctorate degree from the University of Minnesota, I have maintained and expanded this vision to be much more comprehensive. I was prepared to facilitate seminars with teachers in the National S.E.E.D. Project (Seeking Educational Equity and Diversity). Minnesota started a state project which I helped develop and facilitate. SEED has been a catalyst which allows me to excitedly forge my life's journey as a life-long learner in terms of interior as well as exterior growth.

Seeding the Process of Multicultural Education

Gene-Tey Shin

Seeding has not been seeds for me
but rain
and earth
and food
rich and darkly thick with
the life
I needed for those seeds which
had already been planted deep within me
by my mother
by my father
by being asian
by being white
by being male and trying to be
a boy trying to be
a man
by being different
and trying to be the same
by being married and becoming a husband
and gradually becoming a partner
by having a son
and being a father
by having students
and being a teacher
by teaching writing
and discovering my own voice
by learning to listen
to others
to myself
to others within myself
and discovering that rich garden
that Milton thought was lost
that Adam blamed Eve for losing
that Christ, Lao-Tzu, and Buddha tried so hard to plant
but that each one of us can only cultivate
ourselves

our selves
in ourselves
without self-consciousness
self-pity or
self-hate but
selflessly
quietly
in celebration
listening
laughing to
the sound of
grass growing
flowers flowering
trees waving
rain falling to
moisten that
rich
dark soil
thick with the seeds
within.

ABOUT THE AUTHOR

It's really very difficult for me to explain why I wrote a particular piece, because there are usually multiple reasons driving my writing. One of the most significant though, is similar to what Gloria Anzaldua describes in her own process as taking images suggested by her unconscious and making sense and meaning out of them through writing. For me, writing is a way of exploring and discovering the connections between who I am and who I have been, and how these layers of identity operate in and with and through the world around me. In this way, writing has been an increasingly valuable and marvelous key to understanding my experiences growing up a biracial Asian American male in mainstream America, teaching in an independent school environment, and pursuing a doctorate in English Education.

TEACHING
& LEARNING

This has been of the great surprises of teaching: that along with teaching what you already know, you also wind up teaching what you're on the verge of knowing, or want to know, or need to know, and that some of your best, most satisfying teaching comes at that scary precipice. I thought this was a peculiarly personal truth until I read Audre Lorde's words:

Teaching is also learning. Teach what you need to learn.

—*Gail Griffin*

Guess What, Ms. Logan?

Judy Logan

I T IS SPRING, AND I HAVE DECIDED TO OFFER A NINE-WEEK
course called "American Women Making History." I have taught this
class many times before, and—as in past years—I order films and
videos, gather together the books, and print out student assignments.

But sometimes classes don't turn out to be what I thought they
were going to be about. Thirty-five students have signed up, fifteen
boys and twenty girls. On the first day I talk about my vision of inclusiveness and about how we cannot hope to cover the history of American women in nine weeks. I explain that they can work in groups or
individually to pursue some topic of particular interest to them, such
as women in sports, or the history of female Chinese immigrants, or
the Latina experience in California. I explain that they will not only be
writing about their topic, but will also make a presentation to teach
their classmates what they themselves have learned. This presentation
may be in the form of a diorama, play, video, mural, comic book,
model, song, puppet show, or some other form of creative endeavor.
We work out a schedule for presentations and I give them some class
time to work on possible topics. This is only our first day, and I still
think I know what this class is about.

Next we read Jamaica Kincaid's short story, "Girl," familiar from
the SEED project seminars. I set a writing assignment: students are to

write about their own memories of voices or experiences telling them what it is like to be female or male. At our next class, in order to help them feel comfortable reading about what they wrote (and to help them listen across gender lines), I move the furniture aside and ask them to sit on the carpeted floor in two circles, boys on the inside, girls on the outside. "We will begin by listening to the boys' pieces," I say, "and the girls' task is to listen carefully without interrupting." I talk about active listening. "Boys, you may read your whole piece, or parts of it, or you may pass."

I have started with the boys because I am impressed that they have signed up for this class, and I want them to feel that they are in no way less important than the girls in this class, even though the topic is about women. The girls and I listen carefully as the boys read their work. Many, perhaps half, opt to pass. The boys who do read remember voices from their childhood, but their voices are not gender specific. They say things like "Don't slam the door" and "Be nice to your little brother." Going around the boys' circle takes maybe fifteen minutes.

I then ask the students to switch places. I ask the girls, now in the inner circle, to begin. Each girl has written a long piece, and not one of them could be mistaken for a boy's.

Hope: "I was always taught that I could do anything. My parents taught me to be independent and self-sufficient, but of course, I encountered outside influences, telling you to be a nice little girl and a nice, self-effacing wife. In school I was told by teachers that I couldn't play sports as well as the boys, I wasn't as smart as the boys, I wasn't as good as the boys."

Martha: "Don't have sex until you're thirty-five, but if you do, use a condom and respect your body. You can make new traditions—not all the old ones are good, but remember that some are. And wear clean underwear, in case you get in an accident."

Kate: "Never marry a man who leaves the toilet seat up—some day you'll thank me for this."

Charlotte: "My parents never said, 'You're a girl so you can't do that.' But they say stuff, they say 'Don't slurp your milk or how will you have dinner with the queen? Girls who burp are not ladies. Honey, bring that drink over here, you're our own little waitress, sooo cute. Do that little thing you do.' What thing, Mom? 'You know, that little thing you do, that little dance, you're our own little dancer!'"

Susan: "My parents didn't mean to be sexist, but I guess they are in some ways. 'He's too old for you, take off that lipstick, cross your legs—you look like a hooker!'" Other girls in the circle laugh and nod.

Kate: "My parents didn't mean to be sexist, but sometimes they are. My father is way stricter with me than my brothers. I had to wear a dress every day to kindergarten. The first day it was a pink one with a big pink bow, but they were all very feminine. I just wanted to get dirty. And my brothers' rooms were messy, but if mine had just a drop of dust—horrors! And 'Won't you entertain the company?' My brothers just get up and go after dinner, but I have to stay, talk to the guests, say 'good night' to every one in turn. I just want to go 'Later,' and be gone, like the boys."

Not one girl chooses to pass. A strong energy moves between them, and while the boys follow the rules about silent active listening, within their own circle the girls nod their heads, gesture, and sometimes interrupt a speaker with, "Yes, yes, me too, me too." When it was the boys' turn to talk about gender, I had the feeling that they were fulfilling a teacher-imposed assignment, but with the girls the group takes on a life of its own. I can tell that the circle of boys has faded away for these girls, and what they see—what excites them and consumes them—are the mirrors held up by their classmates.

∽ ∽ ∽

Soon, issues of sexual vulnerability begin to surface. Some of the girls tell stories about how their parents refuse to let them stay out at night as long as their brothers can, even though their parents claim to be feminists. "My father says he worries about my getting raped," Marianne says. "But my brother could be mugged or beaten up and my parents don't keep him on a strict curfew." Other girls nod in agreement and complain about unfair restrictions because they are female. After a while I break my own rule about listening without interrupting. "Hmmm," I say. "I sympathize with your complaints. But I also know your parents and I empathize with their dilemma. I, too, sometimes worry about your safety. So what are we to do? How do we negotiate between our need for freedom and our need to be safe?" The conversation shifts from complaints about restrictions to incidents of safety and harassment. These girls are not safe, and they know it. The voices shift from complaints about their treatment to an awareness and analysis of the dangers they face by virtue of being born female.

Marianne: "He can stay out late, do whatever, and I can't, because they say, 'You're a girl and you could get raped.'"

All the girls: "YES!"

"Like when some guy drives by and tries to pick you up."

"I hate that."

"There's a lot of bad stuff that can happen to guys, but no one tells them to stay in."

"They can get hurt by weapons, they can be jumped, kidnapped . . . but *girls* have to stay inside."

Hope: "But I do feel more scared at night because of rape and stuff. I get scared on BART (Bay Area Rapid Transit) and on the street. One in three women are raped before they're eighteen, you know."

Kate: "Guys come up to you, gross guys."

Marianne: "Old guys see you, like twenty-five, and try to hit on you."

"It makes me sad to hear this from you girls," I say. "Is there anything that could be done to change it?"

Susan: "My parents should trust me more. I know when I feel unsafe. It makes me sick that people think I have bad judgment because I'm a teenager."

Hope: "Sexual harassment in school is the worst. It's like if you wear a tight shirt you're asking for it."

Marianne: "They say, 'Don't act like you want it if you don't want to get it.' Like we ever want someone to make degrading comments."

Kate: "In class this person threw me a note, and it was kind of funny, I mean kind of. It was about how my boobs bounce when I run in gym, and it was funny, yeah, but I was really embarrassed. I mean not really, but I was, and I told the teacher and the boy got in trouble; he got really mad. And that really felt good. It was cool that the teacher didn't ignore it."

Charlotte: "They say the boys will stop if you ignore them, but it's not true."

Hope: "There's a guy in gym who always stands behind me and says he likes my butt. I told the teacher, but he just said, 'Oh, he likes you, Hope,' and I don't feel comfortable playing sports now because this guy is always looking at my butt. I didn't want to get into sports at all after that."

Kate: "I wanted to quit track because of the comments about my chest. It was revolting. I feel safer if I wear big clothes. I buy my clothes like three sizes too big and it's the fashion, but it makes me feel better. My mom says, 'Why can't you buy your clothes so they fit?' and I say, 'Mom, Dude, it's because I don't want people commenting on my body. I have to dress like this.' I mean, sometimes you want to be feminine, but you can't because they can see your body if you wear those clothes and you get comments."

Marianne: "Sometimes I want to look like crap, no makeup, no nice clothes, just so no one will bother me."

Susan: "I know five girls who were almost raped by this one guy in this school. I was one of them." Agitated, she gets up. "He pushes your hands up against the wall like this and gets real close to you. I got away. People tell the principal or the teachers, and they say there's no proof; it's that boy's word against yours. It's like, 'Boys will be boys.'"

Marianne: "There's guys I'm scared of here and I walk all around the building to avoid them. Once, though, I turned a corner and saw these guys. One grabbed me and pushed me against the wall. The other one said, 'I'll get her from behind,' and they started trying to pull my shirt open and unbutton my pants. I couldn't even say anything, but I kicked and hit and he let me go."

I note the construction: Not an active, "I got away," but a passive, "He let me go."

Marianne: "You know, I think about it whenever I get dressed. When I'm shopping, I think, 'Would people think I'm a ho if I wear this?' Girls too. Would Susan think I was a ho? Would Kate?"

Susan: "I managed the boys' basketball team this year. This boy walked up during practice and he just reached out and grabbed both my breasts. And this other boy standing there said, 'Did he just touch you?' and I said, 'Yeah,' and he said, 'Darrell, you shouldn't do that.' Darrell said, 'I didn't do anything!' and walked away. And the coach turns to me and says, 'Next time you should really watch yourself.' Like it was my fault! I couldn't believe it."

Kate: "Unless you do like a political thing and make a big deal and try to get everyone in trouble, nothing happens at all. You have to do this huge thing, and even if you do, nothing happens."

All through this dialogue the boys have sat quietly and attentively in the outer circle. I say, "I want to stop here and check with the outer circle. They have been very patient and I would like to hear what this experience of listening to this conversation has been like for them. But I also want to tell the girls, I am not leaving this conversation as it is. There are places we can go from here. This is an important, scary, and profound conversation you're having, and we will continue."

I say, "Has it been easy or hard for you boys to hear this and be able to separate yourself from it, or do you hear the girls and feel persecuted or defensive?"

Dylan: "I can separate myself, but I feel angry at the boys who do that stuff. I feel scared, too, alone at night in the city, though; girls aren't the only ones who feel that way."

Luke: "I understand being afraid because I'm with my sister on the street and there are men who threaten her and I can tell how she feels, the way she gets real stiff. But I'm scared, too, because I've been beat up myself."

Neil: "Boys who do that to girls learn it from their families. Their parents don't say, 'It's not OK to do that.' They think it's OK to act like that."

Dylan: "It's easier for girls to do this assignment because there's more stereotypes about women. That note the boy wrote Kate; it was sick, about how her breasts wiggle when she runs and stuff I can't even say. I mean, I didn't really know it was this bad, and it's kind of changed the way I think. You hear all these girls talk at once and you realize it's a big deal."

I say, "I'd like to point out that I heard allies in the outer circle for you girls. You heard voices who had experienced what you had experienced and agreed with you and you have been taken seriously." (I say these things because by now the girls have been talking for about an hour and a half. The class period is almost over, and I hate to leave them without any sense of closure or accomplishment.) I suggest that some of them might decide to do a project about sexual harassment at our school. "Perhaps some of you might do some primary research, collect stories and experiences, and make them into a book," I say.

Dylan responds with enthusiasm: "I'd like to do that!" Other students nod, look at each other, make pacts with their eyes. Now I know what this class is about.

∾ ∾ ∾

When we reassemble, Marianne brings in a tape of an Oprah Winfrey show on sexual harassment, featuring girls, their mothers, and several experts. The program reinforces the idea that ours are not just isolated stories. Students realize we have plugged into a universal phenomenon.

When we finish viewing the tape, I say, "The other day, I heard a lot about issues of safety and freedom for women, and in particular about safety at Dolores [Middle School]. There's a lot we could do with a class project, based on this discussion. One idea is to write up some of these stories and collect them into a book. You might want to interview teachers, talk to them about what they're observing and feeling on this issue. Or we could develop a presentation for the other teachers, counselors, and students.

"We have to be careful not to assume that all boys engage in this behavior. Boys can take an active part in changing the behavior of others. Because it's not just a female's job to change it, but a male's job as well." I then remind the class that they can do their project on any topic in women's history, not just sexual harassment, but about two-thirds of the class want to work solely or partly on sexual harassment at our school. Students have so much to say that it becomes hard to hear everyone.

Hope says, "It was good to get the feelings out yesterday, but our feelings were so forceful that we excluded the boys, so they didn't get to talk."

Luke asks, "Is sexual harassment if you write a note to someone, but the girl doesn't see it?"

"If you say she's beautiful, it's not sexual harassment; if you say she's got big boobs and she's a slut, it is," Marianne replies.

Hope adds, "Well if you're writing to a friend and you say something racist, it's still racist even if a black person doesn't read it."

Manuel: "It's not degrading, though, because they don't know you wrote it. It's sexist, but it's not harassment."

Hope replies, "Harassment is when you make the person feel uncomfortable."

"It could be sexism if you write a note, but not harassment. I don't even know what harassment is—don't you have to like say it out loud and bother them?" asks Susan.

Luke says, "It's not sexual harassment to write notes, but it can start sexual harassment because it gets around and everyone starts believing it. The note can lead to sexual harassment."

Barbara says, "I think we have a double standard. Sexual harassment happens to girls more, but we go up and feel on guys too, and maybe some of them like it but maybe some don't and they don't want to say anything."

"So maybe it's how the person feels about it, not if the person is a boy or girl?" I interject.

Kate says, "You want to deny it's happening, you don't want to say anything because even though it's happening, it's like you're almost kind of flattered that the guy is paying attention to you. So you say you mind, but deep inside you kind of think it's flirting and you feel you should deny that it's not flirting, that it's something else, and then you realize it's something else and you feel really bad, like you can't believe you thought there was anything good about this. It's confusing. And you don't want to tattle on something so small, or something that makes you feel that way." I love Kate for being able to say this in class.

Pearl says, "You shouldn't have to make the counselors do something about it, but if that's what it takes, then you get in there and keep telling them."

Hope says, "They don't listen."

But Pearl persists, "Well, if it affects you, you want something done, then you keep going in until you make them listen. You can do something about it. You have to do something about it."

As I listen to these conversations, I think of all the things I myself have observed in the halls—boys who come up behind smaller girls and embrace them in a big bear hug, lean on them, and ignore the girls' protests. The boys who push their friends into girls, snatch things from girls, hit them, shove them, and protest they were "just playing" when I come to the girls' aid. I think of all the boys, larger than me, who just walk away when I confront them. Many times I follow through, track them down, write it up. I think of all the things I allow myself to "not see" as I walk down the hall, because, in truth, were I to follow up on every incident of sexual or physical harassment that I see around me, that is all I would do.

I think of my whole history of sexual harassment experiences, and I re-experience some of the rage and sorrow and fear these experiences generated. The problem is so overwhelming in our school. Time and again the girls give examples of asking a teacher or counselor for help, only to be ignored or directed in how *they* can change. Only once does a student tell the story of an experience where there was some resolution: Several boys cornered her and touched her inappropriately. She told her parents, who contacted the school. This student had a counseling session with her parents, the counselor, the principal, the boys, and their parents. She was completely satisfied with the outcome and said that these boys have never bothered her again.

∾ ∾ ∾

Those students who decide to pursue this topic form committees. One committee will research the laws about schools and sexual harassment and phone other school districts and ask for copies of their sexual harassment policies. Another committee decides to design a questionnaire for teachers. Another committee decides to design a similar questionnaire for students and conduct some in-depth interviews. The fourth committee calls itself the "Observation Committee." They develop a list of criteria to look for in the halls during passing time and at lunch in the cafeteria. One student, Corey, is friends with several of the boys who our conversations have identified as perpetrators of sexual harassment. He wants to interview them. I tell him I think this isn't a good idea although I admire his commitment to getting to the bottom of this topic. "I'm afraid that would backfire on you," I say. Fortunately, his mother agrees with me and forbids him to do it, although he never really understands why.

Other students in the class pursue their own interests—women in science, individual women who have captured their interests, etc. But the committees have the most energy. They use class time to confer, report, plan, and share. I continue to show all the videos and movies I ordered before the class started. This soothes my conscience—at least they are learning something that is really about women in history.

∾ ∾ ∾

The time comes for class reports. The observation committee goes first. During class time they have generated a list of specific behavior to look for in the halls, in classes, and on the playground. "During the past weeks we've seen many incidents of sexual harassment, " Marianne reports. "We've heard comments about bodies like 'She has a big butt,' or, 'She's got big, you know, breasts . . . .'"

I sense Marianne's discomfort here. "It's OK to say what you have to say," I assure her. "You are reporting on it, you're not adding to it."

Marianne nods. "These slurs are shockingly common. You don't even hear it because you think it's so normal. People think there's just a few harassers, but we've found that there's a lot more than we thought, making verbal comments. A few that we heard and wrote down are, 'She's got a fat ass,' 'I'm gonna slap that bitch,' 'She's a fat-ass ho,' 'She's a lesbian,' 'Suck my burrito,' 'Eat my hot dog,' things like that."

The class starts to laugh.

"I want to point out that laughing releases tension," I say. (I'd be crazy to fight the tide on this one—I feel laughter coming on, too.) "But I also want to point out that it's disparaging to laugh at things that are serious. Sexual words can be uncomfortable, and sometimes that makes us laugh, but if we were talking about racial slurs we wouldn't laugh."

"There are about ten people who are the main harassers," Marianne continues. "You watch and you see that they wait for certain people; each one bothers about three or four people. And the girls can't do anything. You can see how embarrassed and hurt they are."

"There's a code of silence among the girls?" I say.

"I even heard my own brother on the phone say, 'I grabbed a girl today,' like it was cool," Marianne says. "I couldn't believe it. And some of the people I heard say things were my friends, and that was weird."

"If it's your friend, you don't want to talk about it with him," says Kate. "You think they didn't mean it."

Corey adds, "I didn't notice it at first, but when I started looking for it I really saw it. I didn't used to see it and thought it wasn't a big deal, but now I really notice it."

The policy committee, consisting of two girls and two boys, goes next. The first girl reports on the Supreme Court definition of sexual harassment. "They recognized two forms of harassment: *Quid pro quo*, like you get a promotion for sex; and hostile environment, which is, like, sexual implications, lewd comments, pornographic photos, that kind of thing. In the San Francisco Unified School District, it is listed under Major Big Problems."

Dylan adds, "Near guns and drug abuse."

The students have interviewed the seventh-grade counselor. She tells them that she has the rules on sexual harassment and will enforce them. She has to get all the possible information from the harasser, the victim, and the witnesses, then write out what happened. The first time she lets the parents know; if it continues, there's a warning. If that doesn't work, she determines how serious it is and they have the option to file a police report. Then it goes onto the person's permanent record. If the police are brought in a second time, the harasser can be expelled.

"But she had no approximate number of how many times it's happened," Dylan adds.

"So we don't know if it's daily or weekly or what?" I ask.

Dylan replies, "Only one person has been suspended for one day, for physically sticking a person to a wall and touching her."

The teacher survey committee reports next. They begin by admitting that the heading on their teacher survey, "Hey you, yeah you!" may have influenced whether or not teachers filled it out. "We got three complaints (about the heading) but another teacher thought it got their attention. Not a lot of teachers responded. We handed out seventy-two. We got six back. I saw one teacher write a hall pass to the bathroom on one, then throw it out. Another teacher put it under some papers and didn't even look at it."

The teachers who did respond were the ones who were upset about the problem. When asked about the most and least they'd do if they witnessed sexual harassment, one said, "The most I'd do is have a discussion in class; the least is nothing." Another said, "The most I'd do is bring it to the counselor, and I have. The least I'd do is stop it." Two of the teachers didn't know that sexual harassment was an expellable offense. One of those who did said, "I'd like to see the school follow through for once, so the student body would know we're serious."

Dylan reads the list of activities, gestures, and writings that can get one expelled on the second offense. They include bra snapping, pantsing, unwanted physical contact, spreading sexual rumors, boys grabbing their groins, passing around centerfolds, sexual notes, putting up sexual graffiti, teasing about body development (under-developed or over-developed), making animal noises in public at individuals, girls yelling "Someone has a hard-on," boys bragging about the size of their penises.

"We also called high schools, universities, and law schools to ask about their sexual harassment policies. About half had them. One school said they don't have sexual harassment there. And when we called the superintendent, we talked to him and he didn't even know who the Title IX person was. He gave us to his secretary. And they gave us a number and it was wrong and we made about fifty phone calls before we got the person. It took about three hours."

The survey committee reports next. Susan says, "We handed out over fifty surveys. As we passed out the surveys, we saw guys throw them out and make fun of them. Other guys handed them back and said they weren't interested or it was too personal or it didn't apply to them. On about ninety-five percent of the ones we did get back, they wrote silly or ridiculous answers. When we asked why they harassed, they gave answers like, 'Because she deserved it,' 'Because her butt's big,' 'Because she has big tits.'"

"So in their minds the responsibility for the harassment resides with the female?" I say.

"Yeah. The girls took the surveys seriously, though."

Christine reads the results of the girls' survey. Fifty-six percent of the girls had experienced all the forms of harassment listed (verbal, touching, gestures, pinching). The girls said it made them feel "fucked up, raped of dignity, hurt, disgusted, cheap, dirty, or that it didn't matter and the boys were just playing around."

Susan says, "Forty percent said they were careful of what (clothes) they buy so boys won't harass them and girls won't call them sluts."

Christine adds, "Sixty percent said they thought someone whistling or grabbing girls happened more that twenty times a month. Thirty-eight percent of the girls thought that the boys should be suspended, twelve percent thought they should be expelled, six percent thought they should get a phone call home, and ten percent thought they should get suspended plus a referral and a parent conference."

Charlotte reports: "Some descriptions of personal experience were, 'Comments are always made to me, I hate it, but I can't do anything about it. Guys touch me and girls call me a slut when the guys do, but I don't think it's my fault. Two boys tried to rape me once, but I fought and got away.' 'A boy kept leaving messages on my answering machine saying he fucked me, and the school chose not to do anything about it.' 'A boy pretended to masturbate in class and said he was going to fuck me. I finally said if he ever threatened me again I'd slap the shit out him. He stopped.'"

I say, "In most cases, there seems to be little awareness by the girls that they have the right not to be treated that way."

Christine: "It's like it's hidden and it needs to be brought up."

I say, "Class, remember the Wellesley/AAUW report I showed you at the beginning of this class? Some of you used parts of it for your reports. There's something discussed in that report called the 'hidden curriculum.' That's a term for all the things you learn in school that are not talked about. There is also something called the 'evaded curriculum,' which is a term for the things we see, but school refuses to deal with. We've looked at both of these and you've done a great job gathering information and asking questions."

∾ ∾ ∾

It is June. The next meeting is our last day in this class. The final committee to report is the interview committee, who tell stories that are by now achingly familiar: A girl talks about being followed, whistled at, called "Mamacita," going all the way around the building to avoid the boys, being late to class. Another girl had her hands held over her head so that the boys could touch her. She broke away and ran down the hall. Boys threatening to rape girls.

Hope says, "It's about power trips. And we discovered that it was the same group of guys in every story."

"And the girls are learning certain behaviors," I say. "Looking away, trying not to be conspicuous, trying not to dress a certain way. They learn to become silent, careful, not active or assertive in life. That's what the hidden curriculum teaches."

Karen says, "Most girls thought there was no point in telling the counselor because she wouldn't do anything."

"Most girls thought there was nothing they could do," Hope adds.

This is not the ending I envisioned. "Well," I say, feeling a little sick that this is the last day of class, "reporting to each other is good, but what else can we do?"

Hope suggests, "Let's make a booklet. Maybe we could hand it out to all the students and teachers."

Pearl, about to graduate, says, "We should go around this year to classes and make a presentation. We should say, 'This is sexual harassment and this is what you do about it.'"

"We have to work on getting girls not to be ashamed," Hope says.

It is only a few minutes to the bell. We look at each other. What to do with all of this? "Well, class, this class is over, but the topic is not. I'll be home this summer if anyone wants to work on a booklet on your own time." Several students raise their hands to volunteer.

But I am working until the middle of July, and by then I am too tired to call these students and get them together to write the booklet. I save all the material, though—the reports, surveys, research, interviews. I have the illusion that I will do something eventually with all this paper, all this effort. I comfort myself that the class has learned a lot, even though the booklet is never produced.

∽ ∽ ∽

It is September. Karen and Kate come bursting into my room just a few weeks after school has started. Their faces look like Christmas morning. Each girl has been accepted into an independent high school— one coed and one for girls only. I am anxious to hear how they like their new schools, and they are anxious to tell me.

"Guess what, Ms. Logan, guess what?" they say.

"What? What? I want to hear everything!"

"Our schools are so cool! There are only about ten kids in each class. Every time we write something, we get to read it aloud, and we get to hear everyone else's work!"

"That's wonderful," I agree. "That's how it should be; I'm so happy for you. What a great opportunity."

Then they look at each other as though they have saved the best for last. "What else?" I prod.

"Both our schools have sexual harassment policies!" They say this with such pride and happiness. I stand and give them each a celebratory hug, but I feel teary inside that this is such a big deal for them.

You shouldn't have to feel so lucky about this, I want to say; this should be part of your birthright. You shouldn't have to go to an expensive, private place in order to feel safe. But I keep the teary part inside and the celebratory part outside. After all, this is a step in the right direction.

ABOUT THE AUTHOR

I wrote this article because I thought it showed how sexual harassment is a part of our education system and how a class can change and respond to the experiences and concerns of the students. It is my hope that the reader will consider whether or not sexual harassment is a part of his or her students' experience, to what extent that impacts students' ability to learn, and how to empower both boys and girls to make the school climate safe for everyone. It is also my hope that teachers will write the stories of their classrooms. I have taught in San Francisco, California, schools for over thirty years.

Five or Six Things
I Now *Know For Sure*

Kim A. Wilson

I NEVER *INTENDED* TO TEACH.

∿ ∿ ∿

It's the eighth (and last) period of a fairly long day in February, and college prep sophomore English class has just begun. I see one of the students lean over and whisper something into his classmate's ear. That student's hand goes up and he says, "Miss Kim, would you please tell us why you said you hate the movie *Billy Madison* so much?"

∿ ∿ ∿

Of the five or six things I now know for sure, one of them is that if I tell my students, "We'll talk about it later," they are going to hold me to it.

I knew this was going to happen. About two months earlier I was taking my students through an exercise that asked them to name their three favorite movies while I wrote the titles on the board. The objective was to lead into a discussion about the ways in which the popular

---

Many thanks to Dorothy Allison for *Two or Three Things I Know for Sure* (Penguin Books, 1995)

medium of motion pictures reflects and informs their culture as well as their views of the world. This would frame our discussion of two future films in the course. This particular class was heavily into bombs and bullets, Industrial Light & Magic-type science fiction, slapstick comedy, and Walt Disney.

One of the movies listed was *Billy Madison*, a theoretically funny 1996 Hollywood production starring Adam Sandler of *Saturday Night Live*. At the end of our discussion about the movies they'd named, I made some wisecrack about how much I hated that film and would not be sorry if I never heard it mentioned again in my lifetime.

Big mistake. The students immediately wanted to know why I felt that way. And as much as I wanted to tell them, I just didn't have the energy to make the effort. So I told them that there was not enough time for me to give them the explanation they deserved, but when there was time, we would talk about it. I never intended to bring this issue up again. But I knew this class wouldn't let it rest.

∾ ∾ ∾

So today is the day of reckoning. The students have been very patient, and now *is* a good time for us to talk about it. "OK," I said. "We can do this. But before I answer your question, I have to ask you to do something for me first. And you need to know that what I'm going to ask is probably going to be somewhat uncomfortable for you. But there is a reason for what I'm asking, and I need for you to trust me on that." I then ask them to think about all the messages they receive from the world around them about black women as they complete the sentence, "Black women are . . . ," which I have by now written on the board.

As I expected, the class was stunned into silence and there was a palpable reluctance to even contemplate doing this exercise. I could *feel* the kids thinking, "Uh oh! What have we gotten ourselves into now?" But we do trust each other, so I said to them, "I want you to be really honest as you try to name the things that black women are. I will not take what you say personally, and it's important that you try to do this because it has everything to do with my response to the movie you asked about."

Once they were convinced that I was serious, they began to name things: black women are "opinionated," "hard working," "always taking care of other people," "maids," and "large" are the descriptors I remember best. But they served my purpose. I began telling my students about some of the images of black women in America which have their origins in slavery. I told them about the practice of white slave owners having their black female slaves nurse their own and their white slave owners' babies. I told them that up until the mid-20th century, it was necessary for many black women to become maids since that was the only job available unless they had some formal education. Many a black woman has put her children through college on what she earned cleaning white people's houses.

I told them about how some of those images have become myths and stereotypes perpetuated by popular media today. And the stereotype perpetuated in the film *Billy Madison* is that of the large-bodied, big-breasted black female maid who, "like one of the family," raises this incredibly rich white boy virtually "as her own." She is his sole confidante and she understands him like no one else. So when things get tough and he is metaphorically crying on her shoulder as she is working in the kitchen, she somewhat facetiously asks him, *"Do you want me to open my shirt?"*

I told my class that while the white students watching this film laughed, I was horrified and infuriated. I also told my class that I was convinced that the only reason that scene was allowed to remain was because its producers knew that it was going to be viewed by a primarily white audience between the ages of thirteen and eighteen. I told them that it didn't matter whether or not the audience "got" the historical relevance of that scene; what *was* going to remain with them was the *image* of that older, black, caretaking woman *offering her breast* to her young, white male *"son"/employer*. And that was the reason I never wanted to hear that film mentioned again.

Though I do not often change my day's lesson plans in this manner, when I do, I notice that *all* of my students are riveted on my face. It's as if they are in my mouth as I speak the words. I am struck by how hungry they are for such knowledge of this aspect of U.S. history. My students listen more intently than at almost any other time.

After I'd finished with this "lesson," I told my students that I was really proud of them for not letting this go and for taking the risk they did by finishing the sentence I'd written on the board. I told them that I would not have done this had they not pushed it because it is oftentimes difficult for me to know how to bring some of this into the classroom given that I am the only adult female of African descent in the building. This is knowledge I want them to have; but I struggle with the fact that I am the only one they know who can give it to them. I then asked if anyone had anything they wanted to say. One of the girls immediately raised her hand and said, "I am so glad that you can talk about this. There are a lot of people, some in this building, who feel the same way. But they never talk about it."

～ ～ ～

All my life I've known that I wanted to work with young people, and I knew that it was critically important that my formal education include learning about gender, race, class, culture, sexual orientation, and a host of other ways in which people's experiences are shaped by social constructions of "otherness." For as long as I can remember, I have always been conscious of how I personified "other" in the minds of many people around me. Especially in schools. In my mind, my own adolescent experiences and wants and needs and somewhat unfulfilled expectations of the adults in my life (i.e., family members, guidance counselors, teachers, church elders) were linked to my desire to grow up to become a different kind of adult model for young people. Although I could never have actually told you what that model might look like (after all, I'd never seen it before either), I *never* imagined myself as a classroom teacher.

My seventeen years in the education profession have taken me from college admissions to secondary school guidance counseling to dormitory parenting to secondary school student leadership development training to secondary school administration. But it was in 1990 that I found myself in a situation where the only thing I hadn't done was classroom teaching. It was time. And I knew it. Since then, I've taught high school English at four different schools in three different states. Until recently I had always been an administrator with part-time teaching responsibilities.

It was not until I moved to Minnesota and became a full-time classroom teacher for the first time that I found myself having to really *think* about the personal and professional dimensions of creating curriculum and developing classroom practices and processes for delivering an education that is truly multicultural and inclusive. That education must include giving students the opportunity to think about difference and decide for themselves the degree to which differences would matter in their own personal and professional relationships with others.

～ ～ ～

It's the first day of this school year. I have three sections of college prep sophomore English and two sections of college prep U. S. literature and composition for eleventh graders. I love the sophomores. I always have. So in an effort to get to know them better and be a better teacher for them, I ask them to write an English autobiography. This would include how they feel about their time in English classes since the sixth grade, what they feel are their strengths and weaknesses in English, what their hopes and fears are for this class this year, and how they would define themselves as students of English language (written and/or spoken) and/or literature (reading). I told them that I wanted them to tell me their truth and assured them I would not take what they said personally or punish them for being honest. I hoped that they would take this opportunity to let me know what they needed.

When I collect and read their work, I am thrilled that my students are so honest with me. As I'd suspected, for many of them their greatest fear was of not being able to keep up with the reading, or not being able to do the reading I might ask of them. They feared being bored by the discipline. They feared getting bad grades. And they feared that their writing was not good enough. On the other hand, almost every single one of them saw themselves as someone who tries hard to do well and to learn. Many of them told me that "English had always been their worst subject." Many confessed that they knew their writing skills weren't great, but they did not know how to improve. A few admitted that if they weren't required to be in English, they wouldn't be. Most let me know in no uncertain terms that if they were interested in something, they did better.

I share with my students the highlights of their collective wisdom and thank them for their courage and their candor. I tell them that I cannot promise they will like everything we do this year, but I know we are all going to learn something.

Of the five or six things I now know for sure, one of them is to tell my students up front that they can trust that whenever I ask them what they think, it's because I really want to know.

∾ ∾ ∾

I'm a person who loves to read: fiction, non-fiction, biographies, autobiographies, short stories, cereal boxes. In all of my previous experience with and in schools, my students shared this love of and enthusiasm for reading. So in my first year at this school I gave my students a questionnaire which asked, among other things, what they've read in the past, what they read for fun, and what they like to read in general. Imagine my shock and dismay when I found that almost 70% of my college-bound students had never read a book for fun or finished a book they were assigned to read for any humanities-related class. For them, reading was pretty much a difficult and boring task, something they did as little as possible unless they were reading a favorite magazine or a particular section of the newspaper. Consequently, they had little or no idea of what kinds of books they would like to read if given a choice.

I learned quickly that if I was going to be an effective English teacher for these particular students, I was going to have to come up with some pretty innovative approaches to get them to read and to recognize the importance of reading as a tool for understanding language.

It's still relatively early in the school year, and I've decided that my sophomore students will read *Oedipus the King* by Sophocles. Aside from the fact that this play will allow me to introduce issues of current Western philosophy and culture and their connection to ancient Greek philosophy and culture, I can also begin to generate some thinking about gender politics, economics, privilege systems, and various cultural archetypes. None of this will be totally unfamiliar to them because I began the year by teaching them about the complex nature of various aspects of culture and cultural groups. Since I plan to have them read *Oedipus* aloud in class, this will also be a good way to help many of my students overcome their fear and embarrassment of public speaking. As I distribute copies of the play, I hear several choruses of "Ugh! This is really big." "Ugh! Do we have to read the whole thing?" "Ugh!"

I can't resist teasing them about their response to reading in general. Afterwards I let them know in no uncertain terms that I went to a great deal of trouble to find a translation of this play that would be accessible to them and to make sure that each student had his or her own copy to use. I asked them to please reserve judgment about this until after they were done. Until then, we really had nothing to talk about.

By the time we are halfway through the play, there are not enough parts for the number of students who want to read on any given day. In one particular class on one particular day, there were four parts available and eight students wanting to read. So I split each role so that I could say "yes" to all eight students. As I listened to them reading, I found myself wishing I had an audio or video recorder. None of the eight students *ever* missed a beat. The rhythm was *flawless,* and the power and emotion of the scene they were reading was so clear that their classmates listened with the same intensity I did. When they finished, I praised them with tears in my eyes.

There are five or six things I now know for sure, and one of them is to ask my students to think about literature in the same way you look at a photograph album.

As you flip through the album you find yourself imagining the context out of which any given picture was taken. You find yourself thinking back to the particular circumstances surrounding *that* moment captured by the photograph. For example, you come across a picture taken when you were six years old. Looking at that photo ten years later prompts questions like "Who else was around when that photo was taken? What was the occasion for the picture? What kind of mood was I and/or everyone else in at the time?" You ask the same kind of relevant contextual questions if you're looking at pictures that are not about you.

I tell my students that all literature is created out of a similar context. The story itself is a reflection of a particular author's vision of his or her world at that particular moment in time and space. Therefore, regardless of whether or not the reader likes or dislikes the actual story, it is still possible to find some point of entry through which a connection can be made. The bottom line is this: thinking about the *context* of a story will help you ask more critically relevant questions and make more substantially informed evaluations in general. We can all learn something from any piece of literature, whatever its place of origin.

This approach toward reading provides my students with a rationale for why I have asked them to read a particular piece, and it gives them an opportunity to make the reading a meaningful exercise. They not only finish reading whatever I give them, they ultimately experience significant success in the English discipline through the process of discovering connections to themselves even though the author's story may be totally unlike and/or alien to their own lives. Additionally, creating an atmosphere where it is safe to talk about underlying assumptions (on the part of the author and/or themselves as readers) associated with gender, skin color, age, class, culture, geography, sexual orientation, religious affiliation, language, or whatever, allows my students to further deepen their understanding of themselves and others.

∾ ∾ ∾

I've lived on the East Coast almost all my life. I moved to Minnesota in 1995. My professional life has almost always been in the private school sector. I have always been one of a handful of females of African descent on staff, if not the only one. No matter where I worked or what I did, it has always been an integral part of my work to have strong relationships with young people of different racial backgrounds. Most of these relationships naturally included lengthy discussions about how differences of all kinds are socially constructed to matter in the world in general and in the United States in particular.

While on some level I was prepared for the reality of being one of a few female Americans of African descent on a teaching staff, I was totally unprepared for the radical difference in the dynamic of race relations in Minnesota. Nor was I prepared for the ways in which gender politics exacerbate the racial politics. I learned the hard way that engaging in real, constructive conversation with adults or students about ways in which these or any other differences mattered with regard to personal, group, and/or world perspectives was not going to be easy. What seemed to matter more was defending positions (who's "right" or who's "wrong"), not exchanging points of view.

I had been raised in an academic culture where it was a given that the best kind of learning takes place when individuals exchange points of view about a particular subject, issue, or topic. We were not required to agree on anything and there was never a hint of judgment or censure, just a communal sharing and the collective making of meaning that encourages and nurtures individual thinking.

After having taught in two different Minnesota independent schools, I've found that this is not the norm. I've seen and students have shared with me that they are told what to think, how to think it, and how to reflect back what they have been told to think on the test. They are rarely invited to say what they think about anything, and when they are, it is tacitly understood that the right answer is a re-stating of what the teacher thinks.

Consequently, when (in my initial ignorance) I asked the question, "What do you think?" I received blank stares or noncommittal, middle-of-the-road responses guaranteed to keep the student out of hot water with the teacher and/or his/her classmates.

Similarly, I learned that my simply asking the question, "Do you understand what I am asking of you?" does not necessarily yield a truthful response from my students. This broke my heart because not only did it stop my teaching style in its tracks, but it all too clearly illuminated for me the degree to which many of my students had learned to keep silent out of self-preservation. Taking such risks with a teacher often yielded more trouble than it was worth. It was easier to just go along with the program.

I always tell them that we do not have to agree on anything, that I am not always so much concerned about what their opinion is as I am that they have one at all. I want them to know and believe that I want to hear their voices because in my classroom we all learn from each other.

Of the five or six things I now know for sure, one is that part of my responsibility as a teacher is to help my students find and develop their voices.

I cannot assume that my students have been taught how to express themselves verbally or in writing. Nor can I assume that they have a language/vocabulary adequate to the task of giving definition, form, or substance to all of the things they see relative to difference and differences.

This meant several things for me as a classroom teacher. One, I had to figure out just how deep the socio-historical ignorance trough was for my students.

Two, I had to figure out how to instill in my students enough trust in me and their relationship with me to engage them in the very difficult task of examining their own biases, stereotypes, and prejudices in a safe and non-threatening manner.

Three, I had to figure out how to get them to deal with their own racism where I was concerned. With very few exceptions I was the first black teacher my students had had. No matter how much the world may have taught them that "we are all equal without regard to race, color, creed national origin," I was a living representative of all that they had also been taught to fear, disbelieve, suspect, or mistrust. One white male student told me toward the end of my first teaching year that he immediately wondered what my "agenda" as a black woman teacher was. Another white male student couldn't believe how smart I was. In fact, my intellect "astounded" him.

Fourth, I had to deal with my own increasing anger and disbelief in finding myself in a life experience situation I hated. It was a lot of work to have to reinvent my classroom persona because I could not teach the way I was used to. I didn't know that there were places in the United States where children were kept tragically ignorant of so many things. And that ignorance is supposed to be OK.

Of the five or six things I now know for sure, one of them is that I struggled to find a way to successfully teach my students how to read, write, think, and speak from their own experience while respecting and affirming the same in their classmates. Recognition of this greatly informs the literature and other materials I include in my curricula.

I've also learned how to begin the school year by building a foundation that ensures we all understand that we are going to learn a lot more than English in my classroom. By establishing ground rules for community-centered classroom behavior, I've found ways to create a safe, trusting, non-judgmental classroom atmosphere so that they can really hear me and each other.

I have learned a lot more about the theory and application of racial identity development in white people because 97% of my students are white and 70% of those are male. Virtually none of them have ever had exposure to anyone remotely like me.

Most of them have been exposed to teaching about difference in ways that only establish "victim/victimizer," "us vs. them" scenarios. My students have never learned to see any of these issues as social constructions visited upon us from the time we are born, or as realities born of a legacy of shared history as Americans in the United States.

And I've learned how to pay closer attention to the ways in which the cultural differences between Minnesota and the East Coast challenged my own racial identity development process.

∾ ∾ ∾

Being a teacher in Minnesota has concretized for me exactly how much of who I am was shaped and informed by having grown up to become a multicultural educator in a part of the country so completely different from where I happen to be now. Being able to name what I now know comes out of my struggle with being so completely unprepared for how the regional/cultural differences made me feel about everything I always "knew."

In an inexplicable sort of way, I still feel like a novice in the classroom. But I cannot deny or dismiss the fact that this journey has been worth most of the changes in my personal and professional life. And the truth is that my Minnesota students have taught me a lot about teaching and learning.

Of the five or six things I now know for sure, one of them is that my appreciation of the ways in which multicultural education can and does serve the academic needs and interests of *all* students has expanded exponentially.

ABOUT THE AUTHOR

I wrote this article because Cathy Nelson said, "Tell us what you do in your classroom that makes English work for your students." Through the process of writing this, I came to understand myself better as a teacher and a learner. I had the opportunity to pay homage to my students. My hope is that the reader will similarly identify what they do in their classroom that works with students. I currently teach in a St. Paul, Minnesota, parochial high school. I have lived in Minnesota for three years.

On the Road to Cultural Bias: A Critique of The Oregon Trail CD-ROM

Bill Bigelow

THE CRITICS ALL AGREE: *THE OREGON TRAIL* (1993) IS ONE OF the greatest educational computer games ever produced. *Prides' Guide to Educational Software* awarded it five stars for being "a wholesome, absorbing historical simulation," and "multi-ethnic," to boot (Pride & Pride, 1992, p. 419). The new version, *The Oregon Trail II* (1994), is the "best history simulation we've seen to date," according to Warren Buckleitner, editor of *Children's Software Review Newsletter* (The Oregon Trail II, 1994). Susan Schilling, a key developer of *The Oregon Trail II* and recently hired by *Star Wars* film maker George Lucas to head Lucas Learning Ltd., promises new interactive CD-ROMs targeted at children 6 to 15 years old and concentrated in math and language arts (Armstrong, 1996).

Because interactive CD-ROMs like *The Oregon Trail* are encyclopedic in the amount of information they offer, and because they allow students a seemingly endless number of choices, the new software may appear educationally progressive. CD-ROMs seem tailor-made for the

A version of this article first appeared in *Rethinking Schools* (Fall 1995, Vol. 10, No. 1).

classrooms of tomorrow. They are hands-on and "student-centered." They are generally interdisciplinary—for example, *The Oregon Trail II* blends reading, writing, history, geography, math, science, and health. And they are useful in multi-age classrooms because they allow students of various knowledge levels to "play" and learn. But like the walls of a maze, the choices built into interactive CD-ROMs also channel participants in very definite directions. The CD-ROMs are programmed by people—people with particular cultural biases—and children who play the new computer games encounter the biases of the programmers (Bowers, 1988). Just as we would not invite a stranger into our classrooms and then leave the room, we as teachers need to become aware of the political perspectives of CD-ROMs and to equip our students to "read" them critically.

At one level, this article is a critical review of *The Oregon Trail* CD-ROMs. I ask what knowledge is highlighted, what is hidden, and what values are imparted as students play the games. But I also reflect on the nature of the new electronic curricula, and suggest some questions teachers can ask before choosing to use these materials with their students. Finally, I offer some classroom activities that might begin to develop students' critical computer literacy.

∾ Playing the Game ∾

In both *The Oregon Trail* and *The Oregon Trail II*, students become members of families and wagon trains crossing the Plains in the 1840s or 1850s on the way to the Oregon Territory. A player's objective, according to the game guidebook, is to safely reach the Oregon Territory with one's family, thereby "increasing one's options for economic success" (The Oregon Trail II, 1994).

The enormous number of choices offered in any one session— what to buy for the journey; the kind of wagon to take; whether to use horses, oxen, or mules; the size of the wagon train with which to travel; whom to "talk" to along the way; when and where to hunt; when to rest; and how fast to travel—is a kind of gentle seduction to students. It invites them to "try on this world view and see how it fits." In an interactive CD-ROM, students don't merely identify with a particular character, they actually adopt his or her frame of reference and act as if they were that character (Provenzo, 1991). In *The Oregon Trail*, a player quickly bonds with the "pioneer" maneuvering through the "wilderness."

In preparation for this article, I played *The Oregon Trail II* until my eyes became blurry. I can see its attraction to teachers. One can't play the game without learning a lot about the geography between Missouri and Oregon. (However, I hope I never have to ford another virtual river again.) Reading the trail guide as one plays teaches much about the ailments confronted on the Oregon Trail and some of the treatments. Students can learn a tremendous amount about the details of life for the trekkers to Oregon, including the kinds of wagons required, the supplies needed, the vegetation encountered along the route, and so forth. And the game has a certain multicultural and gender-fair veneer that, however limited, contrasts favorably with the white male-dominated texts of yesteryear. But as much as the game teaches, it *mis*-teaches more. In fundamental respects, *The Oregon Trail* is sexist, racist, culturally insensitive, and contemptuous of the earth. It imparts bad values and wrong history.

∞ They Look Like Women, But . . . ∞

To its credit, *The Oregon Trail II* includes large numbers of women. Although I didn't count, women appear to make up roughly half the people students encounter as they play. But this surface equity is misleading. Women may be present, but gender is not acknowledged as an issue in *The Oregon Trail*. For example, in the opening sequences, the game requires students to select a profession, any special skills they will possess, the kind of wagon to take, and the city from which to depart. Class is recognized as an issue—bankers begin with more money than saddle makers, for example—but not gender or race. A player cannot choose to be a female or African American.

Without acknowledging it, *The Oregon Trail* maneuvers students into thinking and acting as if they were all males. The game highlights a male lifestyle and poses problems that historically fell within the male domain, such as whether and where to hunt, which route to take, whether and what to trade, and whether to caulk a wagon or ford a river. However, as I began to read feminist scholarship on the Oregon Trail (e.g., Faragher & Stansell, 1992; Kesselman, 1976; Schlissel, 1992), 1 realized that women and men experienced the Trail differently. It's clear from reading women's diaries of the period that women played little or no role in deciding whether to embark on the trip, where to camp, which routes to take, and the like. In real life, women's decisions revolved around how to maintain a semblance of community under great stress, how "to preserve the home in transit" (Faragher & Stansell, 1992, p. 190). Women decided where to look for firewood or buffalo chips, how and what to cook using hot rocks, how to care for the children, and how to resolve conflicts between travelers, especially between the men.

These were real-life decisions, but, with the exception of treating illness, they're missing from *The Oregon Trail*. Students are rarely required to think about the intricacies of preserving "the home in transit" for 2000 miles. An *Oregon Trail II* information box on the screen informs a player when "morale" is high or low, but other than making better male-oriented decisions, what's a player to do? *The Oregon Trail* offers no opportunities to encounter the choices of the Trail as women of the time would have encountered them and to make decisions that might enhance community and thus "morale." As Lillian Schlissel (1992) concludes in her study, *Women's Diaries of the Westward Journey*:

> If ever there was a time when men and women turned their psychic energies toward opposite visions, the overland journey was that time. Sitting side by side on a wagon seat, a man and a woman felt different needs as they stared at the endless road that led into the New Country. (p. 15)

Similarly, *The Oregon Trail* fails to represent the *texture* of community life on the Trail. Students confront a seemingly endless stream of problems posed by *The Oregon Trail* programmers, but rarely encounter the details of life, especially that of women's lives. By contrast, in an article in the book, *America's Working Women*, Amy Kesselman (1976) includes this passage from the diary of one female trekker, Catherine Haun, in 1849:

> We women folk visited from wagon to wagon or congenial friends spent an hour walking ever westward, and talking over our home life "back in the states" telling of the loved ones left behind; voicing our hopes for the future in the far west and even whispering, a little friendly gossip of pioneer life. High teas were not popular but tatting, knitting, crocheting, exchanging receipts for cooking beans or dried apples or swopping food for the sake of variety kept us in practice of feminine occupations and diversions. (p. 71)

The male orientation of *The Oregon Trail* is brought into sharp relief in the game's handling of Independence Day commemoration. Students-as-pioneers are asked if they wish to "Celebrate the Fourth!" If so, they click on this option and hear loud "Yahoos" and guns firing.

Compare this image to the communal preparations described in Enoch Conyers' 1852 diary:

> A little further on is a group of young ladies seated on the grass talking over the problem of manufacturing "Old Glory" to wave over our festivities. The question arose as to where we are to obtain the material for the flag. One lady brought forth a sheet. This gave the ladies an idea. Quick as thought another brought a skirt for the red stripes . . . . Another lady ran to her tent and brought forth a blue jacket, saying: "Here, take this; it will do for the field." Needles and thread were soon secured and the ladies went at their task with a will, one lady remarking that "Necessity is the mother of invention," and the answer came back, "Yes, and the ladies of our company are equal to the task." (Hill, 1989, p. 58)

The contrast of the "Yahoos" and gunfire of *The Oregon Trail* to the collective female exhilaration described in the diary excerpt is striking. This contrast alerted me to something so obvious that it took me a while to recognize. In *The Oregon Trail*, people don't talk to *each other*, they all talk to you, the player. Everyone in *The Oregon Trail*-constructed world directs her or his conversation to you, underscoring the simulation's individualistic ideology that all the world exists for *you*, the controller of the mouse. An *Oregon Trail* more alert to feminist insights and women's experiences would highlight relationships between people, would focus on how the experience affects our feelings for each other, and would feature how women worked with one another to create and maintain a community, as women's diary entries clearly reveal.

As I indicated, large numbers of women appear throughout *The Oregon Trail* simulation, and they often give good advice, perhaps better advice than the men we encounter. But *The Oregon Trail's* abundance of women, and its apparent effort to be gender-fair, masks an essential problem: The choice-structure of the simulation privileges men's experience and virtually erases women's experience.

⚭ African Americans as Tokens ⚭

From the game's beginning, when a player starts off in Independence or St. Joseph's, Missouri, African Americans dot *The Oregon Trail* landscape. By and large, however, they are no more than black-colored white people. Although Missouri was a slave state throughout the Oregon Trail period, I never encountered the term "slavery" while playing the game. I found race explicitly acknowledged in only one exchange, when I "talked" to an African American woman along the trail. She said: "I'm Isabella. I'm traveling with the Raleighs and their people. My job is to keep after the cows and watch the children. My husband Fred is the ox-driver—best there is." I wondered if they were free or enslaved, and if we are to assume the Raleighs are white. I asked to know more, and Isabella said: "I was born in Delaware. My father used to tell me stories of Africa and promised one day we'd find ourselves going home. But I don't know if I'm getting closer or farther away with all this walking." The end. Like Missouri, Delaware was a slave state in antebellum days, but this is not shared with students. Isabella offers provocative details, but they hide more than they reveal about her identity and culture.

The Oregon Trail 's treatment of African Americans reflects a superficial multiculturalism. Black people are present, but their lives aren't. Attending to matters of race requires more than including lots of black faces or having little girls "talk black": "I think it's time we be moving on now." (This little girl reappears from time to time to repeat these same words. A man who looks Mexican, likewise, shows up frequently to say, with a heavy accent: "Time is a-wasting. Let's head out!")

Although one's life prospects and world view in the 1840s and 1850s—as today—were dramatically shaped by one's race, this factor is invisible in *The Oregon Trail*. *The Oregon Trail* players know their occupations but not their racial identities, even though these identities were vital to the decisions the Oregon Trail travelers made before leaving on their journeys and along the way.

For example, many of the constitutions of societies that sponsored wagon trains specifically excluded blacks from making the trip west. Nonetheless, as Elizabeth McLagan (1980) points out in her history of blacks in Oregon, *A Peculiar Paradise*, blacks did travel the Oregon Trail, some as slaves, some as servants, and even some, like George Bush, as well-to-do pioneers. Race may not have seemed important to *The Oregon Trail* programmers but race mattered a great deal to Bush: Along the Trail, he confided to another emigrant that if he experienced too much prejudice in Oregon, he would travel south to California or New Mexico and seek the protection of the Mexican government (McLagan, 1980).

And Bush had reason to be apprehensive: African Americans arriving in Oregon Territory during the 1840s and 1850s were greeted by laws barring them from residency. Two black exclusion laws were passed in the Oregon Territory in the 1840s, and a clause in the Oregon state constitution barring black residency was ratified in 1857 by a margin of eight to one—a clause, incidentally, not repealed until 1926.

Upon completion of one of my simulated Oregon Trail journeys, I clicked to see how my life turned out: "In 1855, Bill built a home on 463 acres of land in the Rogue River Valley of Oregon," experienced only "moderate success" and later moved to Medford, "establishing a small business that proved more stable and satisfying." Although *The Oregon Trail* simulation never acknowledges it, "Bill" must have been white because in 1850 the U.S. Congress passed the Oregon Donation Land Act granting 640 acres to free white males and their wives. It is unlikely that a black man, and much less a black woman, would have been granted land in 1855 or have been allowed to start a business in Medford some years later.

Why were whites so insistent that blacks not live in Oregon? The preamble of one black exclusion bill explained that "situated as the people of Oregon are, in the midst of an Indian population, it would be highly dangerous to allow free negroes and mulattos to reside in the territory or to intermix with the Indians, instilling in their minds feelings of hostility against the white race . . ." (McLagan, 1980, p. 26). And Samuel Thurston, a delegate to Congress from the Oregon Territory, explained in 1850 why blacks should not be entitled to homestead in Oregon:

> The negroes associate with the Indians and intermarry, and, if their free ingress is encouraged or allowed, there would a relationship spring up between them and the different tribes, and a mixed race would ensue inimical to the whites; and the Indians being led on by the negro who is better acquainted with the customs, language, and manners of the whites, than the Indian, these savages would become much more formidable than they otherwise would, and long and bloody wars would be the fruits of the commingling of the races. It is the principle of self preservation that justifies the action of the Oregon legislature. (McLagan, 1980, pp. 30-31)

Thurston's argument carried the day. But *The Oregon Trail* programmers have framed the issues so that race seems irrelevant. Thus, once students-as-pioneers arrive in Oregon, most of them will live happily ever after—never considering the impact that race would have on living conditions.

∾ Just Passing Through? ∾

The Oregon Trail programmers are careful not to portray Indians as the "enemy" of westward trekkers. However, the simulation's superficial sympathy for Native groups masks a profound insensitivity to Indian cultures and to the earth that sustained these cultures. The simulation guidebook lists numerous Indian nations by name—and respectfully *calls* them "nations." *The Oregon Trail* guidebook explains that emigrants' fear of Indians is "greatly exaggerated."

> Some travelers have been known to cross the entire breadth of the continent from the Missouri River to the Sierra Nevadas without ever laying eye on an Indian, except perhaps for occasional brief sightings from a distance. This is all well and good, for it is probably best for all parties concerned for emigrants and Indians to avoid contact with each other. Such meetings are often the source of misunderstandings, sometimes with regrettable consequences.

Emigrants often spread disease, according to the guidebook, which made the Indians "distrust and dislike" them. The guidebook further warns *The Oregon Trail* players not to over-hunt game in any one place as "few things will incur the wrath of the Indian peoples more than an overstayed welcome accompanied by the egregious waste of the natural resources upon which they depend."

The ideology embedded in *The Oregon Trail* and *The Oregon Trail II* is selfish and goal-driven: Emigrants should care about indigenous people only insofar as they need to avoid "misunderstanding" and incurring the wrath of potentially hostile natives. *The Oregon Trail* promotes an anthropocentric earth-as-natural resource outlook. Nature is a *thing* to be consumed or overcome as people traverse the country in search for success in a faraway land. The simulation's structure coerces children into identifying with white settlers and dismissing non-white others. It also contributes to the broader curricular racialization of identity that students absorb—learning who constitutes the normalized "we" and who is excluded.

The Oregon Trail players need not take into account the lives of others unless it's necessary to do so in order to accomplish their personal objectives. Thus, the cultures of Plains Indians are backgrounded. The game marginalizes their view of the earth. Contrast, for example, the Indians' term "mother earth" with *The Oregon Trail* term "natural resource." The metaphor of earth as mother suggests humans in a reciprocal relationship with a natural world that is alive, that nourishes us, and that sustains us. On the other hand, a resource is a thing to be used. It exists *for* us, outside of us, and we have no obligations in return.

The consequences of the Oregon Trail for the Plains Indians, the Indians of the Northwest, and for the earth were devastating. In fairness to *The Oregon Trail*, students may hear some of the details of this upheaval as they play. For example, on one trip I encountered a "Pawnee Village." Had I paid attention to the warning in the guidebook to "avoid contact" I would have ignored it and continued on my trip. But I entered and "talked" to the people I encountered there. A Pawnee woman said: "Why do you bother me? I don't want to trade. The things that we get from the white travelers don't make up for all that we lose." I clicked to hear more. "We didn't know the whooping cough, measles, or the smallpox until your people brought them to us. Our medicine cannot cure these strange diseases, and our children are dying." I clicked on "Do you have any advice?" Angrily, she said, "No. I just want you to leave us alone." The implication is that if I just "leave [them] alone" and continue on the trail I can pursue my dream without hurting the Indians.

However, this interpretation hides the fact that the Oregon Trail itself, not just contact with the so-called pioneers, devastated Indian cultures and the ecology of which those cultures were an integral part. Johansen and Maestas' (1979) description of the Lakota language for talking about these pioneers helps us see how they were regarded by the Indians:

> (The Lakota) used a metaphor to describe the newcomers. It was *Wasi'chu*, which means "takes the fat," or "greedy person." Within the modern Indian movement, *Wasi'chu* has come to mean those corporations and individuals, with their governmental accomplices, which continue to covet Indian lives, land, and resources for private profit. *Wasi'chu* does not describe a race; it describes a state of mind. (p. 6)

The *Wasi'chu* cut down all the cottonwood trees found along the rich bottom lands of plains rivers—trees which "offered crucial protection during winter blizzards as well as concealing a village's smoke from its enemies. In lean seasons, horses fed on its bark, which was surprisingly nourishing" (Davidson & Lytle, 1992, p. 114).

The Oregon Trail created serious wood shortages, which even the *Wasi'chu* acknowledged. "By the Mormon guide we here expected to find the last timber," wrote overlander A. W. Harlan in describing the Platte River, "but all had been used up by others ahead of us so we must go about 200 miles without any provisions cooked up." A few weeks later, in sight of the Black Hills, Harlan wrote: "[W]e have passed many cottonwood stumps but no timber . . ." (Davidson & Lytle, 1992, p. 115).

Wasi'chu rifles also killed tremendous numbers of buffalo that Plains Indians depended upon for survival. One traveler in the 1850s wrote that, "The valley of the Platte for 200 miles presents the aspect of the vicinity of a slaughter yard, dotted all over with skeletons of buffaloes" (Davidson & Lytle, 1992, p. 117). Very soon after the beginning of the Oregon Trail the buffalo learned to avoid the Trail, their herds migrating both south and north. Edward Lazarus (1991) points out in *Black Hills/White Justice: The Sioux Nation Versus the United States— 1775 to the Present* that "the Oregon Trail did more than move the buffalo; it destroyed the hunting pattern of the Sioux, forcing them to follow the herds to the fringes of their domain and to expose themselves to the raids of their enemies" (p. 14).

However, wrapped in their cocoons of self-interest, *The Oregon Trail* players push on, oblivious to the mayhem and misery they cause in their westward drive. This is surely an unintended, and yet intrinsic, part of the game's message: Pursue your goal as an autonomous individual, ignore the social and ecological consequences: "look out for number one."

❧ No Violence Here ❧

The Oregon Trail never suggests to its simulated pioneers that they should seek permission of Indian nations to travel through their territory. And from this key omission flow other omissions. The simulation doesn't inform players that, because of the disruptions wrought by the daily intrusions of the westward migration, Plains Indians regularly demanded tribute from the trekkers. As John Unruh, Jr. (1993), writes in *The Plains Across*:

> The natives explicitly emphasized that the throngs of overlanders were killing and scaring away buffalo and other wild game, overgrazing prairie grasses, exhausting the small quantity of available timber, and depleting

water resources. The tribute payments . . . were demanded mainly by the Sac and Fox, Kickapoo, Pawnee, and Sioux Indians—the tribes closest to the Missouri River frontier and therefore those feeling most keenly the pressures of white men increasingly impinging upon their domains. (p. 169)

Wasi'chu travelers resented this Indian-imposed taxation and their resentment frequently turned to hostility and violence, especially in the later years of the Trail. The Pawnee were "hateful wretches," wrote Dr. Thomas Wolfe in 1852, for demanding a 25 cent toll at a bridge across Shell Creek near the North Platte River (Unruh, 1993, p. 171). Shell Creek and other crossings became flashpoints that escalated into violent skirmishes resulting in the deaths of settlers and Indians.

Despite the increasing violence along the Oregon Trail, one choice *The Oregon Trail* programmers don't offer students-as-trekkers is the choice to harm Indians. Doubtlessly MECC, the publisher of *The Oregon Trail*, is not anxious to promote racism toward Native peoples. However, because simulation players can't hurt or even speak ill of Indians, the game fails to alert students that white hostility was one feature of the westward migration. The omission is significant because the sanitized non-violent *The Oregon Trail* fails to equip students to reflect on the origins of conflicts between whites and Indians. Nor does it offer students any insights into the racial antagonism that fueled this violence. In all my play of *The Oregon Trail*, I can't recall any blatant racism directed at Indians. But as Unruh (1993) points out, "The callous attitude of cultural and racial superiority so many overlanders exemplified was of considerable significance in producing the volatile milieu in which more and more tragedies occurred" (p. 186).

～ The End of the Trail ～

Soon there will come from the rising sun a different kind of man from any you have yet seen, who will bring with them a book and will teach you everything, after that the world will fall to pieces.

—*Spokan Prophet, 1790 (Limerick, 1987, p. 39)*

A person can spend two or three hours—or more—playing one game of *The Oregon Trail* before finally reaching Oregon Territory. Upon arrival, a player is awarded points and told how his or her life in Oregon turned out. Yet the game fails to raise vital questions about one's right to be there in the first place and what happened to the people who were there first.

In its section on the "Destination," the guidebook offers students its wisdom on how they should view life in a new land. It's a passage that underscores the messages students absorb while engaged in the simulation. These comforting words of advice and social vision are worth quoting at length:

> Once you reach the end of your journey, you should go to the nearest large town to establish your land claim. If there are no large towns in the area, simply find an unclaimed tract of land and settle down . . . . As they say, possession is nine-tenths of the law, and if you have settled and worked land that hasn't yet been claimed by anyone else, you should have little or no trouble legally establishing your claim at a later time. As more and more Americans move into the region, more cities and towns will spring up, further increasing one's options for economic success. Rest assured in the facts that men and women who are willing to work hard will find their labors richly rewarded, and that you, by going west, are helping to spread American civilization from ocean to ocean across this great continent, building a glorious future for generations to come! (The Oregon Trail II, 1994)

The Lakota scholar and activist Vine Deloria, Jr. (1977), in his book, *Indians of The Pacific Northwest,* offers a less sanguine perspective than that included in the CD-ROM guidebook. People coming in on the Oregon Trail "simply arrived on the scene and started building. If there were Indians or previous settlers on the spot they were promptly run off under one pretext or another. Lawlessness and thievery dominated the area" (p. 53). From 1850 on, using provisions of the Oregon Donation Act, thousands of "settlers" invaded "with impunity."

As Deloria points out, there were some in Congress who were aware that they were encouraging settlers to steal Indian land, and so Congress passed the Indian Treaty Act requiring the United States to get formal agreements from Indian tribes. Anson Dart, appointed to secure land concessions, pursued this objective in a despicable fashion. For example, he refused to have the treaties translated into the Indians' languages, instead favoring "Chinook jargon," a non-language of fewer than 300 words good for trading, giving orders, and little else. Dart's mandate was to move all the Indians east of the Cascades, but he decided some tribes, like the Tillamooks and Chinooks, should keep small amounts of land as cheap labor reserves:

> Almost without exception, I have found [the Indians] anxious to work at employment at common labor and willing too, to work at prices much below that demanded by the whites. The Indians make all the rails used in fencing, and at this time do the boating upon the rivers: In consideration, therefore, of the usefulness as labourers in the settlements, it was believed to be far better for the Country that they should not be removed from the settled portion [sic] of Oregon if it were possible to do so. (Deloria, 1977, p. 51)

Meanwhile, in southwestern Oregon white vigilantes didn't wait for treaty niceties to be consummated. Between 1852 and 1856 self-proclaimed Volunteers attacked Indians for alleged misdeeds or simply because they were Indians. In August of 1853, one Martin Angel rode into the Rogue River Valley gold mining town of Jacksonville shouting, "Nits breed lice. We have been killing Indians in the valley all day," and "Exterminate the whole race" (Beckham, 1991, p. 103). Minutes later a mob of about 800 white men hanged a 7-year-old Indian boy. In October 1855, a group of whites massacred 23 Indian men, women, and children. This incident began the Rogue Indian war, which lasted until June 1856 (Beckham, 1991). Recall that this is the same region and the same year in one *Oregon Trail* session where "Bill" built a home and experienced "moderate success," but, thanks to *The Oregon Trail* programmers, he learned nothing of the social conflicts swirling around him.

Nor did Bill learn that, even as a white person, he could protest the outrages committed against the Rogue River Valley Indians, as did one anonymous "Volunteer" in a passionate 1853 letter to the *Oregon Statesman* newspaper:

> A few years since the whole valley was theirs [the Indians'] alone. No white man's foot had ever trod it. They believed it theirs forever. But the gold digger come, with his pan and his pick and shovel, and hundreds followed. And they saw in astonishment their streams muddied, towns built, their valley fenced and taken. And where their squaws dug camus, their winter food, and their children were wont to gambol, they saw dug and plowed, and their own food sown by the hand of nature, rooted out forever, and the ground it occupied appropriated to the rearing of vegetables for the white man. Perhaps no malice yet entered the Indian breast. But

when he was weary of hunting in the mountains without success, and was hungry, and approached the white man's tent for bread; where instead of bread he received curses and kicks, ye treaty kicking men—ye Indian exterminators think of these things.

—*A Soldier* (Applegate & O'Donnell, 1994, p. 34)

The Oregon Trail hides the nature of the Euro-American invasion in at least two ways. In the first place, it simply fails to inform simulation participants what happened between settlers and Indians. To *The Oregon Trail* player, it doesn't feel like an invasion; it doesn't feel wrong. After one of my arrivals, in 1848, "Life in the new land turned out to be happy and successful for Bill, who always cherished bittersweet but proud memories of the months spent on the Oregon Trail." (This struck me as a rather odd account given that I had lost all 3 of my children on the trip.) The only person that matters is the simulation player. I was never told whether life turned out equally "happy and successful" for the Klamaths, Yakimas, Cayuses, Nez Percés, Wallawallas, and all the others who occupied this land generations before the *Wasi'chu* arrived. The second way the nature of the white invasion is hidden has to do with the structure of the simulation. For a couple hours or more the player endures substantial doses of frustration, tedium, and difficulty. By the time the Willamette or Rogue River Valleys come up on the screen we, the simulated trekkers, feel we *deserve* the land, that our labors in transit should be "richly rewarded" with the best land we can find.

Data Deception and ∾ Thoughts on What to Do About It ∾

In the Beatles' song, all you need is love: in *The Oregon Trail*, all you need are data. *The Oregon Trail* offers students gobs of information: snake bite remedies, river locations and depths, wagon specifications, ferry costs, and daily climate reports. Loaded with facts, it feels comprehensive. Loaded with people voicing contrasting opinions, it feels balanced. Loaded with choices, it feels democratic. But the simulation begins from no moral or ethical standpoint beyond individual material success; it contains no vision of social or ecological justice, and, hence, promotes a full litany of sexist, racist, and imperialist perspectives, as well as exploitive perspectives of the earth. And simultaneously, it hides these biases. The combination is insidious, and makes interactive CD-ROMs like this one more difficult to critique than traditional textbooks or films. The forced identification of player with simulation protagonist leaves the student no option but to follow the ideological map laid out by the programmers.

Nonetheless, my critique is not a call to boycott the new "edutainment" resources. But we need to remember that these CD-ROMs are not teacher substitutes. The teacher's role in analyzing and presenting these devices in a broader ethical context is absolutely vital. Thus, teachers across the country must begin a dialogue toward developing a critical computer literacy. We need to figure out ways to equip students with the ability to recognize and evaluate the deep moral and political messages imparted by these CD-ROMs as they maneuver among the various computer software programs.

Before choosing to use CD-ROMs that involve people and places, like *The Oregon Trail* —or, for example, its newer siblings *The Yukon Trail*, *The Amazon Trail*, and *Africa Trail* —teachers should consider the following questions.

- *Which social groups are students* not *invited to identify with in the simulation?* For example, Native Americans, African Americans, women, and Latinos are superficially represented in *The Oregon Trail*, but the "stuff" of their lives is missing.

- *How might these social groups frame problems differently than the simulation?* As we saw in the foregoing critique of *The Oregon Trail*, women tended to focus more on maintaining community than on hunting. Native Americans had a profoundly different relationship to the earth than did the Euro-American "tamers of the wilderness."

- *What decisions do simulation participants make that may have consequences for social groups not highlighted in the simulation? And what are these consequences?* Although the very existence of the Oregon Trail contributed to the decimation of Plains and Northwest Indians, simulation participants are never asked to consider the broader effects of their decision-making. What may be an ethical individual choice may be unethical when multiplied several hundred thousand times. In this respect, CD-ROM choice-making both reflects and reinforces conventional notions of freedom that justify disastrous social and ecological practices.

- *What decisions do simulation participants make that may have consequences for the earth and non-human life?* Similarly, a simulation participant's choice to cut down trees for firewood may be rational for that individual, but may also have deleterious effects on the ecological balance of a particular bio-region.

- *If the simulation is time-specific, as in the case of* The Oregon Trail, *what were the social and environmental consequences for the time period following the time represented in the simulation?* The wars between Indians and the U.S. Cavalry in the latter decades of the nineteenth century are inexplicable without the Oregon Trail as prologue.

- *Can we name the ideological orientation of a particular CD-ROM?* The question is included here simply to remind us that all computer materials—indeed, all curricula—*have* an ideology. Our first step is to become aware of that ideology.

These questions are hardly exhaustive, but may suggest a useful direction to begin thinking about CD-ROMs as they become increasingly available and begin to cover more and more subjects.

Finally, let me use the example of *The Oregon Trail* to introduce some ways teachers can begin to foster a critical computer literacy. Once we have identified some of the social groups that are substantially missing in a CD-ROM activity like *The Oregon Trail*, we can try to locate excerpts from diaries, speeches, or other communications of members of these groups. We can then engage students in role play where, as a class, students face a number of Oregon Trail problems. For example, class members could portray women on the Oregon Trail and decide how they would attempt to maintain a community in transit. Or they might role play a possible discussion of Oglala people as they confront the increasingly disruptive presence of *Wasi'chu* crossing their lands. Students might be asked to list all the ways African Americans would experience the Oregon Trail differently than Euro-Americans—from the planning of the trip to the trip itself. (It's unlikely, for example, that every white person on the streets of Independence, Missouri, said a friendly "Howdy," to the blacks he encountered, as each of them does to the implied but unacknowledged white male *Oregon Trail* simulation player.) Students also could assume a particular racial, cultural, or gender identity, and note whether the choices or experiences described in the simulation make sense from the standpoint of a member of their group. For example, would a typical African American in Missouri in 1850 be allowed to choose from which city to begin the trek west?

As we share with students the social and ecological costs of the Oregon Trail, we could ask them to write critical letters to each of the "pioneers" they portrayed in the simulation. Some could represent Rogue River Valley Indians, Shoshoni people, or even Mother Earth. For instance, how does Mother Earth respond to the casual felling of every Cottonwood tree along the Platte River? A Native American elder or activist could be invited into the classroom to speak about the concerns important to his or her people and about the history of white-Indian relations.

We could encourage students to think about the politics of naming in the simulation. They could suggest alternative names for the Oregon Trail itself. For example, the historian of the American West, Frederick Merk (1978), aptly calls the Oregon Trail a "path of empire." Writer Dan Georgakas (1973) names it a "march of death." Other names might be "invasion of the West," or "The 20-year trespass." Just as with Columbus's "discovery" of America, naming shapes understanding, and we need classroom activities to uncover this process.

Students could write and illustrate children's books describing the Oregon Trail from the standpoint of women, African Americans, Native Americans, or the earth.

After doing activities like these, students could "play" *The Oregon Trail* again. What do they see this time that they didn't see before? Whose world view is highlighted and whose is hidden? If they choose, they might present their findings to other classes or to teachers who may be considering the use of CD-ROMs.

The Oregon Trail is no more morally obnoxious than other CD-ROMs or curricular materials with similar ideological biases. My aim here is broader than merely shaking a scolding finger at MECC, publisher of *The Oregon Trail* series. I've tried to demonstrate why teachers and students must develop a critical computer literacy. Some of the new CD-ROMs seem more socially aware than the blatantly culturally insensitive materials that still fill school libraries and book rooms. And the flashy new computer packages also invoke terms long sacred to educators: student empowerment, individual choice, creativity, and high interest. It's vital that we remember that coincident with the arrival of these new educational toys is a deepening social and ecological crisis. Global and national inequality between haves and have-nots is increasing. Violence of all kinds is endemic. And the earth is being consumed at a ferocious pace. Computer programs are not politically neutral in the big moral contests of our time. Inevitably, they take sides. Thus, a critical computer literacy, one with a social and ecological conscience, is more than just a good idea—it's a basic skill.

REFERENCES

Applegate, S., & O'Donnell, T. (1994). *Talking on paper: An anthology of Oregon letters and diaries.* Corvallis, OR: Oregon State University Press.

Armstrong, D. (1996, February 23). Lucas getting into education via CD-ROM. *The San Francisco Examiner,* pp. E-1-E-2.

Beckham, S. D. (1991). Federal-Indian relations. *The First Oregonians.* Portland, OR: Oregon Council for the Humanities.

Bowers, C. A. (1988). *The cultural dimensions of educational computing: Understanding the non-neutrality of technology.* New York: Teachers College Press.

Davidson, J. W., & Lytle, M. H. (1992). *After the fact: The art of historical detection.* New York: McGraw-Hill.

Deloria, Jr., V. (1977). *Indians of the Pacific Northwest.* Garden City, NY: Doubleday.

Faragher, J., & Stansell, C. (1992). Women and their families on the overland trail to California and Oregon, 1842-1867. In F. Binder & D. Reimer (Eds.), *The way we lived: Essays and documents in American social history, Vol. 1.* pp. 188-195. Lexington, MA: Heath.

Georgakas, D. (1973). *Red shadows: The history of Native Americans from 1600 to 1900, from the desert to the Pacific Coast.* Garden City, NY: Zenith.

Hill, W. E. (1989). *The Oregon Trail: Yesterday and today.* Caldwell, ID: Caxton Printers.

Johansen, B., & Maestas, R. (1979). *Wasi'chu: The continuing Indian wars.* New York: Monthly Review.

Kesselman, A. (1976). Diaries and reminiscences of women on the Oregon Trail: A study in consciousness. In R. Baxandall, L. Gordon, & S. Reverby (Eds.), *America's working women: A documentary history—1600 to the present.* pp. 69-72. New York: Vintage.

Lazarus, E. (1991). *Black Hills/White justice: The Sioux Nation versus the United States—1775 to the present.* New York: HarperCollins.

Limerick, P. N. (1987). *The legacy of conquest: The unbroken past of the American west.* New York: W. W. Norton.

McLagan, E. (1980). *A peculiar paradise: A history of Blacks in Oregon, 1788-1940.* Portland, OR: The Georgian Press.

Merk, F. (1978). *History of the westward movement.* New York: Knopf.

The Oregon Trail [Computer software]. (1993). Minneapolis, MN: Minnesota Educational Computer Company.

The Oregon Trail II [Computer software]. (1994). Minneapolis, MN: Minnesota Educational Computer Company.

Pride, B., & Pride, M. (1992). *Prides' guide to educational software.* Wheaton, IL: Crossway Books.

Provenzo, Jr., E. F. (1991). *Video kids: Making sense of Nintendo.* Cambridge, MA: Harvard University Press.

Schlissel, L. (1992). *Women's diaries of the westward journey.* New York: Schocken.

Unruh, Jr., J. D. (1993). *The plains across: The overland emigrants and the trans-Mississippi west, 1840-1860.* Urbana. IL: University of Illinois Press.

ABOUT THE AUTHOR

I wrote this article because I worry about educator's romance with technology, including fancy computers, the internet and CD-ROMs. I'm not anti-computer, but it seemed to me that administrators and some teachers have regarded the new technological goodies as progressive and purely benign, even as the magic ingredient in the schools of tomorrow. I wanted to add my voice to those who are urging, "Not so fast." I've taught high school social studies for twenty years in Portland, Oregon—currently at Franklin High School—and co-edit the journal, *Rethinking Schools,* where a version of this article first appeared.

What Color Would That Be, Shirlee?

Perry Andrews

SHIRLEE ENTERS THE ROOM AND MAKES A BEELINE FOR where I'm at. She's got a question for me, same one she asks most days. It's a sure sign that something must be of great importance in the life of a four-year-old when a question can't wait first thing in the morning and comes on a regular basis. Shirlee's question is one I understand differently today. It comes with an awareness of what cultural difference can mean that has begun blowing into my life as a teacher and a member of the monthly diversity seminars in our school, on a strong wind of new filters. Later in my life as a teacher than I would like to believe possible, for what that says.

She comes up with a hug, early morning eyes bright, and asks, "How do you like my hair, Mr. Andrews?"

From readings and conversations, I have learned that in African American culture the names given to hair—straight, wavy, curly, heavy, coarse, soft, nappy, kinky—hold meanings, histories different from my own. I can only imagine the ritual of patience that Shirlee, her mother, and older sisters go through most mornings to brush and braid her hair. It is a morning ritual that costs more of them, and I know there are others that our parents of color go through in preparing their children for the days they spend in a predominantly white school.

"It looks beautiful, Shirlee. I love your braids."

Today there is special meaning in having her hair look good. It's picture day, and in a little while we'll be going upstairs to have that one quick chance at smiling and holding our head in the right spot at just the right moment. Some kids come in dressed for the event while others look pretty much the same as always. Some parents trust us to straighten out the hair of their children closer to the time of the actual event, something that I realize would be almost impossible for Shirlee's parents to trust us to do.

Later we're waiting outside the picture-taking room, and one of the kindergarten girls, another child of color, is trying to do what many of the other kids are easily able to do: use the new red plastic combs that the photographer has passed out to all the kids. Every year the same plastic combs. But this year, as Tiffany sits with tears in her eyes, having given up trying to use the comb that was not designed for hair like hers, but simply to free the hurtful thing from the tangle it's made of her hair, I see another aspect of cultural difference I hadn't given thought to before. I can help Tiffany get the comb out of her hair. And next year I can be sure there are picks available for the children whose hair requires them.

On another morning the dialogue on difference begins and opens between the children and me. We're in a circle, where we start and end our morning together here in pre-K, a time when as the year and the children develop, we begin to feel like a community. It is a time for conversations about many things, these young hearts, these minds working to make sense of their world. To describe with words the questions we grown-ups can't always find the words to ask, or the answers. As a teacher it is one of the most precious times of the day, as these four and five-year-olds try to put into words what they feel, how they think, what they wonder about.

To teach the best I can, I know that I must listen *Now* and be present with them in their questioning. The complexity of these young thoughts can surprise even the most seasoned teacher, no matter how long one has engaged in these conversations. And though the day's routine sometimes threatens to intrude on this time, and though the energy of all the children isn't always directed towards these inquiries, I know we must stay with them, listen, hear these voices and the questions they ask.

Jessie may be fidgeting, Nick playing with Ben's belt, Carey snuggling deeper into my lap with eyes heavy from watching movies late with grandma, but Jonathan has a question that must be heard. His face shows he's working hard to ask it. We are what we teach. We talk about what we value. The kids know this. So I listen. Jonathan has a question.

"My nose is different than Shirlee's. Why is hers fatter and flat?" he asks.

"All of us have differences, Jonathan. There are lots of different kinds of noses here today," I answer, knowing somehow this isn't enough. My own nose, though I am a white man, is wide and flat also, resulting from a couple of breaks as a child. Do I start there, with myself? How do I help us get to what may really be behind the question?

"What else do you see that's different about us?" I ask the group.

There are comments from all around the circle. Comments about hair. Lisa's hair is longer and curlier than mine. Comments about eyes. Dina's eyes have green in them. Comments about size. Jeff's taller than any of us. But Jonathan frowns with concentration and wants more than this.

"Shirlee's skin is black. Is it black underneath, too?"

Shirlee answers this one herself, perhaps having been asked this question before. She's ready to find and offer answers.

"No, it's the same under, all veins and blood and bones. And I'm brown, not black."

We know that for children of color, racial identity begins to matter far earlier than it does for white children. Even as adults, some of us from the majority culture have never had to identify ourselves that way. But for Shirlee, the answer to Jonathan's question is clear. How many of these children in circle this morning have wondered about this? Most of us are white, and though it is still early in the fall, I've wondered how to open this door. But now that the question has been asked, we can begin a dialogue that will be re-visited often throughout the year together.

A few feet from where we sit is our shelf of colored papers. Though I haven't planned for it this morning, it's one of those perfect teaching moments when in seconds I can lay my hands on a pretty full spectrum of the colors that correspond to those of our class community. There is white, cream, sienna, dark tan, red brown, chocolate brown, dark umber, and black.

I pull them from the shelf quickly and come back to circle and lay them out in a sort of value scale from light to dark. The children have been comparing the colors of their skin while I've been getting the paper. Arms held side by side, there is a note of wonder in their voices as they do this, and even before I speak they have the idea and begin to find the color that best matches their skin. Hands placed on paper, arms reaching over arms, crisscrossing over the papers on the floor, laughter, excitement. There is only one child whose hand actually matches the white piece: Josh's hand, white on white, with delicate blue veins beneath the surface. And no one's hand matches the black piece at the other end.

Most of us are finding colors somewhere in between and there are "ohs" and "ahs" in the childrens' voices and wonder again at the spectrum of our colors. And I think, "This is how we begin to talk about these things with children." For right now these four- and five-year-olds are open to the diversity within our class. There is a sense of joy as the children find the paper their hand best matches. A love almost, yes, a love of one another as they compare: your tan to my cream, my red brown to your chocolate. How can we keep and foster this acceptance, this love? How can we make this openness and wonder the values these children always hold toward the differences among us?

Later we've regrouped. Back on our bottoms, as we say in pre-K. The kids are ready to make their work choices around the room. I'm excited to see how this energy will continue through the morning, what the conversations will be around the room as we work and play together. Shirlee's hand has gone up quickly and I call on her, but she's not ready with a work choice. Instead she has a comment. It begins with a drawn out "I" and a big, breathy sigh. She hesitates to go on. "What, Shirlee? What would you like to say?"

Again she begins with a big exhalation of breath, as if its a doozy she's about to give us. Sigh, smile, hand on her head as she shakes it slowly back and forth, she begins again.

"I wish we could all be the same color," she breathes out.

I know what my question is, what it has to be, and yet for one brief moment I think, "Please let us have done this well." Thoughts flash through my head of the stories of African American children identifying with white dolls, somehow at so young an age having realized that they are not of the valued culture and color.

"What color would that be, Shirlee?" I ask, hoping she knows that I value all colors.

"Brown like me."

"It's a beautiful color, Shirlee. I love them all."

She smiles wide. All around smiles as the hands go up again. We call on children to make choices. They move off into the many places of our room. And I am glad Shirlee is who she is and strong. But I know that there can be a price to pay for that strength in a school where white is still the predominate color of the children and teachers. I want all of the teachers Shirlee will have along the way to support her voice, to recognize it, value her. I will work for that. The diversity work we do in our school has given many of us a place to start the work here, a format, a series of filters. We try, many of us. I try, sometimes tripping and stumbling along the way, but open to the talking, risking. I'll keep on taking those risks. Keep on talking. And listening.

ABOUT THE AUTHOR

As teachers we carry the stories of hundreds of children. I am filled with these stories each year as I teach pre-K children at an independent school in Minneapolis. They live in my memory with the clarity of a cold Minnesota winter day, sky bright blue with sunlight. They are cutouts in time. Moments of pure life, of joy and pain, laughter and tears, scraped knees and injured feelings, and epiphanies of discovery in the life story of being human. As a teacher, I have always been a storyteller. Carrying tales learned from other teachers and cultures form a wealth of memory and literature. I have only just begun to find voice for these stories of my life in teaching, to give voice to those whose stories have become part of my voice, my story.

Science Education: An Invitation

Janice Koch

A S TEACHERS BEGIN TO SEE SCIENCE IN MULTIPLE WAYS, students can come to see themselves as "scientific." I used to think it was sufficient to consider other ways of "seeing" science by referring to scientists who were women and/or people of color. I now believe that while these images support a more inclusive vision for scientific work, we need to begin our conversation with our own stories—stories about who we are and how our own racial background, class, gender and culture influence our relationship to science.

∾ The Scientist Within ∾

Where I grew up, in an inner-city neighborhood of New York, summertime recreation was usually afforded by the local park. In addition to playgrounds and sprinklers, there were grassy fields and trees. I often occupied myself by lying in the grass and watching the insects on their journey through the grass and clover. Sometimes an ant would crawl up onto my hand and explore my fingers, my wrist, and my palm.

Adapted from a chapter in *Science Stories: Teachers and Children As Science Learners*. Boston, MA: Houghton Mifflin Co. (1999).

In amazement I would watch this ant as it worked feverishly to find familiar ground, knowing it was not on grassy turf.

The park held many other fascinations for me. In the early fall, I collected acorns from the huge oak trees as well as "polly noses," the winged seeds from northeastern Norway maple trees. Often I would lie on a blanket, look up in the sky, and make up stories about the clouds. Their formations became animals or dragons, depending on the day.

On occasions when my family and I visited a restaurant, I would always mix the salt, pepper, sugar, and ketchup into the glass of water on the table. "Ugh," my father would exclaim, "she's making such a mess." "Don't be silly, dear," remarked my mother. "She is exploring. Maybe she will grow up to be a scientist."

As you can see from this story, my mother, although not herself a scientist, had a feeling about what scientists do, and she "coded" my early explorations as "scientific" (Koch, 1999). We need to consider what it means to "code" everyday behavior as scientific. Making deliberate observations and inferences, designing experiments and testing them out, and revising investigations are all characteristic of scientific processes. Messing about with materials can be a way of exploring them, and so my mother rose to my defense by naming my "messy play" scientific. Whether or not we think about specific behaviors as being scientific is often a product of our perceptions of science and scientists.

◦⌣◦ Who Does Science? ◦⌣◦

Not long ago, two third-grade teachers in a local elementary school were interested in exploring their students' beliefs about scientists. Distributing crayons and drawing paper, they asked each student to draw a picture of a scientist and describe what the scientist was doing. The thirty-nine students' drawings contained thirty-one men and eight women. Further, of the thirty-one male scientists, twenty-five had beards and messy hairstyles. All of the scientists were white.

One boy added a bubble quote for his scientist that said, "I'm crazy." Another third- grade boy described his scientist as follows: "He is inventing a monster. He painted his face green." Still another boy wrote, "My scientist makes all kinds of poisons. He is a weird person." Another caption on the bottom of a drawing said, "Dr. Strangemind," and on the back the student explained that "he does strange things like blow up things and other crazy stuff." Many of the children described their scientists as "blowing things up," "acting crazy" or "goofy," or working with "a lot of potions."

People asked to draw a scientist typically draw a white male with one or more of the following characteristics: wild hair, eyeglasses, a white lab coat, a pocket protector, and some bubbling flasks. Studies reveal that both students and teachers frequently draw this popular image of the scientist (Fort and Varney, 1989). This image is a stereotype because it exaggerates what real scientists look like, and it is reinforced by the scientist images we see in cartoons, movies, magazines, and the popular press. Such stereotypes become part of our belief systems and influence our future behavior. All too often they limit what we do and think. Most of these third-graders, young as they were, had already internalized the stereotyped image of the scientist.

The stereotypes of scientists can discourage individuals who are other than white and male from seeing themselves as truly scientific. Some of the consequences are obvious. For example, substantially fewer females enroll in science courses than do males, beginning in high school and continuing through college. Females are not the only outsiders to science. The marginalization of students of color is profound, since both school science and media images of science really refer to "white western science." Hence, the implicit curriculum message is that the *only* science is white western science. This embedded notion of science is so pervasive that the gap in participation along racial and gender lines persists despite many types of interventions designed to encourage their participation. It is a complex issue, but the way in which we conceptualize "who does science" certainly contributes to the problem.

᥍ Science Outsiders ᥍

My own early research indicated to me that at every grade, cultural norms inhibit the identification of girls with scientific study. When I visited an after-school science club in a grade school in the northeast United States and there were two girls out of twenty students, I wondered what messages were sent out about this club and who should participate. What is wrong with science education that none of the girls are flocking to the club? Events like this are signals to teachers that something is going wrong in the teaching of science.

For example, the assumed squeamishness of girls in the science lab is an example of cultural stereotyping that prevents girls from fulfilling their science potential. While these girlhood stereotypes tell girls they shouldn't get messy, the women they become do the real "messy work" as they maintain the daily fabric of life. The women often get messy with diapers, chickens, turkeys, toilets and the evening meal. One familiar story is recalled by a student of mine. "When I was in seventh grade, we had to dissect a frog. I was so excited to do it, but I screamed the entire time so the boys would think I was acting like a girl." Herein is the challenge . . . to see how acting like a girl means acting scientific.

> Good science teaching needs to encourage, invite, engage, excite, interrogate, challenge and shine, like a beacon, signaling that science is truly for everyone. Seeing the light, girls would flock toward this science classroom, feeling connected, competent and anxious to engage in scientific experiences. (Koch, 1998, 474)

❧ Connected Science Teaching ❧

We need to place the students' questions and experiences at the center of our school science experience. The stories described here reflect a shift in my own thinking as I changed careers from teaching earth science, biology and chemistry in high school to teaching elementary school science, and finally to teaching elementary school teachers at a university. This journey began when I started to wonder, "In what ways must science education change to reflect the lived experience of all members of society? And in what ways can the diverse experiences of different populations of students restructure the content and pedagogy of science education?"

For me, thinking about these questions caused me to reject the dominant mode of science teaching, i.e., lecture and lab requirements where the teacher is the ultimate authority imparting de-personalized, de-contextualized knowledge. These curricula are designed to describe minute parts of nature, and this, coupled with fact-based assessment, alienates many youngsters and adults from science.

Critiques of science education from diverse communities of learners suggest that science is a selective rendering of nature because all of our observations are filtered through the personal lenses of our own experiences. These critiques reject the notion that scientists hold up a mirror to nature. I believe that the "mirror" has inherent biases and that a more honest science requires that scientists describe their respective lenses.

In education, there persists the belief that science education has somehow evaded multiculturalist critique by appealing to a universalist epistemology: that the culture, gender, race, ethnicity or sexual orientation of the knower is irrelevant to scientific knowledge (Stanley and Brickhouse, 1994). Knowing personally that this was not the case, I often invite students of any age to write their science autobiographies (Koch, 1990). The autobiographical data becomes a starting point for constructing the science curriculum. We share our autobiographical science stories and begin to construct definitions of science based on our own experiences with science—in school or beyond the classroom. Those definitions range from viewing science as a way of knowing nature to seeing science as merely a collection of facts to be memorized. Based on their prior experiences, some students reported that they view science as cruel, unfeeling, unforgiving of error and alienating. Others report feeling "disconnected" to school science saying that it had nothing to do with their lives. That is where we begin—with an understanding of who the students are and how they relate to science. Knowing this helps us to create curriculum that will overcome their negative experiences and reinforce their positive ones.

Using students' personal experiences to examine science is central to our efforts to create a science learning community across difference. More importantly, using personal experiences, observations and questions forces us to embrace our experiences with a critical eye so that we could find meaningful ways to connect with people who are different from the culturally-constructed scientist image.

Angie Barton (1998) created this atmosphere in a homeless shelter. She discovered that when science time at the shelter began, the children participated in activities that reflected their lived experiences. These urban students of elementary and middle school age constructed investigations of local pollution, looking for causes, interviewing local business people and residents. They created and enacted plans for picking up trash and planting vegetables and flowers (p. 387). Furthermore, since the children can only have food in the shelter in the dining room when it is served and have no access to eating between meals or after school, they also designed experiments focusing on food, making experimental pizza, pancakes, jelly, and fried rice.

Clearly, the science grew out of the children's experiences. As Barton (1998) has demonstrated, using lived experiences to build science curriculum

> provides space for multiple voices to be heard and explored. When multiple voices are heard and explored, children learn that their experiences do not have to be channeled into defending a particular reality, and that there is room for them to play with their representations of science and their identities within science. (p. 389)

For example, if we create science experiences in our classroom that include us all, we need to look at the practices of aboriginal peoples and take those practices to heart. We learn that many native cultures engage in formal observations of nature. Recollection and consideration of extraordinary natural events contribute to an important database that documents nature's deviations from previous patterns. Snively and Corsiglia (1998) show that it is the descriptive ecological knowledge about nature that First Nations peoples in Canada and Native Americans in the United States have acquired through long years of experience with their natural environment that has been vital to their survival. It is this ecological knowledge that has much to offer Western science because in traditional Western science, detailed attention to native ecosystems has been ignored.

Science is expressed in Native American tradition in many ways, and stories of traditional communities include important data and ecological knowledge. When Native Americans planted and harvested corn, they were acutely aware of the need to plant ground cover after each harvest lest the soil be eroded. Their traditions were based on their need to protect the land by restoring the soil after the harvest.

Formal science education has not made space for those who believe there may be another way to create science experiences in schools. Much of the personal experience that we can bring to bear on school science is undervalued in standards and assessments.

> Once, while doing science with middle school children on a small rural island off the coast of Maine, I learned how to spot a clam in the wet sand off this island coast. The middle schoolers who taught me how to spot a clam were adept at observing the slightest differences in the surface of the sand. The clues to their clams' whereabouts involved an almost intuitive ability to perceive minor changes in their coastal environment. Their skill in this arena is a valuable attribute for scientific study. Nobody ever told them that (Koch, 1996, 308).

So, what do we accept as scientific? What is legitimate knowledge in science education? We need to explore the connections between personal experience and "science." Barton (1998) expresses it as de-centering science—taking science out of the center—as a target to be reached—and placing the children's experiences, wondering, questions and explorations at the real center.

❧ The Science Lab Report ❧

The way that school science operates intentionally denies the lenses and voices of personal experience. For example, high school laboratory experiences are often contrived activities with predictable outcomes. All the students are supposed to come up with the same responses. Often "Did I get it right?" and "Can I copy your lab report?" are familiar questions in the high school science lab. A revision of this rote reporting that legitimizes the personal voice uses the following format:

My name is :

I worked on this lab with:

We were hoping to find out:

This is the procedure we followed:

This is what we thought would happen:

This is what actually happened:

The parts of this process that we were unsure of were:

The parts of the process that we were happy with were:

If we had this to do all over again we would:

As a result of this lab, we reasoned that :

Introducing the first person to the lab report connects the knower to the known, identifies the learner's agenda, and reminds us of the personal, human nature of science.

❧ Keeping a Science Journal ❧

Students can also personalize the experience of doing science by keeping a science journal. This is a journal in which the focus of attention is nature and natural events in the daily experiences of students. Science can be thought of simply as a way of knowing your natural world. Therefore a science journal contains observations as well as questions about nature. Keeping a science journal forces us to take notice of the ways in which nature presents itself to us. Science journals are a way for students to contact their scientific self.

Science journals can also contain items about science in the news or science that you see in a classroom. Students can write about a science show they saw on television. Often there are news items either on television news or in the print media that relate to a scientific breakthrough or recent medical discovery. A science journal can encourage students to ask their own questions, writing about observations that they do not understand. For some, the science journal may be a log, recording the natural events that capture student curiosity.

The following excerpts from my own journal illustrate a type of story that sometimes emerges in science journals. This is the almost-daily log of a bird-watching experience I had in my own backyard. The geographic setting is a heavily treed suburban area outside of New York City. Notice that I did not know how to explain everything I saw; I recorded my questions as well as my observations.

Tuesday: I never noticed the hollow in the middle of the trunk of the low-lying tree in the backyard. Imagine my surprise today when, as I glanced through the dining-room window, I saw a bird fly right out of the tree! I wandered over to the hollowed-out area in the tree trunk and I peeked inside. I counted eight small white oval eggs. Each egg seemed to be about 4 cm long. The baby birds will soon be hatching, I think. I wonder why the eggs are white. Wouldn't it be better if they were a dark color, for camouflage?

Tuesday [two weeks later]: Well, it has been two weeks, and the mother bird continues to fly into and out of the tree periodically. Sometimes, when I glance into the hole, I can see her just sitting there. Yesterday, when I went to pay her my usual visit, she flew out just before I reached the tree. I leaned over to peek at the little eggs but they were gone! In their place were several tiny birds, their necks extended upwards and their beaks wide open. They made soft, small chirping noises that seemed clearly to say, "Feed me." Quietly I stared at them, and then, fearing that the mother bird would return at any moment, I walked away. Now I am wondering what type of bird this is. It's not one that I recognize.

Wednesday: This morning I ran out to the hollow in the tree. The sun was shining at just the right angle into the hole in the tree trunk. The mother bird had just flown away, and when I peeked in, I counted at least eight pink baby birds, eyes closed, with no feathers. They really do look brand new and fragile. I wondered where the mother bird had gone and how long she would leave her hatchlings alone.

An hour later I returned for another glance, and as I looked down into the hole, the mother bird looked right back up at me. Was I surprised! I quickly walked away. But I've noticed that she has a pointed beak and brown feathers. When she flies off, I can see white feathers on her tail. She's a largish bird. I must find my bird book and identify her.

Monday: The hatchlings are still there, a little bigger now. And I've found my field guide to the birds. Combing through the pictures, I spotted several birds that seem to look like the mother bird. She's a little like a catbird, a little like a mockingbird with her white feathers under her tail. But then I found her—and her black necklace. She's a northern flicker, I'm sure of it. I was so excited to identify her.

It can also be helpful to share your journal with others. I took the opportunity to read my journal entries to my students. They all became nearly as wrapped up in the events as I was. Each time they saw me, anxious to hear how the birds were progressing, they asked me, "How are the hatchlings doing?"

Moreover, as I shared my science journal with my students, they began to bring in books and articles about birds that they thought would interest me or that piqued their own interest. It is not unusual for observations of nature to lead to some research, and that is what happened with us. We clipped a local newspaper article on bird watching that featured the northern flicker. We learned that our area has a rare-bird-alert hot line that provides a frequently updated, taped report of what rare birds have been seen lately and where. Some class members contacted the local Audubon Society, which sponsors bird walks, lectures, and other opportunities to learn more about local and migratory birds.

By the end of the class, we had amassed a significant amount of information about local birds and northern flickers in particular. We all understood that this process began with my science journal and the entries I shared with the group. This type of thing often happens when we personalize the experience of observing nature and invite others to share in the event.

Reminders handy as you and your students begin your journal:

- All your observations are important. No observation is silly or too simple.

- All your questions have value; collect them in your journal.

- Note the date and time of all your entries. This information can be helpful later if you want to go back and look for a pattern or connections.

- Entries in your journal can be of any length.

- Watch for interesting science shows on television.

- Make use of any opportunities to find out what other people are thinking about natural events.

- Have fun and write freely.

◠ Science with Fruits and Vegetables ◠

Typically in the third-grade curriculum, children learn about edible plant parts. Students explore the characteristics of fruits to learn that they are the container for the seeds of the plant. They explore the vegetables to learn that they are really the stem, root, leaf, or flower of the plant. In one third-grade class, the teacher invited students to bring in a common fruit and vegetable. The teacher then brought in her own collection of fruits and vegetables. Instead of tomatoes, apples, green peppers and cucumbers, this teacher brought in guava, mango, papaya, okra, avocado, collard greens, black-eyed peas, kiwi, jicama, and turnip tops. After the students explored which had seeds and which ones had no seeds, they went about doing research. Where are they grown? Who eats these? How are they cooked? How often are they eaten?

The diversity of the classroom was reflected in what fruits and vegetables the teacher brought in. This science lesson entered the personal dimension of lived experience and broadened everyone's way of thinking. The fruits and vegetables that we eat are a direct connection to our personal culture, the lives our students live outside the classroom. The question always remains, "What part of the human condition do we miss out on when we construct science from only one cultural perspective?" Perhaps nothing was more thrilling than one little boy's glee upon holding up an avocado and remarking that he eats this at home. Alas! The curriculum connected to his life.

We can only begin to peek at a transformed science education, one that is grounded in the students' own experience. However, if we remain entrenched in old traditions in science classrooms, we will never find the papaya or the avocado. But if we start with the papaya and the avocado, our science classes become an invitation to all our students.

REFERENCES

Barton, A. (1998). Teaching science with homeless children. *Journal of Research in Science Teaching,* 35(4). 379-394.

Fort, D. & H. Varney. (1989). How students see scientists: Mostly male, mostly white, and mostly benevolent. *Science and Children,* 26(8). 9-14.

Koch, J. (1990). The science autobiography project. *Science and Children,* 27. 42-44.

Koch (1996). National science education standards: A turkey, a valentine, or a lemon? In R. Yager (Ed.) *Science/Technology/Society as reform in science education.* Albany, NY: SUNY Press.

Koch, J. (1998). Response to reflections on being female in school science. *Journal of Research in Science Teaching,* 35(4). 473-475.

Koch, J. (1999). *Science stories: Teachers and children as science learners.* Boston: Houghton Mifflin Co.

Snively, G., & Corsiglia, J. (1998). Rediscovering indigenous science: Implications for science education. Paper presented at the National Association for Research in Science Teaching. San Diego, CA, April.

Stanley, W. & Brickhouse, N. (1995). Multiculturalism, universalism and science education. *Science Education,* 78(4). 387-398.

ABOUT THE AUTHOR

I believe that there is a budding scientist in each of us just waiting to be awakened. I wrote this piece because, in my life as a science teacher and a science teacher educator, I have come to understand how exciting it is to have a scientist within oneself who can view the natural world and try to make some personal sense of it. I hope that the reader will evaluate her or his personal connection to science and make it possible for students to feel legitimate in connecting their lived experience to science as a way of knowing the world.

Changing the Subject

Joan Countryman

A YOUNG AFRICAN AMERICAN WOMAN WHO WAS A FRESHMAN at a community college accepted her calculus professor's invitation to make a presentation at a regional professional meeting. With the help of her female teacher, she prepared a brief talk about the concepts behind a procedure in calculus. With only a touch of nervousness, she presented her paper at the student session and successfully fielded a few questions. Then, a male professor at the back of the room raised his hand. "Put your first transparency back on the overhead," he commanded. When she complied he said, "See that 6? It should be a 5."

The calculus professor who told me the story reported that her first reaction was, "How could we have missed that error? We worked so hard," not "Who does he think he is?"

The end of the story is that he was wrong about the 6.

Of course, the real news in the story is that the young woman agreed to make the presentation at all. Girls tend not to advertise their interest and skill in mathematics. That she and her female teacher assumed that it was true that they had missed an error is not surprising, given the propensity of girls to attribute success to luck and failure to lack of ability. An explanation for the behavior of the male teacher is that boys, on the other hand, attribute failure to bad luck and success to their own ability. For him, being wrong was not an issue.

When I think about multicultural education in mathematics and science, I consider the challenge of gender:

- Although girls start school ahead of boys in reading and computation, by the time they graduate from high school, boys have higher SATs in both.

- Girls are more likely to believe they are incapable of doing math and science and to avoid it in high school and college.

- Girls are less likely to take math and science even when they show ability in those areas.

A sixth-grade boy, told that he has failed a math test, will tell you there was something wrong with the test. A girl will decide that she should pursue less challenging math. By the time she reaches high school she has opted out of choices that prepare her for advanced courses. In too many cases, by the time they graduate from high school, students who are not male and students who are not white have concluded that math is not for them.

I also consider the challenge of race:

- In the year 2000 there will be about fifteen million children in elementary school, about ten million in secondary school, half boys and half girls. Four in ten of those under eighteen will be nonwhite, a figure that is three times what it was fifty years ago.

- African American and Latino students still perform below their white peers in math and science and are severely underrepresented in advanced courses.

Would school mathematics and science look different if women and other underrepresented groups were central to our teaching and our thought? Would we still emphasize logic and right answers, or might we focus on collaboration and exploration? Are race and gender issues in math class?

Is there something wrong with these students, or is something wrong with the way we think about math? Addressing that question has led schools to reconsider a number of assumptions hidden in the mathematics curriculum and produced some striking results. In Providence, Rhode Island, Equity 2000, a College Board effort to close the gap in college attendance between white students and students of color, eliminated tracking in middle and high school math and required that every eighth-grader take pre-algebra, every ninth-grader algebra, and every tenth-grader geometry.

The district has replaced all the math books and restructured the curriculum for all grades, emphasizing cooperative learning, concrete materials, critical thinking and problem solving. In 1990, there were 585 students taking Algebra 2, pre-calculus or calculus. This year 1,400 students are enrolled in those courses. Eight years ago 1,560 Providence high-schoolers were enrolled in remedial and general math courses. This year there are none. Eight years ago, 2,262 students were taking Algebra 1, geometry and Algebra 2. This year 4,146 high-schoolers are enrolled in those courses. By the end of the 1996-97 academic year, 72 percent of Providence ninth-graders had passed Algebra 1. In a district with a 76 percent "minority" population this is remarkable achievement, but there is still work to do.

Teachers in the Providence Equity 2000 project learned early on that they could no longer stand in front of a class and lecture to the students. The failure rate was high when they approached the subject in traditional ways, and the project itself might have failed if teachers had not been willing to rethink their beliefs and practices. Facing the really challenging questions —What are the aims of teaching math? Who shapes the math curriculum? What is the role of mathematics in general education? How might math reflect our multicultural society?— takes time and commitment. Nor is the payoff instantaneous, but the results in Providence in this decade should be powerful incentives to anyone who believes that change is both necessary and possible.

The framework for that change must include a commitment to inclusive education at all levels, training for teachers and staff, the expectation of success for all students, a climate that values the diversity of the community, and multiracial, multicultural, gender-inclusive curricular materials. An excellent collection of resources is available on the equity web site of the Eisenhower National Clearinghouse: http://equity.enc.org./equity/.

For example, at that site you will find Marylin Hulme's "Guidelines For Evaluating Mathematics Books For Bias" which includes questions like:

• Do math texts have word problems which include both girls and boys? If so, what topics are they dealing with?

- What language is used to address women and men? To refer to them? When names are used, do they represent diverse cultural groups?
- Compare the number of boys and girls pictured doing as opposed to watching activities.
- Are there members of diverse cultural groups depicted as active in the illustrations? Are there women and men from such groups?
- Do the texts include the contributions to the field of mathematics made by women and by members of culturally diverse groups ?

Many of the Providence ninth-graders who passed Algebra 1 in 1997 are taking upper level mathematics courses. They are succeeding, in part, because they work hard and, in part, because their teachers, believing that these students can learn, have been willing to rethink their own approach to teaching mathematics. Paying attention to gender and race and to the many cultures in the classroom will allow us to change the subject.

ABOUT THE AUTHOR

I wrote this article because I feel that it is important for math and science teachers to include themselves in the conversation about multicultural education. We can change the subject so that everyone is included in the discourse. I head Lincoln School, an independent school for girls in Providence, Rhode Island, and occasionally teach a little math.

Teaching U.S. History:
Room for Imagination

Cathy L. Nelson

WHILE TRAVELING IN AUSTRALIA AS PART OF A U.S. TOUR we asked each other familiar questions when getting to know one another: What's your name? Where are you from? What do you do? When I responded that I was a high school U.S. history teacher, the reaction by the "asker" was strong. The smile left his face, replaced with an expression that I initially thought might mean a medical emergency. With passion, he said, "I hated U.S. history when I was in school!" He then relaxed and added, "But I love it now."

I have encountered such responses often. This sense that U.S. history in particular and social studies classes in general are dull, unimportant, and irrelevant to students' lives is rampant. My own belief that the social studies are broad in content, deep in complexity, and incredibly important is not a perspective shared by most current and former students.

In light of the need for citizens to understand the history of their nation in order to make informed, intelligent decisions about its future, and the equally important process of understanding the ways in which individuals and groups within that nation are shaped by its history, I realized that I had work to do. I began to look at the teaching of U.S. history with a new lens, intent on finding answers. To do so first required posing critical questions: Whose stories are told? Whose perspectives are represented/included? How has my own education interfered with my ability to imagine the teaching and learning of U.S. history in ways that will engage students and connect to their lives and mine?

ᑐ Whose Stories Are Told? ᑐ

I decided to extend the questioning to my students. The questions I invited them to explore were: What have your experiences been so far in your formal education learning about U.S. history, and how do you feel about it? On this, the first day of the U.S. history courses I taught at Fridley [Minnesota] High School, I essentially asked my students to write their own U.S. history autobiography. After the usual questions from students regarding length of the assignment, one student wrote, "History is about dead white men and who cares?"

I was awed by her response. She was articulate, succinct, and observant in ways that I had not been as a student. She had noticed whose stories were told, and they were not the stories of people like her. She quickly added that I shouldn't worry. She was a good student and would do all her homework.

As a student of U.S. history, I did not often notice the absence of women. And when I did, I assumed that if they had done anything important, they would have been included in the textbooks.

My first lens to critique the curriculum was that of gender. Where were the women? The only woman I remember learning about in history class was Betsy Ross, who may or may not have sewn the flag in question. As I was totally uninterested in anything to do with sewing, she and her story did not inspire me or convince me that she was historically significant.

Lerner (1990) has distinguished between history as the unrecorded past and History as sharing in the world and its work. Women have been at least half of history, sharing in the world and its work—central, not marginal. History, on the other hand, was about the few who wrote speeches, laws, won or lost battles or elections; in short, who were involved in those public activities selected to be recorded and interpreted.

The question, "Where were the women?" sent me, among other places, to the National Women's History Project (NWHP) in California where I quickly learned that there were many stories to tell—those of Sybil Luddington, Fannie Lou Hamer, Sarah Winnemucca, and Sor Juana Ines De La Cruz, to name a few. The Project's staff also provided another important lesson—I would need to recognize that women's history is multicultural. This same pervasive silence I had finally recognized regarding women in general applied to all men and women of color, people with disabilities, and other marginalized groups.

I realized that what is being taught, or not being taught, is an important component of multicultural education. We send powerful messages to students about whose lives and activities are important by whom and what we choose to talk about in classrooms. McIntosh (1984) minced no words regarding the importance of the content of the curriculum: "I think that the *main message any school delivers about what counts is delivered through its curriculum*" (p. 8).

As I thought about the U.S. history courses I had taken, I also recognized that discussions of social and political movements focused on the leaders. Individuals were lauded while the stories of collaboration and collective efforts were either omitted or merely alluded to. Hull House *was* Jane Addams. The Civil Rights Movement *was* about Dr. Martin Luther King, Jr. The stories of how people worked together to make history were omitted, replaced by a focus on the individual placed in the center.

This narrow definition of "who counts" leaves most people out, distorts the ways in which history is really made, and disempowers students in the political realm by creating the impression that few people are capable of bringing about change. Another clear message conveyed through the curriculum by omission is that young people haven't been active participants in shaping this country's history. This view is inaccurate and does not serve our interest in encouraging young people to become involved in their neighborhoods, communities, states, and nation.

Which stories get told shows students whose input, ideas, and contributions are valued. Sara Evans (1983) clearly encapsulated how we owe students a history that empowers them to be agents of change and agents of their own futures: "Having a history is a prerequisite to claiming a future. That our power to shape the future comes in part because we know that we have shaped the past" (p. 231).

∾ Whose Perspectives Are Represented/Included? ∾

The first history lesson I remember learning in school was about the arrival of Columbus to "our" part of the world. We learned the names of the ships and the year of arrival and, attesting to the power of mnemonic devices, most adults can still cough up the year 1492 when asked.

One of my dreams is to be on *Jeopardy* and for the final category to be U.S. history. This dream turned into a nightmare while I was working on curriculum related to the then upcoming Columbus Quincentennial. In my dream-turned-nightmare, the subject was Columbus, but I was not required to name the ships or the year of his "discovery." The final Jeopardy answer that I was to provide a question for was: "The indigenous people that Columbus first encounters in the New World." In my dream/nightmare my ignorance about U.S. history was revealed to the nation. But I would have gone home with the money if they had asked me to identify the name of Robert E. Lee's horse.

Although multiple perspectives is an oft-touted cornerstone of social studies education, it is much less frequently reflected in the textbooks or classroom practice. When students are given an opportunity to research and explore historical events from various perspectives and to interrogate the texts, wondering out loud how there can be such divergent views of the same event, the teachable moment has arrived. This notion that such varying descriptions and analysis of events can coexist is something they're very familiar with in their personal lives, for example, as brothers and sisters offer varying responses to parents asking, "What happened here?" In their schooling they also need to see evidence that either/or thinking does not reflect the real world, nor does it accurately capture the story of our nation's past.

Once the window was open for me to see perspective and its absence, the floodgates opened. The "theory" of the Bering Strait (often taught more as fact than theory) never considered the fact that bridges generally allow travel in either direction. The unit named "Westward Expansion" was exposed for its particularity. I saw the narrow perspectives revealed in statements like "Black people benefited from the social struggles of the 1960s" when a more accurate statement would be, "The whole nation benefited from the social struggles of the 1960s."

There is an African proverb that captures "why" so much of U.S. history is written from a Eurocentric perspective: "*Until the lions have their historians, tales of hunting will glorify the hunter.*"

❧ "Brilliant Flashes of the Obvious" ❧

The same year I was first learning about Columbus, I vividly remember my first grade teacher enthusiastically introducing the winter art project of making snowflakes. She kept proclaiming, "There are no two snowflakes alike . . . There are no two snowflakes alike . . . " It became a mantra that day. I was, at that very moment, looking through Minnesota classroom windows at six feet of "no two alike." The little voice inside of me wanted to challenge her account, knowing somewhere deep within me that on this point the teacher was wrong. But I was a good student. I had learned to censor myself, to silence myself, to not challenge the teacher.

It was February, and I had been in school since September. I was learning two important, though inadvert, lessons: (1) If the teacher says it, that's the way it is (As a high school social studies teacher, I confess to sometimes lamenting that students no longer buy into this notion); and (2) School is not a place where questions are asked. Neither of these early lessons has served me well in the world. I was exchanging my questions and understanding of the world for the goodies that being a good student afforded me.

Over the length of my teaching career, I have come to expect and welcome what I call "brilliant flashes of the obvious"— moments when I understand something that, in retrospect, I have a hard time accepting that I didn't know before. They are now perfectly *obvious*.

For example, social studies often is organized in K-12 schools around the notion of the "expanding environment." Students first learn about themselves, then their household, neighborhoods, communities, state, nation, and world. This progression also sends the message that the work done in state, national and international arenas is more valuable than community and local activities. The traditional progression in teaching U.S. history is one of moving further and further from the lives of our students and from the arenas they as citizens might imagine being part of shaping.

In the discussion of community, it is not unlikely to learn about law enforcement officers. Ultimately that translates into a test question something like this: "Law enforcement officers are our _____ (friends)." As a student, I was schooled to know that if I were in trouble, I could count on law enforcement officers to help me. Nothing in my early personal experiences living in rural Minnesota led me to question this. But the moment I imagined that test question from the perspective of the African American children that lived in my new neighborhood in North Minneapolis, the fallacy of this assumption was immediate. Not only can people of color not depend on law enforcement officers to be helpful, but parents specifically instruct their children on how to interact with the police in such a way that they will not be hurt. And once such an initial brilliant flash of the obvious was over, the aftermath was more questions: What other groups might see law enforcement officers differently than I had? What other "knowledge" taught in schools was conflicting with the cultural and daily realities of students? What else was I not seeing?

African American students in a classroom facing that question are being asked to exchange their understanding of their community and world in exchange for the "perks" that academic success offers them. And this is just the beginning of the contrast between their quest for knowledge and their reality. These daily indignities go unobserved, the structural inequities go unnoticed, and perspectives are presented that remain unacknowledged or challenged as *versions* of reality.

I also remember how carefully our teacher placed the first book in our hands. We were told how to open it, how to crease back the pages, how not to dog-ear the flaps, and how we must never, ever, ever write on the pages (but if we must, to be sure to use a pencil.) The only book we were that careful with in my home was the Bible, so I concluded that this must be "sacred," that I could believe what was between the covers of that book, that the printed word was to be believed. This assumption has not served me well in my adult life, nor does it prepare students to think critically.

I also recognized that students just don't buy all of the "facts" we're asking them to learn. On some level they get it that the material often distorts reality, that we are passing on the lies that were passed on to us, that we are faithfully replicating a body of knowledge replete with perspectives we've never been asked to critique. I have taken a private oath to never again diagram "How a bill becomes a law," as that schematic diagram does not accurately reflect the role of power and privilege in our law-making bodies—power and privilege that are inequitably distributed along the lines of race, class, gender, sexual orientation, religion, age, disability, and language. The U.S. history classroom can challenge oppression and highlight the efforts toward social justice.

One of the "facts" I learned as a child was that there were four basic food groups. Not only were we often asked to list them in tests, we planned entire menus around this quartet of food groups. Imagine my surprise when they *changed* this basic scheme! The tentative nature of knowledge is another cornerstone of social studies teaching, but we didn't really believe in it. And we certainly never discussed the political nature of knowledge, such as the influence an industry like the dairy industry could bring to bear on defining "truth." The trick is to see such lobbying not as an isolated event but as just a small example of the role power can play in the social construction of "reality." The trick is to look forward to moments that provide brilliant flashes of the obvious.

∾ ∾ ∾

In 1988 I was traveling to Colorado Springs to attend the National SEED Leaders' Workshop. Flying through the mountains on a day with high winds, I was not feeling safe and needed something to distract myself. So I began reading one of the national, generic newspapers. Buried somewhere in the middle of that edition was a short article titled, "Researchers have discovered two snowflakes alike." I remember wanting to shout at the top of my lungs, "I knew that when I was six!" In addition to reminding me that much of what we know takes somewhat longer for researchers to confirm, this moment serves as a touchstone for me. I do know what it feels like to sit in a classroom and have someone explain the world in ways that I knew deep within myself were not true. I had spent six years looking at six feet of "no two alike" and I knew there had to be two snowflakes alike out there somewhere.

I recognize the tremendous impact my selection of materials, activities, and approaches has in the classroom. Part of my responsibility as a teacher of U.S. history is to challenge the assumptions about what constitutes history and to encourage students to critically ask questions of texts: Whose stories are told? How are these stories told? Who is doing the telling? To ask what stories the students have to share. Whose perspectives are included/represented? How have racism, sexism, classism, and other systems of oppression influenced history and the telling of that history? How can we challenge those systems and actively participate in the making of history? How has that history shaped who we are today as individuals, as members of various groups, and as citizens?

What is required is imagination: weaving scholarship with teaching experience to bring into view the experiences, contributions and perspectives of traditionally understudied groups; transforming our images of what the teaching of U.S. history looks like to be unlike our own experiences in fundamental ways.

I remember seeing a poster once which quoted some words of Albert Einstein: "Imagination is more important than knowledge." Part of imagination is asking ourselves, "What if it really wasn't the way you've been taught it was?" and "How do you imagine this would look like from another perspective?"

As a student and teacher of U.S. history, I am aware that whatever greatness our country has achieved has been because of the diversity of its people, not in spite of it. Accurately telling that story needs to reflect this diversity. To imaginatively create approaches to the learning of U.S. history that engages students, I have more questions to ask, learning to do, and images to create.

REFERENCES

Evans, S. (1983). Toward a usable past: Feminism as history and politics. *Minnesota History*, 48 (6). 231-235

Lerner, G. (1990, Spring). Writing women into history. *Women of Power*, 6-9.

McIntosh, P. (1984). Gender issues for the schools: An interview with Peggy McIntosh. *Independent School*, 44 (2). 6-14.

ABOUT THE AUTHOR

I believe that K–12 teachers have stories to share that will help other teachers to imagine how they can work toward a curriculum that is multicultural. I offer my story to encourage others to write as well. I have taught secondary social studies in Minnesota schools for sixteen years. I am currently the Executive Director of the Minnesota Inclusiveness Program, a nonprofit educational corporation, and the Co-Director of the Minnesota S.E.E.D. Project (Seeking Educational Equity and Diversity), a staff development project that prepares educators to return to their schools and facilitate monthly, three-hour seminars on multicultural education.

Silenced by Shakepeare Class

Emily Style

In high school my hand was always in the air
waving confidently

I never noticed silence, I had much to say
comfortable with being, at home in school

As a sophomore in college, my hand refused to go up
I became silent, studying Shakespeare
in a class where everyone's English was schooled-to-be
smarter than me

To be or not to be?

I was silent, unable to understand even
the questions asked by other students
whose parents had once been in college
where my parents had never been . . . but I became their
    daughter then,
silenced in school, not at-home there

Learning for the first time
the meaning of class,
joining "the silent majority"
on the other side
of the great divide
between those who "participated" in class,
and those who did not . . .

Now, years later, as teacher with classes of my own,
I listen for/in/to multi-cultural silences,
embracing many ways of being,
even Shakespeare's

ABOUT THE AUTHOR

I wrote this poem in a 1993 workshop sponsored by the Dodge Foundation as I wrestled with how to name some of my own experience of classism. I have been a high school English teacher as well as an educator in other settings since 1970. My commitment to education as respectful encounter for all—rather than a silencing of some—is rooted in rethinking my own experience of schooling. With Peggy McIntosh, I have co-directed the National S.E.E.D. (Seeking Educational Equity & Diversity) Project on Inclusive Curriculum since its beginning in 1987.

BUILDING
COMMUNITY

Creating community . . . involves this most difficult work of negotiating real discussion, of considering boundaries before we go crashing through, and of pondering our differences before we can ever agree on the terms of our sameness.

—*Patricia J. Williams*

Building Community in a Diverse Suburban Classroom

Käri M. Anderson Suggs

"**D**IDN'T YOU WEAR THAT SHIRT YESTERDAY?"
"What are you—Black or White?"
"How come you walk so funny?"

Building a sense of community in a sixth-grade classroom is hard work. It was particularly difficult during my fourth year of teaching—the worst of my brief teaching career. Students were name-calling, pushing, fighting, and teasing. Incidents of sexual and racial harassment, bullying, and arguing filled many of our hours together. I was desperately searching for strategies to create a positive learning environment where students could learn and I could stay sane.

I remembered what it was like for me as a student, trying to learn in an unsafe and threatening environment. It was troubling when I realized that I was once again uncomfortable in my own classroom. I knew that I had to create a safe and respectful community, one that would allow students' stories to be shared and their voices to be heard. My responsibility as a classroom teacher included helping students find their voices, tell their stories. This would help build community, a classroom community where all students were valued and where we recognized our links to one another.

As a young girl, I had literally begged my parents to ask me questions at the dinner table. Sometimes it was because I wanted to share knowledge and stories. Other times it was because I wanted to learn new things. The kitchen table in our home was a place where I became the storyteller for brief moments. School rarely afforded me this opportunity.

Like Barbara Kingsolver's Codi in *Animal Dreams* (1990), I returned to teach differently than I was taught. Ironically, I taught in the same district that I grew up in so I was aware of the district's shortcomings as well as its strengths. That year my classroom was home to twenty-nine students representing a range of cultural, religious, and economic backgrounds as well as abilities. This made my commitment to build community even stronger, knowing that teaching to and from diverse perspectives was going to be critical to a successful year. I wanted to provide windows and mirrors for all of my students.

Many aspects of my personal and professional career led me to change my teaching to facilitate students finding their voices. I had been my building's representative on our district-wide multicultural committee for three years. I attended workshops on multicultural education. I learned about the cultural backgrounds of my students. I read articles and books and heard real-life stories from friends and colleagues. But how was I to go about accomplishing such a daunting task?

My professional development had included learning some of the skills and tools that building community would require. I was familiar with active listening skills. I challenged myself to create in-depth, hands-on lessons. I worked with teachers in my own and other schools to create multicultural units. I learned from Nelsen, Lott, and Glenn (1993) that "Kids learn best—both academic and social skills—when classroom management is based on mutual respect" (p. 109). But I was not getting to the heart of the problem. I needed to involve my students to a greater degree in the process of their own learning.

At a graduate school seminar, I met two sixth-grade teachers who shared their ideas with me. That was on a Sunday. On the following Monday I initiated an addition to our academic day that we called "Circle," a time when we pulled our twenty-nine chairs together and shared our stories. We would sit in a circle so that we could all see one another and all have the opportunity to speak, to listen, and to be heard. I knew that a circle symbolically and behaviorally represented equity and diversity. We would start by sharing stories about how we came to have the names we do. I hoped students would be less disrespectful toward one other if they knew more about their own lives as well as others.

Once the tables and chairs were moved to the edges of the room, we took turns sharing what we knew about our own names. Some gave a six-minute soliloquy, while others just said a few words. Most students were able to share something, i.e., who named them, the significance of their middle name, the history of their family name. We learned that some classroom members were named after relatives, others after song lyrics, and one who was named after her father's old girlfriend. We found links between students who shared middle names. Those who were unable to think of anything came back the next day ready to share the name stories they were discovering. The diversity of their name stories helped me gain insight into their lives.

As we shared these personal stories, people passed by our door, wondering what we were doing. The students were acutely aware that this day was different from others. This was our beginning.

My schedule permitted us to allocate a thirty-five minute block of time at the start of most school days for Circle. Occasionally we took more time sharing so that the academic subjects had to be shortened by ten or fifteen minutes. Our topics varied daily as we continued with Circle in those early weeks. Stories came from other stories. We chose topics together, sometimes in advance, other times as we pulled our chairs together on the floor. I was constantly on the prowl for Circle ideas that would stimulate sharing stories and facilitate our getting to know one another better. We talked about family traditions, memorable snow stories, worst gifts, birth stories and neighborhood experiences.

One day a student brought her Cabbage Patch doll to school. Before the bell rang that morning, a fair amount of teasing had occurred. At Circle she was eager to share and the other students seemed equally anxious to make fun of her. Before she began, I asked the students, "How many of you have had Cabbage Patch dolls?" Eighteen hands went up and the stories started pouring out. There were stories of waiting in line to buy the dolls and memorable gift and "birth certificate" tales. Now it was safe for the doll owner to tell her story.

This incident reminded me that telling wasn't enough, so we started to bring items to class to share: baby pictures, old school projects, stuffed animals, knickknacks. We passed collectibles around the Circle: shells, coins, recipes, and artifacts that represented their cultural and family backgrounds. As we heard about fried catfish recipes and baptism and burial rituals, we learned about the experiences of others.

The challenge was creating an atmosphere that valued all people's stories. I was concerned about comments made in Circle, but when we began, I had no concrete approach to insure that language was always respectful. I soon realized that ground rules were needed, so I added the ones I had learned at a diversity workshop: speak only from your own experiences (use "I" statements), let people know when they say something hurtful, keep all stories confidential, and show respect by not interrupting people while they were speaking. These ground rules gave us a place to refer to when students' comments or behaviors were not creating a safe place for sharing.

The stories kept coming every week. Quite often we talked about chronic illness, disease and death—their own, their family members, friends and pets. It was through Circle that we heard breast cancer updates of one student's mother. Circle became a safe place for another student to share about her physical health in relation to living with spina bifida, and where I shared my own experiences of living with a chronic illness. It was also where we learned about the difficulty in growing up and becoming a teenager. One student was very frightened about this new stage of life and worried about leaving the security and naiveté of childhood behind. She knew where she was coming from and what she wanted to become, but somehow the path to get there was not clear enough.

> When students speak authentically of what they know and imagine, others experience the speakers. Entering into another person's life by taking delight in their imaginative responses and through what they are willing to disclose about themselves is one of the joys of belonging to a community of caring people. (Peterson, 1992, p. 51)

Talking about oneself is not an easy task for everyone. It requires trust and acceptance, sometimes rare qualities in a classroom of twelve-year-olds. A winter art project provided a metaphor for the work we were doing together. We had talked about the metaphorical masks we wear for other people. Some masks they wore to fit in with friends, others to gain respect around elders. To emphasize the idea of masks, we actually made them in class.

The afternoon of the mask-making we pushed the tables back and spread newspaper out to cover the floor. We filled a few ice cream pails with warm water and had pre-cut pieces of plaster casting material in piles next to them. Kathy, our sixth-grade teacher assistant, demonstrated the process on a volunteer student. After putting Vaseline on his eyebrows to avoid plaster build up, a piece of plastic wrap was torn off the roll and a mouth hole was cut to allow unencumbered breathing. Once the plastic covering was in place, the student lay down to receive the covering. Kathy then dipped the plaster strips, one by one, into the warm water, squeezed the excess liquid off, and formed them to the contours of his face. As they anxiously waited for their turns, the other students watched as his face magically appeared,

This art project was another big step towards building a bridge of trust with my students because they were actually covering up noses and mouths, sometimes of classmates they did not get along with so well. But my fears were calmed quickly. They were excited about creating these faces, their faces. Students paired up and very carefully covered their partner's face with the plastic wrap and the plaster strips and began to create.

The words of Judy Logan (1993), writing about the process of creating quilts with her students, echoed my thoughts about making our masks: "I take time out now and then to notice and appreciate what is going on. The energy in the room is calm and relaxed, but focused and productive. Students are self-directed and supportive of one another" (p. 8).

It was wonderful to watch my students create each other, literally, as they shaped and formed their partner's mask. They sat in spoke fashion in the center of the room, like the wheel that had been holding us together. We manipulated the plaster strips, usually used for making casts for broken limbs, and watched as they started to harden and thicken. The plaster warmed as it covered their faces, creating a comforting covering, not unlike a blanket. As each mask was finished, a fresh-faced student appeared, blinking at the now bright fluorescent bulbs overhead. We then gathered the masks and set them to dry on the back counter where they waited for us to finish the decorating process. When dried, we decorated them with paint, glitter, yarn, fringe, and plastic jewels. The mouth openings seemed to yell, "I have a story that needs to be told!" These voiceless masks hung from our ceiling for five months, watching over us, looking down on us, not missing a single Circle.

Now that our ceiling was appropriately filled by the students themselves, we returned to our Circle. Many mornings I knew there were stories waiting to be told by how my students walked in the door at 8:35 a.m. Sometimes Circle was a place for me to share my experiences or a time to talk about school rules or playground behavior. It even allowed a time and place for visitors to be welcomed, whether they be family members, pets, or visiting teacher friends. On the days when we didn't have time for Circle or I was not able to be there, it had to wait for the next day. I had learned by experience that a substitute teacher did not have the same relationship with my students. I also knew that the idea of letting the stories come forth from the students was working successfully when students started requesting (begging, actually) that we hold Circle.

As the year progressed, the importance of Circle became more evident. The personal glimpses into the students' lives helped inform me as their teacher and formed the basis for mutual respect in our classroom. A journal entry of mine stated it best when I wrote, "I feel drained some days thinking of all the things I know about my students' lives. Knowing that I don't have a lot or any similar experiences, I sometimes feel left out or find it a challenge to really understand. My work becomes to understand, to tell, to wonder, to know . . . and help." For me, Circle was one place where I felt most myself. I became a real participant in the learning process with my students. They learned about me as we learned about each other.

Circle was a place and time when emotions were permitted to take center stage. Voices were heard, tears occasionally flowed, and laughter periodically pealed off the walls. After reading "Eleven" by Sandra Cisneros, students took turns sharing their memories of prominent school experiences. The stories they shared were poignant and brought with them a wealth of feeling and emotion that still shaped their day-to-day experiences at school. One child remembered being injured at school and being taken to the hospital. Another remembered presenting a project in front of the class and being shamed by a classmate, someone who was in our classroom that very year. Two others remembered tying their first grade teacher's shoes together and how fun it was that she played along with their prank. Circle provided the space to constructively express emotions rather than having those same emotions bounce off the walls all day.

Hearing the stories of those who did not like school helped me to better understand what it was like to be a student who chooses to "not learn." When a student shared about having "play" fights with his cousin that often turned violent, it wasn't just me asking questions or giving advice. Classmates were becoming resources and sounding boards for each other.

One of my students was a Jehovah's Witness who had experienced a lot of teasing from his classmates because they did not understand his family's religious beliefs and practices. One day he told me that he had a video we could watch if we wanted to. It was during our unit on World War II and the video, *Purple Triangles,* was a wonderful fit with our curriculum. It described what it was like for a Jehovah's Witness family living in Europe during that war. This not only gave all of us an important historical perspective, but it also helped us better understand one of our classmates. For at least one day of his sixth-grade experience he could share the story and the history of the religious group he identifies with.

At other times Circle became a stage for performing. We may not have known what a talented singer was in our midst without Circle. Another time a student pulled out a folded piece of paper from her pocket and read the two poems that she was submitting to a local contest.

As the volume of stories mounted during the year, we started a writing project to capture these oral memories on paper to be a lasting remembrance of this hard work. This also provided an outlet for those less comfortable with public speaking. This part of our day I called "Autobiography." When the topic of neighborhood play stories or moving to a new school came up, we would later write our own versions and add them to a growing story folder. I shared picture books, asked questions, and told stories to generate writing ideas for their expanding student story folder. As the end of the year approached, students organized, word processed, and edited these stories.

When the writing was completed, students placed these stories inside handmade, fabric-covered, painted and bejeweled books, and we decided to host an open house for the students' family members and friends. These finished, bound books were impressive, containing slices of their lives to date. They reflected hours of writing, thinking, editing, word processing, and living. Their stories explored issues of parental separation, sibling relationships, health concerns, childhood games, toys, friends and dreams.

The students formed committees to organize the event: invitations, decorations, program design, food and beverage, and room arrangement. Black, purple and silver balloons and streamers hung from the doorway and ceiling. A food table was covered with veggies, chips, bars and sodas. The front of the classroom looked like the setting for an impromptu poetry reading. Five chairs and stools of differing heights were gathered from around the building. The students decided that they wanted to read in small groups instead of standing alone to face their new audience. Our room was again being transformed.

The thirty family members and friends at each of the two readings listened attentively and clapped enthusiastically. We bore witness to the embodiment of their hard work. Student faces beamed with pride tinged with nervousness as they shared a chapter of their choice from their books. This was a celebration of who they were and what they were learning. This memorable finale to their autobiography work highlighted my students' ability to organize, plan, and author. What amazing writing! Absolutely no comparison to textbook-led drill and grammar practice.

Most importantly, we were building community. Students did listen to each other more often and waited until classmates were attentive before speaking in Circle. They had an audience, a voice, a story. Though not perfect, their behavior reflected a definite improvement from the start of the school year.

To finalize this year's Circle, we pushed aside the tables and pulled our chairs together one last time an hour before the sixth-grade graduation ceremony. I began by passing a ball of yarn across the circle, holding tight to the beginning of the skein. We literally connected ourselves as each person shared a memory from the past year. Some were funny: admissions of the real antics during field trips, memories of my slipping off a chair, reminders of other silly classroom behavior. Others were painful: reflecting about the loss of this special time and place called elementary school and thoughts about hurtful and wasted time spent in fights with close friends.

When the web was completed, we shook it, freeing those memories. Then the yarn doubled back on its path as we stated one thing we hoped and dreamed of for the next year as seventh graders. The ball ended back in my hand, carefully rerolled. I wrapped the yarn around my wrist once, passing it to the student to my left. This process was repeated around the circle. When everyone was connected, we cut the yarn between us. We all left our piece of yarn on our wrist or tied it to our ankle or clothing as a reminder of our year together. I wore my yarn until July. There were students who wore theirs just as long as I did.

I learned much more about my students than I could have from cumulative files and tests. The sharing of diverse experiences had permeated our classroom and characterized our days. Even though I still had tough moments and hours, days and weeks, I found that Circle was one part of my curriculum with this group of students that helped me not only endure but thrive.

By the end of the year my students were comfortable telling and writing about their own lives. They had an attentive audience every day. Circle had been a vehicle for problem-solving and conflict resolution. The connection of these two portions of our days was inextricable from the tapestry of my students' lives. I had worked hard at this thing called "teaching."

I had lived what Herbert Kohl (1991) suggested when he said, "Risk-taking is at the heart of teaching well" (p. 47). I now had a deep connection to my students' lives, and their stories are what I remember most from our year together. As I look at their class picture I am able not only to remember their names but how they got those names, as well as personal snapshots of their experiences of growing up.

As the year continued, I was hesitant about taking our masks down from the ceiling. Whenever students asked if they could take them home, I would quietly suggest, "Let's leave them up just a little while longer." That was all I had to say. These masks hung as protectors of the students as our Circle continued and autobiographies were formed.

Finally, though, the quiet plaster masks came down from the ceiling. Students quickly commented on how empty the room felt, as if they were taking down and removing themselves and their voices from our classroom. Each student left the building with his/her own mask in hand, hopefully ready to face the next challenge, that first step beyond elementary school.

Through the sharing of stories we came to know one another. We took the stories we shared and heard and left our classroom sanctuary. Now these stories have a life outside their original four walls. It is a basic form of learning and building community, this sharing of stories.

I can already hear next year's students asking as they enter my room in the fall, "Do we get to write an autobiography and have Circle?" Judy Logan (1993) said it best: "We probably will, because we have so many stories to tell and we're such good writers" (p. 75).

REFERENCES

Kingsolver, B. (1990). *Animal dreams.* New York: Harper Perennial.

Kohl, H. (1991). *I won't learn from you!* Minneapolis: Milkweed Editions.

Logan, J. (1993). *Teaching stories.* St. Paul: Minnesota Inclusiveness Program.

Nelsen, J., Lott, L. & Glenn, H. S. (1993). *Positive discipline in the classroom: How to effectively use class meetings and other positive discipline strategies.* Rocklin: Prima Publishing.

Peterson, R. (1992). *Life in a crowded place: Making a learning community.* Portsmouth: Heinemann Educational Books.

ABOUT THE AUTHOR

Through my teaching I have learned that it is necessary to change my practices to open the door to learning. The telling of stories is one change that has become integral to my teaching. Through this change many people benefit—students, teachers, families, and the community. I write to reflect on my teaching and to remind myself to change my classroom practices. I have taught sixth grade for six years in a first-ring suburb of St. Paul, Minnesota, and will keep working to change what happens around me for many years to come. In addition to being a teacher, I am a wife, a step-mother, a daughter, a sister and an aunt who enjoys living in Minneapolis.

Breaking the Silence: Interrupting Bias

DeBorah Zackery

A VETERAN TEACHER AND FRIEND OF FIFTEEN YEARS CALLED asking for my help. At that time I was the diversity coordinator for the Rochester, Minnesota, public schools. Her third-graders were saying things to each other that she refused to repeat on the phone. "It's not just race!" she emphasized as she tried to find the words to explain the problem. "The boys say sexist things to the girls. The girls say sexist things to the boys and to each other. Everything is a joke. They tease each other about culture, hair color, and even the ability of one little boy to speak clearly. He has a hearing loss."

"I don't know what you can do to help," she continued. "But if this does not change, I will not be able to make it through the year."

When I told my friend I would help, I knew I had books on my shelf that might give me some ideas. We set a time to visit with the entire class the following week, and I began to create the exercise I will describe here.

I introduced myself to the third-grade class as the multicultural coordinator for the school district. I explained my position by saying that sometimes I try to help people see how their words and actions hurt others. I told them I had been invited by their teacher because some of the words they were saying and actions they were doing were hurting people.

With that I gave each student a 5x7 card. On the front of the card, I asked them to write down three things they could not change about themselves. I told them I would not ask them to do anything that I would not do myself. "As you write, I will tell you three things about myself I cannot change," I said. "I cannot change that I am a female. I cannot change the color of my skin. I cannot change that I need to wear glasses."

After the students had each completed the task, I asked them to turn their cards over. "Write on the back how you feel when someone teases you about the things you cannot change." Again I stressed that I would not ask them to do what I would not do. And I explained how it felt to be teased about the things I could not change about myself.

"I don't like to be told I can't do something simply because I am female. It makes me feel left out, as if I won't be given a chance. I feel angry when someone teases me about the color of my skin. I felt humiliated when the other kids called me 'four eyes.'"

When the students had finished writing their feelings, I asked them to share with the class one thing about themselves they could not change and how they felt when they were teased about it.

I gave empathetic and reflective responses to the students as they shared their differences. However, when they shared their feelings, I listed the feeling words on the board. A few of the feeling words they shared were: angry, hurt, alone, embarrassed, mad, felt like crying, felt left out, felt alone, felt like fighting. As students repeated the same or similar feeling words, I began to tally the number of times each word was repeated.

In concluding this part of the exercise, I summarized that it appeared that no matter what the difference, we experienced similar feelings when we were teased. We all know how it feels to be singled out for things about ourselves we cannot change.

The next part of my work with students was equally important to creating a positive school environment. I shared with the students several ways to be an advocate. I defined an advocate as a person who adds his/her voice to such exchanges. I asked students to raise their hand if they could not respond right away when they were teased. All but two or three students raised their hands. I explained that it was very common to be silent when someone hurts you. The hurt is so deep you cannot think of anything to say at the time.

"Have you ever had the experience of knowing exactly what to say a little while later?" I asked. Many of the students could identify with that experience as well. "That is why I need you to practice adding your voice. Sometimes you will hear someone singled out because of something s/he can't change. The person may not say anything, but that does not mean it didn't hurt. When that happens, I want you to add your voice. I want you to be an advocate. I am going to give you several ways to do it. One thing you can say is, 'We don't tease people about things they cannot change.' For the next few weeks I want this to be your class rule. If you hear someone being teased and you know it is about something they can't change, I want you to say the class rule.

A second way to add your voice is to ask the person how they would feel if someone teased them about their difference. 'How would you feel if . . . .'

Another way is to tell the person how you would feel if s/he made that comment to you. 'I would feel . . . .'

Fourth, you can always give accurate information to correct a mistake. 'The truth is . . . .'"

In groups of three, I then asked students to role play one of the examples from their cards. One person was to be the victim, one the perpetrator, and one the advocate. For approximately five to seven minutes, they created and practiced their roles. When the students indicated they were ready, we began to share with the large group. I explained to the students that in each role play I would say the words that hurt. Their role was to practice stopping, interrupting, and correcting me.

Each triad approached the front of the room and whispered to me the role I was to play. The most memorable scenario was the one Rhea shared. The words she whispered for me to repeat were, "Hey, Diarrhea, let's play." In a pleading tone, she said, "All I want is for them to call me Rhea. Not Diarrhea, just Rhea." As requested, I stepped back and repeated the words she said hurt her so deeply. Although her eyes told me she knew it was a role play, her face turned red with pain again. Her bottom lip began to quiver and she bit it to make it stop.

From her side her advocate began to speak. "Mrs. Zackery, you would not like it if someone teased you because you are brown." Gesturing to Rhea she said, "Her name is Rhea. She does not like to be called Diarrhea. It hurts her. In our class, we don't tease people about things they cannot change. Her parents named her. She can't change her name." Rhea looked at Andria as if to say, "You have a friend for life."

The girl who played the role of Rhea's advocate was very soft-spoken. She expressed herself in a conversational tone, a point I had stressed to the students before we began. Her words and the way she spoke them were equally important.

With each role play, I highlighted the method the student chose to interrupt bias. Andria was a good example of using my own difference, skin color, to help me empathize with Rhea. She informed me of Rhea's correct name, she let me know what Rhea preferred, she told me I had hurt Rhea, and she told me the class rule.

I then asked the students to put an *x* in the upper right-hand corner if an adult is around when they are teased. I explained that often students are waiting for an adult to make the people hurting them stop. Afterwards, I collected the cards and quickly tallied the results.

Only one student said an adult was present when they were teased. However, all thirty students gave an example. I explained that there was one chance in thirty that I, another teacher, parent or adult would be there if they were teased.

"You know, when I teased my brother or called him a name, I was smart enough not to do it when an adult was around, too," I told them. "This is your classroom. The only person who can make it a fun place to be without put-downs is you." Holding the cards in my hand, I gestured with them and said, "You just told me that only one of you has ever been caught."

In a conversation with the classroom teacher after the exercise, she explained that Andria was a quiet student who rarely spoke in class. For the class to hear Andria correct me brought the message home in a special way. This was the most the class had heard from Andria in two months of school.

In the weeks that followed this classroom exercise, a number of positive things happened. Andria was included more by her classmates. Her fellow students seemed to accept her silence and smiles as part of who she was. The classroom teacher reported the students spoke about being an advocate for each other daily.

About two weeks after the exercise, I entered the school building and two little girls screamed my name down the hall. "Hi, Mrs. Zackery! Mrs. Zackery! I was an advocate yesterday. We were outside on the playground and a boy we don't know called Kim a name. She was so upset she could not speak. You know that's how you feel when someone makes fun of you. Well, I was her advocate. I told him her name was Kim and we don't tease people about things they can't change. Heather was there, too, and she said, 'Yeah, we don't tease people.' The boy mumbled he was sorry and walked away."

I met Rhea outside of school once after the exercise. She noticed me in the dentist's office. I smiled hello, but that wasn't enough. She went over to her father and insisted that he walk over and meet me. "She's the one who made all the kids stop calling me Diarrhea," said Rhea. The father's face went from one of polite, anonymous greeting to a smile reserved only for family and friends. As Rhea went in for her dentist appointment, her father explained how helpless he felt when his daughter was teased. He said he did not know how much it hurt her until Rhea talked about my coming to class. Rhea had explained each way to interrupt bias and why it was important. He thanked me and wanted me to know that Rhea hated school until the name-calling stopped. Every day she would make excuses not to go.

Bias is rampant in our schools. We all have a responsibility to recognize bias. We all have a responsibility to interrupt bias. Given an opportunity to practice breaking the silence and interrupting bias, I believe students and adults would be more likely to do so.

Creating a bias-free environment that fosters diversity requires preparation and practice. Good will and a good heart are not enough. Those are the attributes of bystanders. People who believe they will be ready to interrupt the bias that crosses their path are often puzzled as to why they did not say or do anything. They often lament that they did not know what to say or do.

Acquiring a skill requires practice. To be a good writer, you write. To be a good reader, you read. To play a piece of music with precision, you have to do more than look at it and talk about it. The same is true for interrupting bias.

The classroom teacher reported that having the opportunity to practice interrupting bias made an impact on the entire third-grade class. Consequently, the exercise was repeated in several buildings in the school district. Out of over 600 students, only four placed an *x* on the card to indicate an adult was around when they were teased. That one piece of data is reason enough for me to continue to empower young people to use words and actions that interrupt bias and break the silence, because when bias confronts them and hurts them, I will not be there. Only the lessons I have taught them give them the resources they will need to interrupt bias.

ABOUT THE AUTHOR

This article was intended to encourage any reader to be open to the voices of difference. Each time I retell this story, the memory of the children's

faces of pain and discovery come to mind. My students are my best teachers. They constantly show me a new detail on the landscape of learning
that I have missed. As a teacher for over twenty years working with students in grades K-12, this teaching story has been one that has changed
me professionally. I am currently principal of Edison/PPL Elementary
School, a Minneapolis Partnership School.

Honoring Student Diversity: Understanding Dakota and Ojibwe Family Life

Marion Helland

A S A NON-INDIAN SCHOOL TEACHER, I REMEMBER THE FIRST American Indian student in my fifth grade class in the mid 1950s. That year I read the social studies text, the reading books, and other teaching materials that mentioned American Indians through more critical eyes. At first an inner voice kept asking, "But how will this sound to Larry?" Previewing films brought on the same nagging question. Eventually the voice boomed out, "How does this sound to anyone?"

My solution at that time was to skip offensive chapters and eliminate offensive stories. In later years I used such stereotypical passages to teach bias recognition skills while continuing to search for accurate replacements.

School texts and curriculum filled with stereotypes and misinformation regarding American Indians spurred a team of American Indian educators to create a curriculum guide for Minnesota teachers.*

---

*The team included Joanne Donald, Tribal Education Director, Bois Forte Reservation; Jacqueline Fraedrich, Director of Indian Education, Robbinsdale Area Schools; Loretta C. Gagnon, Program Manager, Indian Education, St. Paul;

For nearly three years the team worked to include American Indian world view, culture content, and teacher background information with model lesson plans for primary, intermediate, middle school and high school levels. The goal was to align the curriculum with the Minnesota graduation standards, to focus on the history, language and culture of the Dakota and Ojibwe of Minnesota, and to provide a teacher-friendly document.

With great interest and anticipation decades later, I accepted the task of writer with the American Indian Learner Outcome Team. One of the areas of information included in the project and that teachers need to be especially aware of is American Indian family life.

༶ American Indian Family Life[†] ༶

The family, the roles played by family members, the functions of the family, the customs surrounding family life and the spiritual dimension of family are the center of American Indian culture. Understanding American Indian culture promotes more effective cross-cultural communication in a diverse society.

Traditionally American Indian families include a wide circle of relatives who are linked together in mutual dependence and who share resources and responsibilities as an extended family. *Family* includes more than parents and children. *Families* include grandparents, uncles and aunts, cousins and many others. Grandparents and other community elders have always played a major role in rearing and educating the young. It is customary in many tribes for the grandparents to raise one or more of their grandchildren. The grandchild is an extension of

---

Verna Graves, Director of Education, Red Lake Reservation; Nora L. Hakala, Supervisor Indian Education Section in Duluth; Carol Jenkins, Director of Education, Leech Lake Reservation; Dave Larsen, Lower Sioux Community; Jeanne McDougall, Education Director, White Earth Reservation; Dr. Thomas Peacock, State Board of Education; Michael Rabideaux, Superintendent, Fond du Lac Education, Fond du Lac Reservation; Jerry Staples, American Indian Education Committee; Doyle Turner, White Earth Reservation; George Weber, Superintendent of Schools, Mille Lacs Band of Ojibwe; and Marion Helland, Curriculum Specialist, Robbinsdale Area Schools.

[†]This is an adaptation of a longer version that is included in the *American Indian History, Culture and Language Curriculum Framework.*

the grandmother and grandfather. This type of shared responsibility for parenting is a family and community strength.

There is also a spiritual dimension to the idea of family. The Dakota use the phrase *mita-kuyapi-owasin* which means *all my relatives*. *All my relatives* includes not only the Dakota, but all human life, plant life, animal life and all things of this Earth. The Ojibwe use the term *indinawe maaganag* which can also be translated *all my relatives*.

American Indians use the symbol of a circle to describe the kinship and interrelationship of all of nature. The family is a circle with each member playing a reciprocal role. The life passages through which we all move is a circle. The seasons of the year form a circle.

Since the appearance of the Europeans on the American continent, American Indians have been struggling to retain the right to freedom, land, tradition and a way of life, that is, for Indian values. This struggle for cultural survival has never been easy —not during the days of colonization nor today during economic competition and culture clash. The majority of American Indians have been forced to live in poverty during the past 300 years. Poverty is corrosive and destructive to culture and the values embedded in the culture. The well-known results of poverty include family disintegration which deteriorates the social structure and social fiber, a shared value system which shapes individual and group attitudes.

It is a foremost interest of parents to equip their children with the tools of survival. It is obvious that the survival of the children and the survival of the culture are related.

∾ Dakota ∾

Among the Dakota, each child born into the family is called by a kinship term that states his or her gender and birth order. The first born if a female is called *Winuna* which literally means *first born female*. The first born if male is called *Chaské* which literally means *first born male*. There are four other names for female children and four other names for male children that also state the birth order. The children are always called these names by family members.

The Dakota call other relatives by kinship terms that are different from those used in the Euro-American kinship system. For example, father's brother is called *father* rather than *uncle* and his children are called *brothers and sisters*. Brother and sister terminology is also more specific, reflecting not only the gender of siblings but also age differences between them. A woman would call her older sister *Aconna* but a much older sister she would call *Micun*. She would address her younger sister by a different term, *Tanksi*.

A Dakota husband generally came to live with his wife and her family after marriage. Dakota women were considered the owners and managers of the home and they decided where each member would sit or sleep. The couple observed the custom whereby a husband never talked directly to his mother-in-law nor a wife to her father-in-law. This practice is considered a sign of respect among family members.

Dakota parenting traditions demonstrate the belief that children should be loved and cherished. Love is shown by parents and other family members who provide for the child's needs. There are stories told that long ago, when food was scarce, the elders voluntarily went without food so the children could be fed. Dakota parenting traditions also include the belief that children should not be disciplined too harshly or subdued too strongly because such action would destroy the spirit of the child. Through encouragement and gentle discipline, children learned to be responsible.

❧ Anishinabe ❧

In the Ojibwe language there are kinship terms for children and other family members. In the Anishinabe kinship system, younger siblings are not distinguished by gender. They are called *Nii-she-may*[*]—my younger sibling. Older brother is called *Nii-sa-yay* and older sister *Nii-mi-say*. Aunts and uncles are distinguished according to whether these aunts and uncles are related through the mother's or father's side of the family. Maternal uncle, for example, is called *Nii-zhi-shay*, and paternal uncle *Nii-mee-shu-may*. Great grandchildren are called *Inda-ni-kubi-ji-gan*, which literally means two pieces of rope spliced together or "*what I have spliced.*"

Many Anishinabe children have more than one personal name given at different times. Children may receive one or more names when they are small. The name may be given by an elder. Parents customarily bring tobacco to the elder whom they want to name their child. The name comes to the elder in a dream. The parents then prepare a ceremonial feast. After receiving a name, the child and elder are bonded in a special relationship. They call each other *nii-ya-wé e,*

---

*A double vowel system of spelling is used.

meaning *my namesake.* A child may be given a nickname rendered either in Ojibwe or English, revealing something about the child's special character.

Examples of naming occasions include birth name, formal name, nickname, name given during illness, and name given at puberty—named after one of their personal attributes. A child's name may be that of an elder who has passed on.

Family refers to an even wider circle of relatives who belong to the same clan. A clan is symbolized as a species of bird, animal or fish. There are many bands or divisions of the Anishinabe nation. Within this large nation are twenty or more clans. One definition of family is the Ojibwe word *indo-daim* meaning *my clan.* Those who belong to the same clan consider one another close relatives.

In the past as well as today, children are cared for by a circle of relatives. Grandparents, aunts and uncles, and fathers as well as mothers take responsibility. Like the Dakota, Anishinabe child-rearing includes the conviction that harsh discipline destroys the child's spirit. Positive discipline takes place through adult example, encouragement and community recognition of the child's accomplishments.

❧ The Community Way of Teaching a Child ❧

Traditional American Indian approaches to teaching and learning provide a powerful model for a constructive learning environment. Learning in the community is vastly different from what usually happens in a formal classroom. In these next two paragraphs, Jane Deborah Wyatt (1978) provides a description of the contrast:

> In the community the usual way for a child to learn a skill from an adult is to observe carefully over long periods of time and then to begin taking part in the activity. The way in which a native child learns the technology of fishing is a good example. By accompanying adults on fishing trips and by listening and observing, a child learns places for fishing and how to set nets, use a dip net, and prepare the fish for eating. A child also learns names of different types of fish, parts of the fish, types of nets and assorted gear, and styles of preparation. All of this is learned by watching and doing with a minimum of verbal preparation or interchange. Similarly it would be unusual for an adult to ask a child to verbalize what has been learned; whether or not the child had taken in and retained the information would be evident in the next fishing trip. A child may, of

course, ask questions about the skills being performed, and the adult may supplement the actual performance with verbal commentary. However, verbal instructions without demonstration and participation, a frequent occurrence in the schools, are rare in the community.

Story-telling in a community setting is also quite different. During a fishing trip a story about other trips or about the history of the area might be told, or the same information might be told weeks later in a totally different context. In either case, once the story was started, it might continue for hours. It would be considered stifling to limit a story-teller to twenty minute sessions. Yet this is precisely what is done in school. During story-telling sessions in the community children are expected to listen quietly. At the end no one asks them to recite the names of the main characters or to answer questions about plot, motivation and moral. In the school classroom the essence of learning is the articulation of information and skills in verbal and written form according to a predetermined timetable, and quizzing to determine if students have retained information. (p. 12)

⌘ Role of Elders ⌘

Elders have a very special place in the community and in the family. According to Basil Johnston (1990), "It was the elders, grandmothers and grandfathers, who taught about life, through stories, parables, fables, allegories, songs, chants and dances. They were the ones who had lived long enough and had had a path to follow, and were deemed to possess the qualities for teaching wisdom, knowledge, patience and generosity" (p. 69). Grandmothers teach young women their roles and responsibilities. Grandfathers teach the young men. Grandmother or *Nokomis* has a special place in the teachings and stories of the Anishinabe people. Most of the stories begin with Nokomis and her grandson. Nokomis raised her grandson, who is Waynaboshoo/ Winnebozhoo/ Nanabozho.* It is not unusual today for grandparents to continue to raise grandchildren. It is also traditional for aunts and uncles to help with the discipline of the children.

⌘ Effects of Government Assimilation Polices ⌘

The assimilation policies of the federal government were purposeful and part of a systematic effort to remove the traditional values, lan-

---

*Different spellings are used by people in different areas.

guages, history and culture from American Indians. These policies have had a tremendous detrimental effect on American Indian culture and language. Some of these policies include:

- creating a reservation system

- making a relocation policy (government efforts to transfer American Indians from reservations to urban centers)

- instituting an allotment policy to break up the American Indian land base

- sending young American Indian children to federal and mission boarding schools

Many of the children sent to boarding schools were not allowed to go home except for periodic visits. In these schools, the history of American Indian tribes was not included in the American story; pre-contact history was treated with a few paragraphs in most texts. Children in boarding schools seldom learned the oral history of their tribes from their elders and storytellers. This had a serious effect on the self-worth and self-esteem of American Indian children. Many of them had a sense of alienation from the political, social and economic make-up of the country. Unfortunately, this practice of exclusion continues today in many history texts and schools. Public school education may have a similarly negative impact when not inclusive of an American Indian world view.

With the implementation of the federal policy of sending young children to federal and mission boarding schools, a link between the elders and the young was broken. Children came back from these schools unable to speak their traditional languages with any degree of sophistication. In many cases they had been led to believe the language should not be spoken at all. As the children of these schools became adults, many chose to not teach their traditional language and culture to their children. Their own memories of the punishment for speaking their language at these schools was much too painful. Many had been put into isolation and beaten for doing it, and the only future they saw for their own children was to completely assimilate into the American way of life. This is a common element of many invaded groups (Freire, 1970):

> For cultural invasion to succeed, it is essential that those invaded become convinced of their intrinsic inferiority. Since everything has its opposite,

if those who are invaded consider themselves inferior, they must necessarily recognize the superiority of the invaders. The values of the latter thereby become the pattern of the former. The more invasion is accentuated and those invaded are alienated from the spirit of their own culture and from themselves, the more the latter want to be like the invaders: to walk like them, dress like them, talk like them. (p. 151)

It should be noted that some individuals had positive experiences in these schools and can relate instances of friendships formed, skills learned, and needs for food, clothing and shelter met.

The policy of assimilation also affected some American Indians' views about leadership. In the past, the tribal community was able to draw upon the perceived wisdom of elders and other persons of knowledge. With the decline in the number of elders who practiced traditional lifestyles and beliefs, the decline in respect for tradition, and the encroachment of leadership styles based upon political power, many reservation communities saw a decline in the number of traditional leaders.

In many boarding schools, boys were trained to be farmers and girls to be homemakers. With this process of Americanization, they were implicitly taught that men and women were not equal. This conflicted with traditional ways. Before the coming of the European immigrants to this land, women were considered the equals of men among the Anishinabe and Dakota.

The policy of assimilation did not wane until well into the 20th century. Until recently, social service authorities often placed American Indian children in need of such services into Euro-American foster homes. The Indian Child Welfare Act finally set guidelines whereby if American Indian children were removed from their homes, every effort had to be made to place them in American Indian homes.

ᩇ The American Indian Family Today ᩇ

In the American Indian family today, parents continue to teach children in the old ways. Many parents expose their children to traditional story-tellers whenever possible and make efforts to tell the old stories. The traditional behavior management techniques are still in use in many families, albeit not as effective when young people are bombarded from all sides by media, materialism, and social issues like racism, poverty and chemical dependency. While most American

Indian infants are no longer carried in cradleboards, parents understand the need to be close to infants and to provide nurturance to them. Many American Indian families understand the need to maintain harmony and balance in the home and to be at one with the environment. This way of life can be described in the following quotations from Wahacanka Ska Win Gough that appeared on the poster by Des-Jarlait titled "Young Child—Old Spirit:"

> In many Indian cultures, young children are considered sacred gifts to the family and to the tribe.

> Each child is to be treated with personal respect, as an individual bearing special traits.

> Each adult generation is to acknowledge the sacredness to young children, and to care of the coming generation. . . .

I could have used the information documented by this team back in the 1950s, but I can use it today as well. We could all benefit from reading, reflecting, and learning more regarding American Indian history, language and culture, given the level of miseducation that has historically taken place.

Processing this knowledge and information on American Indian family life can be part of becoming a wiser, more sensitive teacher. Inspired by this knowledge, teachers will behave differently and plan more wisely in relation to students. Nurturing the little voice that asks, "But how will this sound to Larry?" Discovering the booming voice that questions,"How does this sound to anyone?"

REFERENCES

Freire, P. (1970). *Pedagogy of the oppressed.* New York: Continuum.

Johnston, Basil. (1990). *Ojibwe Heritage.* Toronto, Canada.

Wyatt, J. D. (1978-1979). Native involvement in curriculum development: The Native American teacher as cultural broker, *Interchange,* 9 (1). 10-14.

ACKNOWLEDGEMENT

The American Indian Learner Outcome Team would like to acknowledge the support of the Minnesota State Board of Education in the development of the American Indian Curriculum Frameworks. The

Team further notes that this project could not have been completed without the support and commitment of the tribes of Minnesota. Megwetch!

ABOUT THE AUTHOR

The questions I am most frequently asked: "So, what do you do for a living, then?" "I teach, have taught and will teach." "I thought you were retired." "I am. I am retired from a position but not from teaching." "How is that?" "Well, I teach so that I can learn and I learn so I can teach. I simply am not finished yet." "But how long are you going to be doing these things?" "As long as there is a need for improvement in human relations. The way things look, it'll be awhile."

Multicultural Educators as Change Agents

Mary James-Edwards

THE TOPIC IN THE SENIOR SOCIOLOGY CLASS I WAS TEACHING was race relations. In a school district struggling with issues of race, this can be a very heated discussion. Michelle, a white student, was sharing her views on race with the class. Everyone appeared to be listening, with some students jotting down notes while others were shaking their heads in agreement or disagreement.

Shawn caught my eye. His body language told me he did not agree with *anything* she was saying. His hand shot up several times, and I signaled to him that I saw his hand and would give him a chance to respond. When Michelle finished speaking, I turned to Shawn and asked if he would like to respond. This was the moment he had been waiting for. I said, "Before you respond, paraphrase what Michelle said." Shawn turned to Michelle, paraphrasing what he had heard and ending with the question, "Did I hear you correctly?" Michelle replied that he had not and proceeded to restate what she had previously said, paying particular attention to clearing up the areas he had heard inaccurately.

As a classroom teacher, I have witnessed discussions about race result in shouting matches with tempers flaring and no listening or understanding occurring. What was different about this class was that I had learned that creating an environment where difficult discussions can take place and a diversity of opinions can be expressed and heard requires skills and strategies. The exchange between Shawn and Michelle provided a "teachable moment" for my students. We discussed what could have happened if Shawn had not paraphrased what he had heard and Michelle had not been able to repeat what she had shared. Shawn shared what he was feeling as he "listened" to Michelle and what had prevented him from hearing what she had really said. We talked about the value of active listening and how to use these skills when we discuss topics that provoke strong emotions and feelings.

◌ Being a Change Agent ◌

After this sociology class was over, I reflected on the reasons our classroom conversations on race were much different than in previous years. An important reason was that I was on my own journey as a teacher.

I agree with Linda Lantieri and Janet Patti, authors of *Waging Peace in Our Schools* (1996), who wrote, "One of the most pressing problems in schools and among youth in general is cultural and racial bias" (p. 89). My challenge, then in the classroom and now at the district level, is helping students and teachers communicate across culture by examining their feelings around racial and cultural difference.

When I was first introduced to the notion that an equity change agent was someone who would work within the school setting to bring about equity, I imagined I would be the facilitator, helping children to learn about each other and how to get along. Valuing diversity would be about educating children. I did not think in terms of examining my own biases about people who were different from me. What I have learned is that before I could authentically work with others to overcome bias and bigotry, I must first do my own internal work. Part of that work included how I handled conflict around these issues and inadvertently contributed to the escalation of these conflicts.

I had to acknowledge that my attitudes and feelings about people who were "other" had been influenced by those who had raised me. Sometimes those messages were loud and clear, other times quiet and subtle. But they conveyed to me how I should feel, what I should think, and whom I could and could not trust. The "teachings" included personal experiences, hearsay, and stories handed down to them and on to me. Having internalized many of those messages and having experiences of my own which confirmed those notions led me to conclude that those who had raised me were right. Their truth had become my truth.

Many people reject the notion that they have been influenced at all by these so-called messages. But when given time and opportunity in a non-hostile environment that allows for reflection, there is acknowledgment of the influences of those who raised them. Some buy into the bias and bigotry as I did and act accordingly. Others choose to break the cycle early on and cross the invisible boundaries that keep us from interacting with others who are different from us. Crossing those boundaries allows us to challenge stereotypes that we have learned.

Realizing that ignorance and prejudice have informed our view of the world and its people often causes us to struggle within ourselves. This is the place where we begin to consider becoming a change agent by working on ourselves first. That work includes unlearning the myths that have kept us disconnected from people who are different from us and beginning to discuss and understand how power and unearned advantage serve as tools of oppression.

Once we have accepted the challenge to work on self first and acknowledge that it is a lifelong journey, we can begin to help others we meet along the way. I now define a change agent as someone who has the skills and commitment to enable others to behave differently by offering them opportunities to learn and grow in positive ways, who acknowledges that lasting change takes time and allows for self development, and who helps to facilitate personal, professional, and systemic change in ways that promote and foster social responsibility, equity, and justice.

Rethinking Conflict
∾ Around Issues of Diversity ∾

Difference is at the center of most conflicts. When we consider multicultural education, too often the concept itself creates fear, controversy, excitement and conflict. Conflict within the context of multicultural education can come in various form of philosophical debates. For a school district courageous enough to truly embrace multiculturalism, conflict may come in the form of resistance from within.

Conflict is viewed by many educators as something to avoid at all costs and is often handled in ways that allow for the least amount of constructive learning. Educators facilitating classrooms where expressions of difference occur must come to grips with conflict as a tool of change. It must be viewed as an opportunity for growing and learning. Before that can happen, it is necessary that educators facilitating those classrooms revisit and analyze the messages they received growing up about conflict .

As part of my work with teachers, I invite them to remember the messages they received, particularly when they were young, about conflict. Their responses include: "Don't talk back," "Never disagree in public," "It's not what you say but how you say it," "Just walk away," and "Don't be afraid to share your views." There were gender-specific remembered voices: "Ladies don't fight," "Let your husband have the last word," and "Don't hit girls." Note the tendency to equate conflict with violence.

There were culturally specific responses as well: "Never argue with white people," and "Don't argue with those people because they'll get violent." There are cultural groups for whom a boisterous exchange of ideas is not considered conflict.

On a nonverbal level, teachers often share that the overriding messages they received were that nothing good came out of conflict and to avoid it at all costs. Nonverbal messages were as powerful, if not more so, than verbal messages.

After hearing the messages teachers recalled, I would ask the group, "What impact have these messages had on how you handle conflict today?" Many stated that they had never taken the time or had the opportunity to think about these messages. One said, "I deal with conflict every day, and I've never thought about how I feel about it."

When I ask these same teachers about messages they give their children about handling conflict, verbal and non-verbal, their messages ranged from "Fight back" to "Avoid." When I ask the teachers to share with each other how these messages help or hinder their work with students, their responses often indicate that their personal reactions to conflict get in the way of their work with students. They agree that this is an area we need to talk more about and work on.

Before I could create an environment where expressions of difference could occur, I also had to gain a better understanding of my own conflict style. I had to develop new skills and behaviors that would not shut down dialogue but allow it to open up. I had to be willing to intervene and interrupt bias when it occurred. Learning new skills was relatively easy. Using them was a challenge. Internalizing them took time.

I was approached one day by a teacher who viewed multicultural education as "one more thing to do" that "will pass like other programs that come and go." Frustrated by having to do "one more thing," she blurted out, "I don't have time to teach about every ethnic group in my class!"

That statement provided incredible learning for me. First, it helped me to understand her definition of what multicultural education is and how it was to be delivered. Second, it gave me the title for a workshop that would offer the skills and strategies that are necessary if multicultural education is to be delivered in an authentic way. Rather than seeing multicultural education as something that has to be done whether we like it or not, multicultural education is and should be viewed as a gift, a wonderful opportunity to learn about ourselves and others by recognizing that we are all experts on our own lives and experiences.

The challenge is to rethink our views and explore our feelings of discomfort when thinking about working toward education that is multicultural. What is getting in our way? My experience has been that a large part of the resistance is the "how to," the delivery of such a program when teachers are already feeling overwhelmed and believe, as one teacher put it, there is "no room in the curriculum."

Staff development programs that provide time and space for self-reflection, acknowledge that we are all at different places in our journey, and that devote adequate time to build the trust necessary for honest, deep discussions around difference are all too rare. These opportunities to learn about self and others, to build community, can help educators become culturally competent. A culturally competent educator is one who takes responsibility for learning about his/her students and the experiences they bring with them into the classroom. The challenge is to incorporate their experiences and ways of knowing into their learning environment. In addition to knowing students individually and collectively, they also must learn skills and strategies to challenge racism and oppression as it exists in educational institutions.

In my experience, staff development is a key component in helping teachers teach and communicate across cultures. The one-shot, two-hour staff development session sends the message that learning in this area is not important and does not provide the time necessary to do the internal work necessary for change.

Creating Educational Environments
❧ That Are Multicultural ❧

Creating a respectful environment where learning can take place is the first step in embracing multiculturalism. It is in this respectful environment that trust can be developed, feelings can be expressed, and the sharing of ideas and experiences can begin.

Multicultural education is about learning many perspectives. Understanding points of view helps to de-escalate conflict and allows room for other stories and "truths" to be explored. These skills, strategies, and concepts are staples of most conflict resolution programs. Establishing rules for discussion and learning to use "active listening" skills help to develop a feeling of safety within small and large groups. Using "I messages" to express one's ideas and feelings allows room for many perspectives to be shared and heard. Paraphrasing information for clarity and acknowledging feelings that may surface allow communication to continue as individuals discuss and work through difficult, emotional topics.

Challenging messages that students bring with them into the classroom requires effective educational strategies that encourage young people to determine their own "truth." It is crucial that students have opportunities to understand and appreciate their own culture and make connections to and appreciate the culture and experiences of others. The price we pay for not allowing this growth and opportunity is the perpetuation of stereotypes, misunderstanding and miscommunication that can often result in conflict that can lead to acts of violence. The environment that was created for Shawn and Michelle, the two students I mentioned earlier, came about because of direct teaching of conflict resolution skills and the infusion of multicultural concepts into the curriculum.

School districts across the country continue to struggle to find ways to help young people. Lantieri and Patti (1996) describe a new vision of education that includes improving the social and emotional competence of children by teaching them life skills.

> This set of skills and understandings is essential for every child, that a child's emotional and social well-being should not be attended to only when emotional outbursts, physical fights, or racial slurs occur; we believe that the teaching of these skills and competencies in our schools is critical for our future survival. (p. 6)

REFERENCE

Lantieri, L. & Patti, J. (1996). *Waging peace in our schools*. Boston: Beacon Press.

ABOUT THE AUTHOR

I currently work for the South Orange and Maplewood School District in New Jersey as the Diversity Coordinator. In this role I also serve as the Site Coordinator for the Resolving Conflict Creatively Program (RCCP) which has been in our district for six years. In working with the school community, I have learned that working on the self around diversity issues is the most difficult and painful. Time and support for those willing to begin doing their own internal work is vital if a true understanding of others is to be achieved.

Harvest Home

Bettye T. Spinner

In the ideal
It is a harvesting,.
this work we do—
a reaping of crops grown
from ancestral seeds,
a gathering of first fruit
from vines that trace their sources
   beyond geography,
    beyond gender,
     beyond the bleach
     and blush
      and black of skin
and root themselves in watery grace,
in knowledge that nurtures us all.

In the ideal
our classrooms fill, like cornucopia,
overflowing with the bounty of our grange.
Life stories, heaped among the texts,
spill into hallways of our schools,
crowd the sidewalks or the subways
or ride yellow buses home,
altering the form of knowing,
changing heads,
   changing hearts,
    changing history,
bring harvest
home.

ABOUT THE AUTHOR

I retired last December after twenty years at Moorestown (NJ) High School, having taught English, creative writing, speech, and theater in five states, as well as Heidelberg, Germany. I'm enjoying my new freedom to write, particularly to write poetry, a primary interest since 1986 when I became a teacher advisor to the Geraldine R. Dodge Program. As a Dodge poet and freelance consultant, I conduct writing workshops and readings in schools, libraries, and bookstores throughout the state, often combining poetry and issues of diversity from my national SEED training back in 1992. I have published two volumes of poetry—*Whispers of Generations* and *In the Dark Hush.* "Harvest Home" was my response to a question on the Leader's Report that first year I co-facilitated a SEED group in my school district.